Explaining Behavior

Explaining Behavior

Reasons in a World of Causes

Fred Dretske

A Bradford Book
The MIT Press
Cambridge, Massachusetts
London, England

This book was set in Palatino by Asco Trade Typesetting Ltd., Hong Kong, and printed and bound by Halliday Lithograph in the United States of America.

Library of Congress Cataloging-in-Publication Data
Dretske, Fred
  Explaining behavior.

  "A Bradford book."
  Bibliography: p.
  Includes index.
  1. Psychology—Philosophy. 2. Human behavior. 3. Causation. I. Title.
BF38.D675   1988   150   87-26158
ISBN 0-262-04094-8

To Judith
Reason and Cause

Contents

Preface

It sometimes seems as though persons and their bodies march to the beats of different drummers.

What I do, or much of what I do, is elaborately orchestrated by what I believe and want, by my intentions and purposes, by my *reasons* for doing the things I do. Often when I move, I have a reason for moving. I go to the kitchen because I want a drink and think I can get one there. If I didn't have those reasons, if I didn't *want* this and *think* that, I wouldn't move. At least I wouldn't move *when* I do, *where* I do, and in quite *the way* I do.

My lips, fingers, arms, and legs, those parts of my body that must move in precisely coordinated ways for me to do what I do, know nothing of such reasons. They, and the muscles controlling them, are listening to a different drummer. They are responding to a volley of electrical impulses emanating from the central nervous system. They are being *caused* to move. And, like all effects, these same bodily movements will occur in response to the same causes, the same electrical and chemical events in the nervous system, whatever I happen to want and believe, whatever reasons might be moving me toward the kitchen.

If, then, my body and I are not to march off in different directions, we must suppose that my reason for going into the kitchen—to get a drink— is, or is intimately related to, those events in my central nervous system that cause my limbs to move so as to bring me into the kitchen. My reasons, my beliefs, desires, purposes, and intentions, *are*—indeed they must be—the cause of my body's movements. What appeared to be two drummers must really be a single drummer.

But does this mean that my thoughts and fears, my plans and hopes, the psychological attitudes and states that explain why I behave the way I do, are to be identified with the structures and processes, the causes of bodily movement, studied by neuroscientists? If so, aren't these scientists, as experts on what causes the body to move the way it does, also the experts on why we, persons, behave the way we do? How can their explanation of why my body moves the way it does be different from my explanation of why I move the way I do? But if these are, indeed, at some deep level, the same explanatory schemes, then the apparently innocent admission that neuroscientists are (or will someday be) the experts on why our *bodies* move the way they do appears to be an admission that neuroscientists are (or will someday be) the experts on why *people* move the way they do. If there is really only one drummer, and hence only one beat, and this is a beat to which the body marches, then one seems driven, inevitably, to the conclusion that, in the final analysis, it will be biology rather than psychology that explains why we do the things we do.

What, then, remains of my conviction that I already know, and I don't have to wait for scientists to tell me, why I went to the kitchen? I went there to get a drink, because I was thirsty, and because I thought there was still a beer left in the fridge. However good biologists might be, or become, in telling me what makes my limbs move the way they do, I remain the expert on what makes me move the way I do. Or so it must surely seem to most of us. To give up this authority, an authority about why we do the things we do, is to relinquish a conception of ourselves as human agents. This is something that we human agents will not soon give up.

It is the business of this book to show how this appatrent conflict, a conflict between two different pictures of how human behavior is to be explained, can be resolved. The project is to see how reasons—our beliefs, desires, purposes, and plans—operate in a world of causes, and to exhibit the role of reasons in the *causal* explanation of human behavior. In a broader sense, the project is to understand the relationship between the psychological and the biological—between, on the one hand, the *reasons* people have for moving their bodies and, on the other, the *causes* of their bodies' consequent movements.

In pursuit of this end, it is absolutely essential that one proceed carefully in the beginning, in describing exactly what is to be explained: behavior. Too much haste here, in a description of what reasons are supposed to explain, can and often does vitiate the capacity of reasons to explain it. It is for this purpose that roughly a third of the book is devoted to behavior itself. Only after we gain a better understanding of what is to be explained, and in particular a better understanding of the difference between bodily movements and their production (and, hence, of the difference between a triggering and a structuring cause of behavior), will it be possible to show how some of the things we do are explained—*causally* explained—by the reasons we have for doing them.

I am grateful to the National Endowment for the Humanities for the year, free from teaching, it took to write the first draft. The Research Committee of the Graduate School of the University of Wisconsin helped to make that year possible, and I also thank them.

I used some of this material in graduate seminars at Duke University, the University of Wisconsin, and the University of California at Berkeley. The students who attended these seminars are, in good measure, responsible for making the next two drafts better than the first draft. I want especially to thank Shelley Park at Duke; Bradley Greenwald, Robert Horton, Angus Menuge, Martin Barrett, Naomi Roshotko, and Greg Mougin at Wisconsin; and Kirk Ludwig, Gene Mills, and Dugald Owen at Berkeley for helpful criticism and discussion.

I am, as always, grateful to my colleagues and good friends at Wisconsin, Berent Enc, Dennis Stampe, and Elliott Sober, for their criticisms, their encouragement, and (since I am sure I stole some of them) their ideas. After many years of fruitful exchange, it is sometimes hard to know who thought of something first. So I apologize, in advance, for inadvertent thefts.

Besides my colleagues at Wisconsin, I am indebted to others for saying and writing things, and sometimes doing things, that helped me in important ways. In this regard I want especially to thank Jerry Fodor, Susan Feagin, John Heil, Rob Cummins, and Claire Miller.

Explaining Behavior

Chapter 1

The Structure of Behavior

A dog bites your neighbor. That is a piece of canine behavior, something the dog does. It is something that happens to your neighbor. Clyde loses his job and Bonnie gets pregnant. These are things that happen to them, not things they do. These things may happen to them, as with your neighbor, *because* of something they did, or failed to do, earlier, but that is a different matter.

The difference between things we do and things that happen to us feels familiar enough. As Richard Taylor (1966, pp. 59–60) observes, it underlies our distinction between the active and the passive—between power, agency, and action on the one hand and passion, patience, and patient (in the clinical sense) on the other. For that reason alone it is tempting to use this distinction in helping to characterize the nature and structure of behavior. With certain clarifications and refinements (a business that will take the rest of this chapter to complete), I think this is indeed a useful basis of classification. Animal behavior is what animals do. Human behavior is what humans do. If plants and machines do things, then whatever they do is plant and machine behavior.

1.1 Internal and External Causes

When a rat moves its paw, that is something the rat does, a piece of rat behavior. When *I* move its paw, the paw still moves, but the rat doesn't move it. There is no rat behavior. Indeed, I could be moving the paw of a dead rat, and dead rats do not behave. This suggests that when movements are involved, the distinction between an animal's behavior and the things that happen to it resides in the difference between *the cause* of these movements. If the cause of movement lies in the animal, then it is doing something, behaving in some way, moving (say) its paw. If the cause of movement lies elsewhere, then something is happening or being done to it: its paw is being moved.

Let us, for the moment, greatly oversimplify and think of *all* behavior as involving some kind of bodily movement, and of each such movement as having some more or less unique cause. These are oversimplifications because, first, not all behavior involves movement. A person waiting for a bus, a bear hibernating for the winter, a chameleon changing color, and a chicken playing dead don't have to move to do these things.[1] It is, furthermore, naive to think of bodily movements as each having some single, unique cause. We know that the production of even the simplest behaviors is enormously complex, often involving the integrated action of hundreds of millions of nerve and muscle cells. Such processes take time, and they may not exhibit a simple linear causal arrangement. The control structure may be hierarchically organized, with delicate feedback mechanisms coordinating ongoing activity with constantly changing conditions. Far from being linear, such feedback mechanisms have a cyclical (closed-loop) causal organization.

One must, however, start somewhere. Refinements will come later. We are now concerned, not with fine structure, but with gross morphology. And, given the simplifying assumptions, the suggestion is that behavior is endogenously produced movement, movement that has its causal origin *within* the system whose parts are moving.[2] Letting C stand for a cause of some sort (internal or external as the case may be), M for bodily movement, S for the system (person, animal) in question, and arrows for causal relationships, this can be represented as in figure 1.1.

A bee's stinging a child qualifies as bee behavior, as something the bee does, not simply because M (penetration of the child's finger by the bee's stinger) occurs. For this can happen without the bee's doing anything—if, for example, the child accidentally pokes its finger with the stinger of a dead bee. This would be a case of some external (to the bee) event's causing M. To get bee behavior, to have something the bee does, the cause of M (stinger penetration) must come from within the bee.

For the same reason, the dog's attack on the neighbor counts as a piece of dog behavior: something *in* the dog causes its jaws to tighten around the neighbor's leg. And the difference between Clyde's *losing* his job (something that happens to him) and his *quitting* his job (something he does) resides in the locus—*in Clyde* or *in his employer*—of the cause of termination.

1. I shall return to it later in the chapter, but the point about the possibility of behavior without movement is meant to be a *logical* point, not a factual claim about the actual occurrence of movement in hibernating bears and limp chickens. It may turn out, for example, that in waiting for a bus subtle compensatory movements are continually being made in the muscles and joints in order to maintain a stable posture. And surely animals go on breathing while they wait, hide, hibernate, and play dead. But these facts are irrelevant. It is certainly no contradiction to suppose that someone waited for a bus *without* moving.
2. Here I ignore a distinction that will become important later in this chapter: the distinction between *a movement* which is produced by some internal cause and the *production* of that movement. I will often speak, for ease of expression, and in a way that I will later reject, of the movement as the behavior.

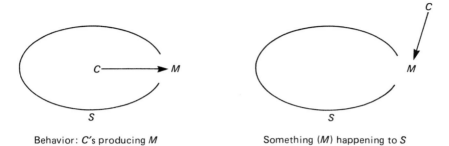

Behavior: *C*'s producing *M*   Something (*M*) happening to *S*

Figure 1.1

Despite its apparent crudity, the simple contrast between internally and externally produced movement captures the basic idea underlying our classification of behavior. *If* we have a well-defined ordinary notion of behavior—and, aside from the vague contrast between things we do and things that happen to us, I am not sure we do—it is, with a few refinements, equivalent to internally produced movement or change. The refinements are important, though, and to these I now turn.

1.2 Action and Behavior

To identify behavior with internally produced movement is not to deny that *some* behavior requires internal causes of a rather special sort.[3] Some of the things we do are purposeful. We intend to do them, and we do them in order to achieve certain ends. In other words, some behaviors are voluntary, the result, or so it seems to the agent, of conscious, deliberate choices.

Voluntary behavior, though, is only one species of behavior. What we are here concerned with is a much more general notion, one that applies to animals, plants, and perhaps even machines in very much the same way it applies to people. It applies to people, furthermore, when there are no purposes or intentions, those factors that allegedly qualify a system as an *agent* and its purposeful activity as voluntary. People shiver when they get cold. That is something they do. They also perspire when they get hot, grind their teeth when they are asleep, cough, vomit, weep, salivate, blush, tremble, hiccup, inhale, exhale, choke, fumble, stammer, fall asleep, dream,

---

3. It should be understood that *internal* does not simply mean inside or underneath the skin, fur, fins, feathers, or whatever. It also includes the idea of a proper or integral *part* of the system exhibiting the behavior. If A swallows B, for instance, we should not give the swallow*er* credit for behavior that properly belongs to the swallow*ee*. But just *when* the one becomes part of the other may not always be clear. I am grateful to Eugene Mills for calling my attention to this point.

wake up, and a great many other things that are in no way voluntary, deliberate, or intentional.

Some of this is reflexive behavior, behavior that is reliably elicited by certain stimuli. Though reflexive behavior is not generally regarded as intentional, it *is* behavior. I instinctively pull my hand from a hot surface. I do this *before* my brain is notified that my hand is in contact with something hot, *before* I have conscious reasons for behaving in this way. This is not something I do *because* of what I believe and desire. It is, nonetheless, something I do. An infant sucks and grasps. A suitably aroused cat turns in the direction of a touch to its muzzle. Another touch to the snout causes the cat to open its jaws in preparation for a lethal bite. These behaviors, though occurring only when there is suitable central stimulation, are, like the sucking and grasping reflexes of the human infant, automatic and involuntary (Flynn 1972; Gallistel 1980; MacDonnell and Flynn 1966).

Spinal animals (those whose spinal cords have been severed to remove all neural connections to and from the brain) can still do a great many things. Nobody scratches a spinal dog's back for him. He does it himself even though, when suitably stimulated, he can't help performing this reflexive act. Cats (Shik, Severin, and Orlovsky 1966) can walk; they can even change the way they walk (in response to altered conditions) without guidance from the brain. Male roaches continue copulating after decapitation by the female.

We can ask, and we expect behavioral scientists to tell us, how and why animals, including humans, do these things. If the answer to the *why* question doesn't always lie (as in these cases it seems clear it doesn't) in our intentions, purposes, and plans, then it lies elsewhere—perhaps in our hormones, perhaps in our genes or the motor programs for which genes are responsible. But the fact that some behavior doesn't have a certain kind of explanation, what we might call an *intentional* explanation, an explanation in terms of the agent's reasons and purposes, doesn't mean it isn't really behavior. If the lowly cockroach doesn't have a mind, doesn't have purposes and intentions, and therefore doesn't exhibit what we think of as intentional behavior, this doesn't mean the poor creature doesn't do anything. To suppose it does mean this is to illicitly constrict behavior to behavior that has a special kind of explanation.

A squirrel buries his nuts. He searches for a hiding place, then digs a hole, deposits the nut, tamps it down with his snout, and covers it with earth. This is something squirrels do. No one manipulates them, marionette-fashion, by invisible strings. To learn that this behavior, at least in the European red squirrel (Eibl-Eibesfeldt 1975, 1979), is what ethologists call a Fixed Action Pattern (FAP)—a behavioral sequence that, like a reflex, is innate, unlearned, and involuntary, and that will occur even when it serves no function (e.g., on a solid hard floor with no dirt)—is not to learn that it isn't really behavior. It is simply to learn that the explanation for this behavior is quite different from what we suspected.

Still, it is one thing to say that all behavior is internally produced movement and quite another to say that all internally produced movement is behavior. Perhaps some of the involuntary responses that behavioral scientists identify as reflexes can be more or less naturally classified as behavior.[4] There are, however, other internally produced changes that are not so easily classified in this way. We grow up. Our hair grows out, and our toenails grow in. We breathe, we sweat, and we get pimples. Our heart beats and our pulse throbs. These bodily movements and changes may be very slow (or very small), but they are movements and they are internally produced. Do we *do* these things? Males get erections. Is this something they do? Females menstruate, and during child delivery and care a fetus is expelled from the womb and milk flows from the mammary glands. Is this female behavior? The thermoregulatory system automatically induces shivering and constricts blood vessels to compensate for temperature changes. Do *we* do this?

Although the issues are not always clear, philosophers tend to be more conservative. They prefer a classification in which growing hair, a beating heart, and a bleeding cut do not count as the actions of the person whose hair grows, whose heart beats, and whose cut bleeds (see, e.g., Taylor 1966, pp. 57–58, 61; Thalberg 1972, pp. 55–63; Wilson 1980, p. 50). Hair, hearts, and cuts may behave this way, but not people. There is even some sympathy for the view that reflexes should be denied the status of behavior: von Wright (1971, p. 193) asserts that salivation and the flexion response of the knee are reactions to stimuli, and that "only people who have had their talk perverted by behaviorist jargon would think it natural to call such reactions 'behavior' of a dog or a man." Perhaps, von Wright grudgingly concedes, such reactions are the behaviors of a gland or a knee.

I say the issues are not clear here because philosophers are typically interested, not in behavior *per se*, but in a particular species of behavior: *action*. Although there is no settled view about what, exactly, an action is, the general consensus seems to be that (ignoring niceties) it is either itself something one does voluntarily or deliberately (e.g., playing the piano) or a direct consequence, whether intended and foreseen or not, of such a voluntary act (e.g., unintentionally disturbing one's neighbors by intentionally playing the piano). Taylor (1966, p. 61), for instance, explicitly contrasts the beating of one's heart and perspiring under the influence of fear with *voluntary* behavior. And it seems quite clear that Thalberg, Wilson, von

---

4. There may be some question about whether, in *very* simple (monosynaptic, for example) reflexes, the movement isn't in fact caused, not by the internal neural process, but by the eliciting *external* stimulus. I shall return to this point shortly.

Wright, and others are concerned, not with the general idea of behavior, but with some special class of behaviors. For this reason it is hard to evaluate the apparent disagreements about classification. We are comparing apples and oranges—or, better, we are comparing fruit (the genus) with oranges (a species).

It is certainly true that there are some—perhaps a great many—internally produced bodily movements (or changes) that we do not ordinarily think of as things we do. Though we may be said to *let* our hair grow (longer) by not cutting it, we don't (at least I don't) speak of *growing* our hair. I *get* rashes, I don't *do* them. Yet, there are a great many other things, equally involuntary, that we nonetheless speak of as things we *do*. We shiver when it gets cold, cough when our throats get irritated, adjust our posture when we begin to fall, inhale and exhale (i.e., breathe), blink, hiccup, snore, dream, urinate, and defecate. These are not—not in Taylor's (1966, p. 57) sense, anyway—things with which we have anything *to do*, since they are things we are helpless either to prevent or to make happen in any direct way. We can, up to a point, sometimes choose a time and a place. We can *hold* our breath for a bit. After toilet training, we can determine *when* and *where* we will defecate; however, we can't, any more than in the case of breathing, choose *whether* to do it at all. Some behavior is voluntary, some isn't.[5]

Classification is always a bit arbitrary, if not about central cases then around the edges. And it is often responsive, as it should be, to the purposes for which the classification is undertaken. Therefore, although our ordinary ways of speaking sometimes tug in a slightly different direction, there are, I think, good reasons to adopt a more liberal taxonomy, a taxonomy that is, I think, more in accord with the usage of behavioral scientists. Clinical psychologists, sociologists, and economists, because of their special interest in human (and generally voluntary) behavior, may have a restricted notion of what behavior is, but when one listens to behavioral biologists, embryologists, endocrinologists, and pharmacologists the picture changes. These behavioral scientists have no trouble classifying as behavior—and by behavior I mean human and animal behavior, not merely the behavior of glands and organs—such things as respiratory and cardiovascular activity (Engle 1986), penile erections (often said to be part of an animal's "display behavior"), the secretions of endocrine and exocrine glands, muscle spasms, convulsions, seizures, involun-

5. Thalberg's (1972, p. 59) list of *reactions* (yawning, hiccuping, wheezing, shuddering, blushing) and *breakdowns* (fumbling, tripping, stammering, collapsing, snoring, fainting) is an excellent partial inventory of behaviors that are not actions. I think, in fact, that Thalberg's argument that there are activities (like the above reactions and breakdowns) that are neither actions nor things that happen to us is an excellent argument for regarding action as a *species* of behavior.

tary eye movements, the regulatory activities of the autonomic nervous system, and all sorts of reactions, *including reflexes*, whose internal production remains well below the level of conscious or voluntary control. If this way of talking does not always mesh very well with our ordinary ways of talking, does not always sound quite right to our untutored sense of things we *do* (versus things that happen to us), the same could be said about the way physicists, chemists, and astronomers carve up our material surroundings or the way botanists and zoologists group living things. Sometimes the purposes of explanation and understanding are best served by not talking the way our grandparents talked.

This is not to say that there is general agreement within behavioral science about what, exactly, is to be counted as behavior. One expects, given their different explanatory interests, approaches, and professional training, to find differences between marine biologists and pharmacologists, on the one hand, and clinical psychologists, sociologists, and economists on the other. They may all be interested in behavior, to be sure, but they are interested in very different kinds of behavior. And it makes a difference to what one sees as behavior whether one spends one's life studying urban teenagers or sea slugs. Donald Griffin, a biologist, is impressed with the versatile behavior of some protozoa (Griffin 1984, p. 31); however, it is doubtful whether a criminologist would even be willing to call this behavior, let alone be impressed with its versatility.

The fact is that insects, worms, snails, crickets, leeches, and even paramecia behave in quite interesting ways. They aren't stones, whose fate is completely at the mercy of external forces. If we ask why the activities (to use as neutral a word as possible) of even the simplest living creatures are regarded as behavior by those who study them, the answer seems obvious. It is not because such movements are thought to be voluntary. It is not because it is thought that leeches and sponges have *reasons*—beliefs, desires, purposes, and intentions—for doing the things they do. No, these activities are deemed behavior for the same reason that certain rhythmic movements of embryos (Preyer 1885), the growth pattern in roots (Evans, Moore, and Hasenstein, 1986), and (to sample the other end of the spectrum) the purposeful acts of human beings are regarded that way: because these movements, these changes of state, are internally produced. Individual scientists may differ when they are called upon to give formal definitions of behavior, but collective practice reflects their use of this criterion as the basis for identifying some changes, but not others, as behavior.

Some descriptions, to be sure, have special implications about the character of the internal cause. Some verbs, as Davidson (1971, p. 45) rightly points out, describe behavior that cannot be anything but intentional: asserting, cheating, and lying, for instance. The descriptions are *theory-*

loaded. To understand the general idea of a theory-loaded description, think about describing something as a *wound*. As Norwood Hanson (1958, p. 55) originally put it, to describe something as a wound is to imply something about how it was brought about. Surgeons don't wound patients—at least not if they are doing their job right—even though their cuts may leave scars that are indistinguishable from those left by genuine wounds. Some descriptions of behavior are like that: they imply something special about the causal origin of motor activity. To ask a question, a common way of describing what someone has done, is to produce meaningful sounds with a certain *intention*. To ask a question is not merely to have the relevant movement of the lips, tongue, and larynx produced by *some* internal cause, any more than to be a wound is to have the scar produced by *some* puncture of the skin. It is, rather, to have these vocal activities produced by a *purpose*, an *intention*, or a *desire* to obtain information. Unless the internal cause of speech is some such intention or purpose, the resulting behavior does not qualify as *asking a question*. It might, rather, be rehearsing a line in a play, reading aloud, telling a joke, or giving an example.

The same is true of *stalking, hiding*, and *pretending*. To stalk another animal is not merely to retain spatial proximity to it, but to do so with a certain lethal purpose. If a cat's movements do not have a special kind of etiology, then the cat isn't *stalking* a mouse. The same is obviously true of an enormous number of the verbs we use to describe animal behavior: hunting, avoiding, chasing, protecting, threatening, and so on.

If one took such descriptions of behavior as the rule, one might be tempted, as some philosophers have been tempted, into mistakenly supposing that to qualify as behavior (and not just a particular kind of behavior), the motor activity, M, must be produced, or at least partially determined, not just by some internal cause, C, but by an internal cause of a very special character—an intention, a goal, a desire, or a purpose. It is this way of looking at behavior, I suspect, that leads some people to deny the status of behavior to involuntary reflexes.

One can, however, acknowledge the point that some behavioral descriptions presuppose a particular kind of internal cause—a specific purpose, intention, desire, belief, plan, or goal—without supposing that, were the internal cause to lack this character, there would be no behavior. No, the animal would still be *doing* something. We just couldn't describe it that way. Let us suppose, for the sake of argument, that stalking a prey *requires* certain intentions and purposes on the part of the hunter. Let us also imagine that it turns out—for whatever reasons, philosophical or scientific—that spiders and lions do not have intentions and purposes. Then it will turn out that spiders and lions do not stalk their prey. Nevertheless, they certainly do *something* to earn their supper, and that—whatever more specific description we may end up using for it—is lion and spider behavior. A cat lover may be wrong in thinking that a cat is sulking, but the cat may indeed be sitting under a chair and looking away.

1.3 Plant and Machine Behavior

Though it may sound odd to speak of plants and machines as performing *actions*, it does not sound odd to speak of them as *doing* things. Though they are quite literally rooted, plants can do things that are remarkably like the things that animals do. But even when plants do not behave the way animals do, this is no reason to ignore their efforts. It is, after all, still behavior: *plant* behavior.

Most people, I suppose, are familiar with the behavior of climbing plants. Perhaps, though, they are not aware that the mechanisms responsible for this behavior are mechanisms (e.g., negative geotropism and positive phototropism) that are also used by some animals (protozoa and primitive invertebrates) to solve similar orientation problems (Staddon 1983, p. 22). There are, furthermore, carnivorous plants (perhaps the best-known is the Venus flytrap) which capture insects and digest them with enzymes. Fungi attack other living things. They capture small roundworms, for instance, by producing a small loop which swells rapidly, closing like a noose, when a worm rubs against its inner surface. To use the words of the botanists Raven, Evert, and Curtis (1981, p. 224), from whom I take the example, these predacious fungi "garrote" the poor worm. Some plants throw (shoot? discharge?) their seeds as far as 15 meters.

Plants, just like animals, exhibit circadian rhythms (24-hour cycles of activity) that are now thought to be endogenous—i.e., internally controlled. And plants, just like animals, have to breathe. Small openings (stomata) in the leaves of a plant open and close in response to environmental and physiological signals, thus helping the plant maintain a balance between its water losses and its oxygen and carbon dioxide requirements.

All this *seems* properly described as plant behavior, as things plants do. All this *is* properly described as plant behavior by botanists. I belabor the point only for the sake of those, if any, who want to restrict the idea of behavior to some special class of behaviors—e.g., the behavior of *animals*, or the *voluntary* behavior of animals, or the voluntary behavior of certain *kinds* of animals.

There is, however, no reason to be so stingy. Letting a plant or an animal *behave* is not conceding much. It certainly doesn't require free will or a mind, if that is what worries people. Plants behave for the same reason animals behave: some of the changes occurring to them are brought about from within. In this respect, these changes contrast with things that *happen to* trees, flowers, and plants. Houseplants get moved around; that is something that happens to them just as it does to certain household pets. Some flowers change color as the season progresses; that is something they do just as (but, of course, not for the same reason as) cephalopods (e.g., squid and octopi) change color under threatening conditions (Grier 1984, p. 287). Some trees shed their leaves in late autumn, and most trees defend themselves from injury by walling off damaged areas. These are things trees do. They also get struck by lightning, attacked by beetles, and cut down. These are things that happen to them.

In each case the underlying basis for distinguishing what the plant does from what happens to it is the same as it is for animals: the locus, internal or external, of the cause of change. Shedding its leaves is something a maple tree does, a form of tree behavior, because the primary cause of leaf removal comes from within the tree. Certain chemical changes occurring within the tree cause a weakening of the mechanical bond between branch and leaf, with the result that the leaves, under the constant force of gravity, eventually fall. If the leaves had departed because of external causes—if a woodsman had plucked them from the branches or a hurricane had blown them from the tree—the tree would not have *shed* its leaves. This wouldn't be something the tree had done; it would be something that had happened to it. Though we do not do so commonly, we can describe hair loss among men in a similar way. If someone pulls a man's hair out or cuts it off, then, as when a tree loses its leaves in a storm, this is something that happens to the man. If the loss occurs in the normal way, however, as the result of internal physiological processes, it is something a man does, a piece of behavior. If snakes get credit for doing something when they shed their skin, and if molting is a form of bird behavior, why shouldn't we get credit for doing something when we shed our hair? It isn't deliberate, as we all know, but that is irrelevant.

What I have said about plants can be said about instruments and machines. If I bend over and pick up a piece of lint, that is something I do, part of my behavior. But a vacuum cleaner also picks up things. This is something the vacuum cleaner does, part of *its* behavior. It gets credit for picking up the dust from the carpet for the same reason I get credit for inhaling smoke from my pipe or a butterfly for sucking nectar from a flower: the vacuum responsible for the respective effects—for getting the dust, smoke, or nectar in—is generated within the systems to which the behavior is attached. Of course, I push the vacuum cleaner around (thus, I get credit for cleaning the house); but *it* picks up the dust from the carpet.

Thermostats turn furnaces off and on, alarm clocks wake us up, and industrial robots now do many of the tiresome, repetitive things that human beings once had to do. Things also happen to these objects: they break, rust, and get repaired. The difference between what they do and what happens to them is, I submit, exactly the same as the difference between what plants and animals do and what happens to them—a difference in the locus, internal or external, of the cause of change.

It is certainly true that with very simple objects, or objects that have no real "articulation" to their internal composition, the distinction between things that happen to them and their behavior, the things they do, begins to collapse. Almost everything starts to count as behavior. Or, depending on your point of view, nothing counts as behavior. What does a stone *do* when you put it in water? It sinks. That, we might say, is the way objects behave in a less dense medium. And if we asked physicists about the behavior of electrons, they might tell us, among other things, that they tend to swerve in magnetic fields. Of course, some of this "behavior" depends on the properties of the object in question (the density of the stone, the charge of the electron); but there is no real basis for saying (in order to salvage our description of behavior as *internally* produced change or movement) that the cause of the downward movement of the stone or the curved trajectory of the electron is internal.

This is merely to concede that our basis for distinguishing between a system's behavior and the things that happen to it is really applicable only to systems that exhibit enough structural complexity and internal articulation to make the internal-external difference reasonably clear and well motivated. When it isn't, as it isn't with pieces of lint, photons, and drops of water, the biography (as it were) of these objects consists, indifferently, of all the events in which they somehow participate. If some of this is described as behavior, as it surely is, we must remember that, at this level, behavior no longer means what it does with animals, plants, and more highly structured inanimate objects. Behavior, as it is being used in this work, contrasts with what happens to an object, plant, or animal. This is not the way the word "behavior" is always used in (say) physics and chemistry. There is no difference, as far as I can tell, between what *happens to* an electron in a magnetic field and what an electron *does* in a magnetic field. There definitely *is* a difference between what happens to an animal placed in water and what it does when placed in water.[6]

1.4 Movements and Movings

Something must be said about a notion that I have so far taken for granted: the notion that there is, for every movement or change, some *unique* cause, either internal or external. My use of the definite article, my way of speaking about *the* cause of movement, betrays this assumption. It is, of course, quite unrealistic. Most (perhaps all) effects depend on a great many other events and conditions. How is one to choose among them? How is

---

6. My thanks to John Heil for helpful discussion on this point.

one to say which of them is the cause? Unless one can make a principled choice about the cause of M, one will have no way, at least no principled way, of saying what is and what is not behavior.

This is an issue that must be faced, but before we face it (in the next section) there is an even more pressing problem. Even if we suppose that all behavior involves some kind of bodily movement, it isn't clear whether one should identify the behavior with the movement or with something else. Shall we identify a rat's moving its paw with the movement of the paw? With the internal cause of movement? Or, if this is still a third possibility, with the one thing's causing the other? Or something else?

There are a variety of reasons one might choose to identify behavior with the movements by means of which things get done—e.g., why one might want to identify a rat's pressing a key with the paw movements by means of which the key is depressed. For some there are methodological motives. If psychology is the study of stimulus-response relations, then both the stimulus and the response should be *observable* (see Taylor 1964, chapter IV). The rat's paw movements are observable. And, if we ignore philosophical quibbles, so is the fact that these paw movements sometimes have certain effects (key movements) that are relevant to classifying the movements as key depressions. So if the rat's behavior, its response to the stimulus, is to be observable, it should be identified with these observable outcomes.

There is, furthermore, a related methodological point about the proper way to describe the data, that body of facts that it is the business of science to explain in some systematic way. If behavior is what we are trying to explain, then behavior itself should be described in a theory-neutral way (or, if that is asking too much, in as theory-neutral a way as possible). It should be described in a way that does not presuppose the correctness of any competing theoretical explanation of it. If a rat's pressing a key is not simply the rat's movements in pressing the key, if this piece of behavior (so described) involves internal antecedents of a particular sort (intentions? purposes? expectancies?), then a rat's pressing a key is not a proper datum for behavioral science. It carries along too much theoretical (and obviously suspicious) baggage in its very description. It presupposes that the observable paw movements have a particular etiology and, hence, a particular theoretical explanation. It would be like an early physicist's describing the behavior of iron filings in the presence of certain metals as "aligning themselves with the magnetic field." That may be what the bits of metal are doing, but that is not the way their behavior should be described for purposes of evaluating alternative explanatory theories. For this purpose, their behavior is better described in more theory-neutral terms—in terms, say, of their orientation relative to some external (observable) frame of reference. And for the same reason, behavior should be understood as "colorless" movements (Hull 1943, pp. 25–26).

Despite these commendable motives, there appears to be an obstacle to identifying behavior with bodily movements. There is, as already noted, a difference between

(1) a rat's moving its paw

and

(2) a movement of a rat's paw.

Since the rat's paw can move without the rat's moving it, there may be something to which (2) refers when there is nothing to which (1) refers. The rat isn't doing anything if I move its paw. It is doing something if it moves its paw. Hence, if it is rat behavior we are interested in, we should be in the business of explaining (1), not (2).

This point, though important, has never been an obstacle for those wishing to identify behavior with bodily movements. All it shows is that behavior, *if* it is to be identified with movement, must be identified with movements of a particular kind: movements having the right cause. According to this line of thinking, then, the right equation is not between (1) and (2), but between (1) and

(3) a (paw) movement *produced by* some (appropriate) internal cause.

Just as a woman *is* a mother if she stands in the right kinship relation to another person, so a movement *is* a behavior if it stands in the right causal relation to an internal process.

This is, to be sure, a compromise on the methodological scruples mentioned earlier, but it is not a major capitulation. Behavior is still observable in one sense. We can still see the movements with which behavior is identified. What we can't do (although this will depend on one's theory of knowledge) is *know* (see) *that* these movements are behavior, since this requires knowing (seeing) that the visible movements *have* the right etiology. It is like seeing my handiwork, the chair I made that is directly in front of you. You can see the chair (which is my handiwork) without being able to see that (and therefore without knowing whether) it is my handiwork. It may be obvious that I made the chair, that it is my handiwork, just as it may often be obvious that certain movements are internally produced, but the fact remains that what makes the visible thing into the thing it is (my handiwork in the case of the chair, behavior in the case of the movements) is something "hidden," something not visible (and so, in this second sense, not observable).

The equation of (1) and (3) presents a compelling picture of behavior. As far as I can tell, it has gained wide acceptance among behavioral scientists.

It is also a view to which many philosophers, including G. E. M. Anscombe (1958) and Donald Davidson (1963), subscribe—often for quite different reasons. Davidson, in fact, claims that there are no actions *other than* bodily movements (1971, p. 23). Part of the appeal of this view lies in the simple fact that it is hard to see what else behavior could be. If painting my house isn't the set of movements I execute in applying paint to my house (all brought about, of course, by the right internal causes), what else could it be? By presupposing that an action is a species of bodily movement, Colin McGinn's (1982, p. 84) question "What is the difference between a bodily movement that ranks as an action and a bodily movement that does not?" gives expression to exactly this feeling.[7] The question is not *whether* behavior is movement, but *what kind* of movement it is.

Of course we describe much of our behavior, many of the things we do, in terms that imply nothing about the particular bodily movements involved in the doing. I cancel an order. She refuses his invitation. He sues his doctor. These are descriptions of things people do, but they are not descriptions of, nor do they imply anything about, bodily movements. There are no particular bodily movements that must occur for one to cancel an order, refuse an invitation, or sue someone. Indeed, circumstances can even be imagined in which no movements at all need occur for these things to be done. Nevertheless, aside from such mental activities as planning a trip, trying to remember a telephone number, or worrying about a leaky roof, the things one does are usually achieved by some change (or internally caused absence of change[8]) of one's body. One initiates a lawsuit by calling one's lawyer (and this, in turn, by lifting the telephone, and so on), cancels an order by nodding when asked, and refuses an invitation by writing a note. Or one does it in some other way. But *the way* always involves some bodily movement or change. And the above account of behavior, the identification of it with bodily movement, is intended to be an account of this basic kind of behavior, the kind of behavior (to echo a distinction in action theory) *by* which, but not *for* which, other things are done. *Basic* behavior, the fundamental form of behavior, is bodily movement.

We can, however, accept the equation of (1) with (3), the identification of behavior with movements produced by internal causes, without accepting the identification of behavior with movements. For (3) is ambiguous. It can be interpreted to mean either

---

7. McGinn, however, later (p. 97) retracts this supposition by identifying bodily movements with *constituents* of actions.

8. This qualification should always be understood, since I will often omit it. One doesn't have to "move a muscle" to do something. Saying nothing, which is not the same as *doing* nothing, in response to an urgent question might easily qualify as rude, possibly immoral, behavior. I return to this point in section 6 of the present chapter.

   (3a) a movement *which is* produced by some internal cause

or

   (3b) a movement's *being produced* by some internal cause.

(3a) identifies behavior—in this case, a rat's moving its paw—with an event—a paw movement—that has a particular etiology; (3b), on the other hand, interprets this behavior as a more complex entity: the *production* of this movement. The latter, unlike the former, has the movement as a part.[9]

   It would be an elementary confusion to identify, say, a rat's paw which was moving (= a moving paw) with the paw's movement. The first is an object, a paw; the second is an event, a movement. It is the same confusion, though not at so elementary a level, to confuse movements which are brought about by internal events with their being brought about by these events. The former is an event, a movement, something that happens to (say) a paw. The second, I shall argue, is a piece of behavior, possibly an action, something the rat *does*. Identifying behavior with bodily movements is, I submit, a conflation of the very real difference between (3a) and (3b)—a difference that is critical to a proper understanding of behavior and what makes it, but not the events composing it, explicable in terms of an agent's *reasons*.

   Behaviors are, like events, datable. It makes perfect sense to ask *when* someone did something (e.g., moved his arm). And it makes perfect sense to ask when something happened (e.g., when someone's arm moved). Though it isn't always obvious with such basic behavior, these times are not the same. And therein lies one reason for refusing to identify behavior with movement, or indeed with any other event that is a constituent of the behavior.

   A bird cannot fly (migrate) to Siberia without, sooner or later, getting to Siberia. If it never arrives, there may have been a time when it was *flying to* Siberia, but there is no time when it flew to Siberia. The time the bird *arrives* in Siberia is not, however, the time it *flew* to Siberia. The migration *took time*; the consummatory event, the arrival, occurred *at a time*.

   The time at which a rat depresses a lever is not the time at which the

---

9. Irving Thalberg (1977, especially pp. 65–71) has a "component" analysis of action that makes an action (a species of behavior) into a complex entity that includes whatever associated bodily movements may be involved. Colin McGinn (1979) also has, as his "preferred" theory, actions as complex events containing, as parts, both tryings and movements. If I understand her, and I'm not sure I do, Judith Thomson (1977) also has something like this in mind when she identifies actions with agents causing movements.

   In this connection it is interesting to note Tinbergen's (1951, p. 2) definition of behavior as "the total of movements made by the intact animal." Is this to be understood as the movements *made* by the intact animal, or as the intact animal's *making* them?

lever moves. The rat can *start* to depress the lever—efferent signals being sent to the muscles, muscles contracting, and pressure consequently being applied to the lever—*before* the lever begins to move. The temporal differences with such simple behaviors are slight, but they are real nonetheless. They are especially evident in the case of ballistic movements (fast movements like jumping and kicking which, once begun, run their course without modification or feedback). Although a praying mantis aligns itself with its prey by using visual feedback, its strike is entirely ballistic and unguided (Staddon 1983, p. 71). Though the mantis hasn't *struck its prey* until contact is made, the insect's causal contribution to this result (forcible contact) is effectively over *before* this event occurs. Likewise, when one kicks a ball, one's leg is "flung" by the muscle. The muscle ceases its activity *before* the leg completes its movement (Sheridan 1984, p. 54). From the point of view of the motor control system, the kick is over before the leg has moved enough to make contact with the ball. But this doesn't mean one has kicked the ball *before* the foot makes contact with the ball. All it means is that the behavior—kicking a ball—*begins* before the occurrence of some events—e.g., the foot's making contact with the ball—that must occur for one to kick a ball. In this sense, kicking a ball is no different from migrating to Siberia: you have to start doing it *before* those events (arriving in Siberia, making contact with the ball) occur that are required for the doing. These events are *required* for the doing because they are a *part* of the doing.

Philosophers have been especially intrigued by examples of killing and dying. The fascination comes from the potential, and often the reality, of large temporal disparities between, say, the act of shooting someone and the event (the victim's death) that makes the act an act of killing. Though Booth did not succeed in killing Lincoln, and hence did not kill Lincoln, until Lincoln died, this does not mean that Booth killed Lincoln at the time of Lincoln's death. The deed began long before the beginning of that event, Lincoln's death, whose occurrence is necessary for the behavior to *be* a killing of Lincoln. Booth no more killed Lincoln *when* Lincoln died than he killed Lincoln *where* Lincoln died.

Though the principle is dramatized in such examples, the same principle is at work even in elementary forms of behavior. You *begin* to move your arm, flick the switch, and turn on the lights *before* those events—arm movement, switch toggle movement, and light's going on—begin to occur which must occur for you to move your arm, flick the switch, and turn on the lights.

Some philosophers, including Hornsby (1980), have been impressed by this line of reasoning and have sought to identify actions (and thereby, by implication, behavior) not with the overt movements in which behavior typically culminates, but with the internal *causes* of these movements. A rat's moving its paw is identified not with paw movements *which are* brought about by internal causes (3a), and not with their *being brought* about this way (3b), but with the internal events that bring them about. In the case of actions (deeds for which the internal event is allegedly some *trying*), the rat's moving its paw is identified with its trying to move its paw (when the trying actually results in paw movement).

This view, unlike the identification of behavior with overt movement, is, on the face of it, implausible. Nonetheless, certain temporal considerations can be enlisted in support of it.[10] The arguments go something like this: I damage your reputation by spreading scurrilous rumors about you. After I initiate these rumors, but before they have spread sufficiently to damage your reputation, I sit back and wait for my activities—poison-pen letters and whispered innuendos—to have their desired effect. While I am "sitting back" I'm not (according to this line of thinking) *doing anything*. I could be asleep. I could be dead. Your reputation is about to be damaged, but I am no longer doing anything to damage it. Hence, if it turns out that I damaged your reputation, as it certainly will once your reputation is damaged (as a result of my activities), then damaging your reputation must be something I did *before* your reputation was damaged. I finished doing it when I finished those activities—spreading rumors, writing and sending letters—that resulted in your reputation's being damaged. I damage your reputation *today* although your reputation will not be damaged until *tomorrow*. The same reasoning leads to the conclusion that Booth killed Lincoln *before* Lincoln died.

If this argument is accepted, a minor extension of it brings us to the conclusion that, just as I can damage your reputation *before* your reputation is damaged, a rat can move its paw *before* its paw moves. What else, other than the internal cause of movement, could be identified with the rat's moving its paw if this is something that can occur, something the rat can finish doing, *before* the required paw movements occur?

This position represents one of two extremes, both of which are unacceptable. They are unacceptable because they locate behavior in the wrong place—either wholly after it begins or wholly before it ends. Behavior, to be sure, requires some internal C to produce M, but that fact doesn't require us to identify behavior with either the M (which is caused) or the C (which causes it). One can, as we have already done, identify behavior with a *process*—C's causing M—that begins with C and ends with M. This avoids the paradoxes of both extreme views by making behavior begin where it should begin (with those efferent activities that bring about bodily

10. See Hornsby 1980, p. 29. For good general discussions of this, and related temporal arguments, see Thalberg 1971 (particularly chapter 5), Thomson 1971 and 1977, and Bennett 1973.

movement) and end where it should end (with those external events or conditions that the behavior requires for its occurrence). A person's moving his arm is then a piece of behavior that begins with those internal events producing arm movements and ends with the arm movements they produce. If we are talking about a more "extended" piece of behavior (a pitcher's striking out a batter, for instance), the behavior begins, once again, with those internal events producing arm movement. The behavior ends, though, not with the arm's movement, but with the batter's missing his third swing at the ball. It is for this reason that striking out a batter isn't something that begins after, or ends before, the ball leaves the pitcher's hand. And it is for this reason that Booth didn't kill Lincoln before Lincoln died (i.e., at the time Booth shot him) or after he shot him (i.e., when Lincoln died).[11]

But does this mean that we can say of the assassin, as he lies comfortably in his bed after shooting his victim, that he is killing someone? Does it mean we can say of the pitcher, struck by lightning at the moment he releases his notorious slow ball, that he (now a pile of cinders on the mound) is striking out the batter? Can dead people do things?

Can J.R. be divorcing Sue Ellen while he lies sleeping on the couch? Why not? It may sound odd to point at him and *say* that he is divorcing Sue Ellen. This makes it sound like he is engaged in some kind of curious legal ceremony: dissolving a marriage by taking an afternoon nap. But J.R. has done all that he can do. The matter is now in the hands of the lawyers, and J.R. awaits the judgment of the court. There is no reason he need be rushing about, huffing and puffing, expending energy, moving his limbs, or moving *anything*, in order to be doing what these words describe him as doing. He had to initiate proceedings, of course; but now that he has done that, he awaits a certain result—a result that, when it occurs, will mean that he has divorced Sue Ellen and that will furthermore mean that during this interval, including the time he spent on the couch, he was divorcing her but hadn't yet divorced her. The same is true of publishing a book (waiting for someone else to print it), selling a house (waiting for the realtors to close the deal), fixing an appliance (waiting for the glue to dry or the solder to harden), and many other acts in which there is a substantial delay between

---

11. Donald Davidson (1963, 1967, 1971) identifies all action with what he calls primitive action: action involving bodily movement of some sort. So, for example, hitting the bull's eye is no more than doing something that causes the bull's eye to be hit (Davidson 1980, p. 21). In reaching this kind of position, Davidson uses the principle (1980, p. 58) that doing something (shooting someone, throwing a dart) that causes X (a death, a bull's eye to be hit) is identical with causing X (killing someone, hitting the bull's eye). I do not think a cause of X is the same thing as a causing of X. The former is typically over before X occurs; the latter cannot exist until X occurs.

one's active contribution and the result whose occurrence makes the activity the activity it is.

There is, to be sure, an unmistakable air of paradox attending certain descriptions of such behavior. Normally we avoid the present progressive tense in such cases—especially when there is a long delay between initiating and consummatory events and when the agent is, during this interval, engaged in other pursuits. It is sometimes hard to know what to say during this interval. How shall we describe the assassin after he shoots his victim and before the victim dies? Often this interval is very short, so we don't really confront a problem about what to say, but there is, nevertheless, always an interval about which such questions can be raised. Shall we really say that during this interval the assassin *is killing* his victim? That doesn't sound right—not if the assassin is no longer engaged in activities designed to bring about his victim's death. But can we say that he *has* killed his victim?[12] Surely not yet. That he *will* kill him? That, too, sounds wrong; it makes it sound as if the assassin *will do* something—something else, that is—that will result in his victim's death. But he has already shot him. There is nothing more for him to do but *wait* for his victim to die. When his victim dies he *will have killed* him, but until he dies there seems to be no convenient way to describe the behavior that will later be describable as a killing. To make matters worse, we can imagine the assassin, with a change of heart, actually trying to *save* the life of his dying victim.[13] Should these efforts prove futile, he will have killed the person; but does this allow us to say that the assassin is killing his victim as he applies bandages and calls an ambulance? Surely he is not killing him *by* applying bandages and calling the ambulance. By what, then, is he killing him?

Analogous "paradoxes" are familiar in the philosophy of perception. Normally, the things we see are close enough so that, given the speed of light, there is little chance for something dramatic to happen between the time light leaves the object and the time it stimulates our visual receptors. But when we think of the moon, the sun, and the stars, puzzles arise. Suppose a distant star was emitting light up to the time of its destruction. Eight years later this light reaches earth and stimulates an observer's retinal cells. He says, as a result, that he sees a star. But how could he see a star? The star from which this light came no longer exists. It ceased to exist eight years ago. How can one see what no longer exists? How can one see into the past?

Here, once again, there is a causal relationship (between an object's

12. This is a result that appears to follow from theories that identify the killing with the bodily movements (e.g., the shooting) that result in death. See Davis 1979 for a balanced discussion of various attempts to cope with these unpalatable consequences.
13. My thanks to Angus Menuge for this dramatic way of putting the problem.

emission or reflection of light and its effect on some sensory system)—a relationship whose consummation, as it were, takes an unusually long time (at least in comparison with most of the things we see). This gives the philosopher time to imagine all manner of strange things happening for which we, given our ordinary ways of describing things, are unprepared. Linguistic choices have to be made. Strange things have to be said. Either we must say that we *do* see into the past, in the sense of seeing something that hasn't existed for eight years, or we must say (also contrary to common sense) that we really can't see the sun, the moon, and the stars. Take your choice. One is going to end up talking funny, like a philosopher, no matter which choice one makes.

When we turn from input to output, we find the same problem, or a similar one. The problem is the same, or similar, because behavior, like perception, is a causal *process* whose completion can take a very long time. And when it *does* take a long time, we can imagine things occurring that disrupt our natural ways of describing things. Turning on the lights normally occurs in a twinkling. You really don't have time to do anything else after you flip the switch and before the lights go on. But locate the bulb on Neptune and the switch on earth. Now you have time to go to bed *after* you flip the switch and *before* the lights go on. Are you turning on the lights while snoring in bed? What if you die before the lights go on. Are you turning the lights on after you die? Can dead people do things? But if you didn't turn the lights on, who did? Science fiction fans will have no trouble imagining a story of the same kind being told about a basic act. A giant squid, a malevolent mutant bent on conquering the universe, has tentacles stretching from Earth to Neptune. Is this monster doing something, grasping Neptune in its tentacles, *after* Earthlings kill it?

These puzzles can easily be multiplied, because behavior, consisting as it does of one thing's causing another, spans a temporal interval, the interval between the cause and its effect. To identify behavior with a temporally extended process, with one thing's causing another, is not to say that behavior isn't datable, that it doesn't occur *at a time*. Certainly it does. I turned on the lights at 7:00 P.M., called my brother at 7:15, and watched TV for the rest of the evening. But behavior, like any protracted event, condition, or process, is no more precisely datable than its (temporal) extremities permit. The picnic (game, battle, ceremony, etc.) took place on July 4 but not *at* 3:00 P.M. It was *in progress* at 3:00 P.M., but it went on all day. Understood as something J.R. did (and not as something that happened to him or as something the court did—granting him a divorce), J.R. divorced Sue Ellen in 1979. That is about as specific as one can get about *when* he did it, *when* this behavior occurred. He filed the papers in January, of course, and the divorce was awarded in December (while he was vacationing in Mexico). J.R. was, as we sometimes say, *in the process* of divorcing her in January, in March, and in December, but he didn't divorce her *in* any of those months. The temporal coordinates we use to locate behavior must have a "thickness" commensurate with the temporal spread of the behavior being located.

If we observe this simple constraint, we can take some of the sting out of the objections described above. The assassin killed his victim in March—to be more precise, in the first week of March 1974. Given a delayed death, though, there is no day (much less an hour, a minute, or a second) of that week on or at which he killed him. To insist that there must be is as silly as insisting that because events and behavior occur *in places*, there always be some perfectly precise place where they occur. Oswald shot Kennedy in Dallas. Perhaps we can be more precise about the place in Dallas where this occurred. But this place must be large enough to encompass both actors in this drama—both Oswald and Kennedy. So this place is, of necessity, much larger than a breadbox. It is certainly larger than the room from which Oswald fired the fatal shots or the hospital in which Kennedy died. For the same reasons, the *times* at which we do things are, often enough, larger than the minutes, hours, and days on which occur the events (the shootings, the deaths, the movements) that such behavior encompasses. Since this is so, there are necessarily times (just as there are places) at which it doesn't make sense to locate behavior—to say of the behavior that *it* is occurring *now* or *here*. To ask whether Oswald was killing Kennedy after he shot him but before Kennedy died is like asking whether he killed him in the room from which he shot him. This time (a time that is shorter than the interval between the shooting and the dying) and this place are just too small to contain the behavior. We need times and places that are suitably large to *overlap* the constituents of the actions and processes ("scattered events," as R. A. Sorensen [1985] calls them) that we are locating at a time and a place.

Behavior, then, is to be identified with a complex causal process, a structure wherein certain internal conditions or events (C) produce certain external movements or changes (M). If M itself brings about some further event or condition, N, then, assuming the transitivity of the causal relation, C's causing N is also behavior. The rat not only moves its paw; it also presses the lever, releases a mechanism, and awakens the lab assistant. It does so because C produces not only M but also (through M) more remote events and conditions (movement of the lever, release of the mechanism, awakening of the lab assistant).[14] No matter how remote the effect may be (there is, in principle, no limit to how remote it might be), though, the behavior is being identified not with the internal cause (C) and not with the

14. The nested structure of these behaviors will be examined more fully in chapter 2.

effect—proximal (*M*) or remote (*N*)—but with a temporally more extended process: the one thing's *causing* the other.

1.5 The Primary Cause of Change

I have so far been doing a lot of pretending. I pretended that the distinction between external and internal was clear and precise. I also pretended that every movement or change had a *single* isolable cause—that if *C* caused *M*, there were no other supporting conditions that were equally involved in (and necessary to) this effect. Furthermore, I ignored the fact that causes themselves have causes. If *C* causes *M* and *B* causes *C*, is *B* or *C* (or neither, or both) *the* cause of *M*?

Though in ordinary affairs we speak of *the* cause of an event, there are obviously many factors involved in (in the sense of being necessary to) the production of any effect. Bodily movements are no different. How is one to say which of the many conditions on which an event depends, and without which it would not have occurred, is its cause? When Bonnie gets hit by a truck, we think of this as something that happens to Bonnie, not as something she does. But surely part of the cause of the collision, or at least a necessary condition for its occurrence, was Bonnie's *being* on that street corner at that precise time. And *that* fact, the fact that she was there, is presumably the result of internal causes—earlier choices and decisions by Bonnie.

There is, furthermore, no hard and fast line separating internal from external causes. Even if every event has, *for any given time*, some unique cause, internal (and external) causes themselves have causes. Hence, by tracing the causal sequence far enough back in time, one can, sooner or later, find external causes for *every* change or bodily movement. Which link in the causal sequence is to be designated as *the* cause of movement? We think of the vacuum cleaner as picking up the dust because *it* generates the vacuum that causes dust to be forced into it. In some vague sense of primary, the *primary* cause (of dust removal) lies in it. But, as we all know, a vacuum isn't created unless the motor is running, and the motor won't run unless electricity is flowing. And that doesn't happen unless the machine is plugged in, and the switch turned on, something *we* do. So who or what is the cause of dust removal? Perhaps we should concede to electrical power companies the validity of their boast that *they*, or their generating equipment, cook our eggs, turn on our lights, clean our house, and wake us in the morning.

A similar story could be told about a rat pressing a bar and a person waving to an old friend: the appearance of a certain stimulus—a red light for the rat, an old friend for the person—causes limb movement in each case. An old friend appears around the corner, the person sees and recog-

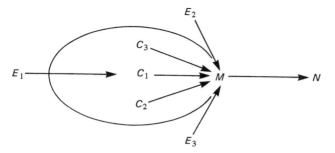

Figure 1.2

nizes him, and as a result the arm is raised in greeting. Why isn't the appearance of the old friend the cause of this arm movement? With simple reflexes there may be only a single synaptic connection between stimulus and response. Why designate the internal event as the cause, as we do in classifying the response as behavior, and not the immediately preceding *external* stimulus? But if the external stimulus is identified as *the* cause of bodily movement, then (on the present account of things) we don't *do* anything.

A more realistic (but still oversimplified) diagram for the causal production of bodily movement would look like figure 1.2. The movements M (and, hence, the more remote effects N) are dependent on a variety of internal (C) and external (E) circumstances. Suppose, for instance, that M is the lordosis reflex—the posture (a rigid, downward-arched back) a female cat adopts when approached by a male during estrus. E_1 is the approaching male; C_1 is the event occurring in the female's visual cortex produced by the approaching male. The female cat doesn't assume this posture all the time (though pet owners may wonder about this)—only, let us say, when it sights a male. C_2 and C_3 are various other hormonal and neurological events that are necessary to the production of M. It is known, for example, that M is dependent on high levels of estradiol in the female's bloodstream. Without this hormone, the female will not be receptive to the male and may even turn aggressive. E_2 and E_3 are various *external* physical factors or conditions influencing the occurrence of M: the medium *in which* the movement occurs, the obstacles in the way of its occurrence, and so forth. If the cat is ear-deep in water or the temperature is close to absolute zero, M isn't likely to occur no matter what favorable internal conditions exist.

So what, exactly, is to be designated as the cause of M, the posture of the female cat? The approach or proximity of the male? Her perception of the male? The female's hormonal state? The fact that she is not ear-deep in water (or concrete)? The fact that the temperature is in a normal range? Unless there is a principled way of saying which causal factor is to be taken as *the* cause of movement or orientation, the present system of classification provides no principled way of saying whether the cat is *doing* anything. It gives us no way of telling what is, and what isn't, behavior.

There is, finally, one further troublesome complication before we try to pull things together. There is a problem, already noted in passing, about distinguishing things a system (whether it be an animal, a plant, or a machine) does from things its parts or components do. Neurophysiologists speak of the behavior of the individual neurons in our nervous system. There is, I hope, no particular problem about distinguishing their behavior from our behavior (although with very simple organisms this might be a problem). But with larger parts there may be a question. Sherrington (1906) describes the way a fly, settling on a dog's ear, is reflexively flung off *by the ear* (my italics). Is this something the ear does, or something the dog does? Or perhaps both? Shall we count the pathological tremors of someone with Parkinson's disease as *human* behavior or, say, *hand* behavior? Our eyes execute periodic jerky movements (saccades). Is this something our eyes do, or something we do? If the heart, not the person, is credited with circulating the blood, why aren't the lungs, not the person, credited with inhaling and exhaling? Many lizards and snakes twitch their tails to distract predators. Some have evolved a tail with a very fragile connection to the rest of the body; under attack the tail breaks off and continues to thrash wildly on the ground, keeping the predator's attention as the lizard escapes (Greene 1973). Who, or what, is to receive credit for this behavior?

I have nothing particularly original to say about how one identifies *the* cause of something from among the many events and conditions on which it depends. It seems fairly clear that this selection is often responsive to the purposes and interests of the one doing the describing. What one person describes as the cause of an accident (e.g., wet pavement) another may think of as merely a contributory condition—*the* cause being the speed of the vehicle or the negligence of the driver. Kathy is overweight. Is the cause of this condition her caloric intake (the fact that she eats too much), or her diminished caloric output (the fact that she doesn't exercise enough)? Which is the cause may well depend on whether it is Kathy giving excuses or someone else apportioning blame. This is merely to say that what is selected as the cause is often the event or condition on which the effect depends (without which the effect would not have occurred) which is, *for one reason or another*, taken to be of primary interest to those doing the describing or explaining. Causal conditions may be out there in the world, independent of our purposes and interests, but something's status as *the* cause is, it seems, in the eye of the beholder.

Fortunately, this arbitrariness in the specification of causes (if that is, indeed, what it is) does not really matter. At least it doesn't matter to me. The important point, for my purposes, is this: *if* something is classified as the behavior of S, then certain movements, changes, or conditions of S are being classified as the result of events occurring *in* S. Something happening *in* S is, for whatever reason, being picked out as the contributory cause of special salience, interest, or relevance—as *the* cause of whatever external movement, change, or condition is associated with the behavior. And this internal event's *causing* this movement, change, or condition (*not* the movement, change, or condition it causes) is being identified with S's behavior. Whatever arbitrariness or context sensitivity there is in the identification of an event's cause will reappear in the identitication of behavior. It will, for example, reappear in disagreements about whether something happened to S (e.g., someone knocked him down) or whether he did something (e.g., collapsed or fell down). It will also reappear in disagreements about whether it was S that did something (flung the fly off its ear) or some part of S (the ear) that did this.[15]

I have no philosophical interest in playing umpire in these disputes, no interest in trying to decide specific questions about what is and what isn't behavior. My interest centers on what it is that one is identifying something *as* when, and if, one identifies it as behavior. It may be arbitrary whether something should be classified as behavior or not, but not at all arbitrary that, once so classified, it is a causal process of the sort described in the preceding section. The project is to understand how behavior is to be explained, and, specifically, how it is, or how it *can* be, explained by reasons. For this purpose it is not essential that, for every *X*, we agree about whether *X* is an apple or an orange; it is enough if we can agree about what *X* must be *if* it is an apple.

It is not always clear how to classify things. Should we say that Clyde moved himself from here to there (behavior), or was he moved (something done to him)? Our uncertainty about what to say reflects an uncertainty about identifying the cause of movement. Suppose Clyde sits motionless in a vehicle as it moves from Madison to Chicago. Is Clyde's movement from Madison to Chicago to be classified as Clyde behavior, as something Clyde is doing, as it clearly is when we describe Clyde as going, traveling, or driving from Madison to Chicago? Or is it something that is happening to

---

15. There are additional complications when we try to distinguish between the behavior of a system and the behavior of its parts. A lot depends on the way we describe the behavior (obviously the dog's ear doesn't fling the fly from *its* ear). It should also be emphasized that there is nothing to prevent certain movements or changes being the result of behavior by *both* the system and its parts. Quite the contrary. Internal (to the system) causes will also be internal to some component or organ of the system and, therefore, capable of constituting not only system behavior but also component behavior. In moving my arm, my brain, nerves, glands, and muscles *do* a great many things. *My* behavior is generated by the behavior—generally quite *different* behavior—of my parts. I exhale; my lungs expel air. I cry; my tear ducts produce tears.

him, as is implied by saying that he is being taken, carried, or conveyed from Madison to Chicago? For most purposes it doesn't make much difference how we classify Clyde's movements. This will depend, as specifying *the* cause of something always does depend, on the interests and purposes of those doing the describing. The vehicle's movement is, of course, the immediate cause of Clyde's movement. We can, nonetheless, classify this as something *Clyde* is doing if we can find, within Clyde, either a cause of the vehicle's movement (he keeps the accelerator pedal depressed) or a cause of his being *on* or *in* the vehicle whose movement he shares (he bought a ticket and boarded). In the first case he is *driving* to Chicago; in the second he is *taking* the bus to Chicago. In each case he is *doing* something. In this case we think of the cause of his getting to Chicago as residing in him, and we think of the vehicle as an instrument, like a hammer for pounding nails or a key for opening doors, that enables him to do this. If Clyde was knocked unconscious and tossed into a baggage car, he might *be on his way* to Chicago, but this wouldn't be something he was doing. It is for this reason that, as I am a passenger on the planet Earth, my ceaseless orbiting of the sun is something that happens to me, not something I do. I don't have a foot on an accelerator, I didn't buy a ticket, and I can't get off.

Our classification of reflexes illustrates this principle. Despite their involuntary nature, and despite the fact that we sometimes classify a response as the behavior of some bodily part (the *leg's* response to a light tap on the knee), we often classify reflexes as behavior. We do so because the reaction to a stimulus, although perfectly reliable, is quite unlike the body's Newtonian response to a shove (where acceleration is proportional to net impressed force). The reflexive behavior exhibits a change in form, direction, or magnitude. If one lightly touches a dog's back, the dog's leg executes a vigorous sequence of circular motions. Neurologists speak of the *gain* of the deep tendon (knee jerk) reflex, a variation in the *strength* of this response that is regulated from within (by the motor cortex). As Sherrington (1906, p. 5) observed, the stimulus acts like a "releasing force" on the organism in the sense that the energy expended in the response far exceeds the energy provided by the eliciting stimulus. Such responses remind one of a vacuum cleaner springing into action, sucking in air and dust, at the merest flick of its switch, or of a computer, after a touch on a key, transforming huge amounts of text in some systematic way. Obviously internal processes, drawing upon their own power supply, are at work, transforming the input into the output. Since internal processes are obviously at work, they *can*, depending on our interests and purposes, be given credit for causing the output. The activity *can* therefore be classified as the result of internal processes: *the dog* is scratching, *the vacuum cleaner* is sucking in air and dust, and *the computer* is renumbering footnotes. Even simple organisms (plants, single-celled animals) that reflexively *withdraw* from a touch or from light will be, or *can* be, credited with doing something if the response exhibits any dependence on internal processes. Perhaps, unlike one's response to a shove, a slight *delay* in the reaction will be enough to exhibit the dependence of the reaction on internal mechanisms. Internal events will then be causally relevant to the movement. Since they are causally relevant, they can, depending on our interests and purposes, be deemed the cause of movement. We can, therefore, credit the system with behavior, with *doing* something.

For a similar reason, getting sunburned can be classified as something that Amy does, not just as an unfortunate thing that happened to her. It is possible to classify it as behavior if the cause of burned skin lies in the person whose skin is burned. Of course, *the sun* is the proximate cause of Amy's burned skin. But, like catching a train to Chicago, if choices and decisions lying within Amy caused her to *be* where the sun (the train) could affect her in this way, then these internal factors can be given credit—remote but nonetheless *primary* credit—for the effect. As long as the outcome *can* be classified as the effect of internal causes, the production of this effect *can* be classified as behavior. In this respect, getting sunburned is no different from warming one's hands by a fire. The fire warms the hands, but internal factors cause the hands to be where the fire warms them. So *you* end up doing something: warming your hands by the fire.

This is *not* to say that such things *must* be classified as behavior, only that they *can* be. Even when Amy had no relevant intention, one *could* regard her getting sunburned as a piece of careless or irresponsible behavior. To regard it as behavior is, as already argued, to classify the result (burned skin) as the result of internal events and conditions. It is, furthermore, to stop speaking of the result (M) that was caused in this way and to start speaking of the process ($C \rightarrow M$) that brought it about. Often, however, there is no reason to classify things in this way. In most normal circumstances it would be most natural to classify it as something that happened to Amy *while* swimming, not as something she did *in* swimming (like frightening the fish or getting her hair wet). Though her decision to stay out swimming an extra hour was a contributory cause of her skin's being burned, it would be treated, like a decision to visit a place *where* one contracted a disease or got hit by a truck, as, at best, a contributory cause, and not as the primary cause of the result.[16]

16. Thalberg (1972, pp. 45—47) despairs of making the distinction between behavior (or actions) and things that happen to one on causal grounds. He points out, correctly, that one often makes a causal contribution to the things that happen to one: a politician campaigns hard (something he does) to get elected (something that happens to him); a skier, by reckless behavior, sets off an avalanche that sweeps him away. These are nice examples, but they do not show that behavior is not to be distinguished from things that happen to one on causal

1.6 Facets of Behavior

In an effort to suggest the enormous variety and diversity of animal and human (not to mention plant and machine) behavior, I have tried to give examples that were representative of the entire spectrum. It is worth emphasizing, though, if only for the record, that many things that pass as animal and human behaviors are structured sequences of more elementary behaviors. Everyday human activities like shopping, driving to work, and reading a paper can be analyzed, almost endlessly, into simpler behavioral components. And, of course, animals have their own richly textured behaviors—a beaver building a dam, a male grasshopper courting a female, a salmon returning upriver to spawn, and so on. If the analytical magnification is turned up enough, even such apparently simple human maneuvers as picking up a pencil can be made to exhibit behavioral components (reaching, grasping), each with its own control structure (Jeannerod 1981).

I will, when examining the way reasons figure in the explanation of behavior, return to this important point. For the moment I merely acknowledge that most of the things we describe ourselves as doing exhibit this internal complexity. How it affects the explanation of *why* we do what we do will become apparent later.

I have, for convenience of exposition, always spoken of behavior as involving movement of some kind. Although movement often occurs, it is clearly not necessary. Hatching eggs is a perfectly respectable form of bird behavior that doesn't require movement. The fact that a bird moves, and, given its physiology, cannot avoid moving during this period is irrelevant. The point is that such movements are not logically *required* for the hatching of eggs. Standing erect (something my mother nagged me to do), guarding, resting, sitting, sleeping, hiding, hibernating, holding, waiting, watching, listening, and blushing are all things we do that do not *necessarily* (although they always do in fact) involve bodily movement. It turns out that, as a matter of fact, one cannot *watch* something, even a stationary object, without some movement of the eyes. Without periodic eye movement (saccades), a peculiar blindness, produced by a "stabilized image" on the retina, occurs and *nothing* is seen (hence, nothing is watched). Once again, this is irrelevant. It is merely a fact about the mechanisms we use to watch things. Maybe extraterrestrials, with quite different visual receptors, watch things without moving their eyes.

Acknowledging that movement is not necessary to behavior does not require us to change anything. We simply note that *M* in figures 1 and 2

---

grounds. They only reflect the arbitrariness in specifying the cause of something. If getting oneself elected by distributing bribes is something people *do* (unsavory behavior, as we like to say), then getting oneself elected by campaigning hard is also something one can do.

can stand for things other than bodily movements. It might be a change in color, temperature, or pressure, changes which may require movements at the molecular level but not what we ordinarily think of as movements of the animal. M can even stand for the *absence* of movement. *Non*-movement also has its causes, and when the cause is internal, the person is standing still, holding her breath, waiting, resting, pointing, aiming, watching, hiding, or whatever. If, on the other hand, the primary cause of non-movement is external, then no behavior is occurring. If Blackie is buried in concrete, his arms and legs are prevented from moving by external, not internal, causes.

For this reason it is important to distinguish between C's not causing M and C's causing not-M. The latter is behavior because the external condition, in this case the absence of movement, has an internal cause. An animal "freezing" in response to an electric shock, a chicken or a possum playing dead in response to capture by a predator, and the constant muscular adjustments occurring in vertebrates to *maintain* (i.e., *not* change) *posture* or to aim a gun are all instances of internal mechanisms *causing* the body *not* to move. As Gallistel (1980, p. 304), citing the work of Gallup (1974) on the "playing dead" behavior of chickens, puts it: "It cannot be too strongly emphasized that playing dead is a behavior! ... [It] involves strongly *de*potentiating the entire motor system [i.e., causing the body to go limp—F. D.] in response to capture." Such behavior is to be contrasted with states (such as paralysis, coma, trance, and death) in which internal processes and mechanisms, like those in the behaviors described above, do *not* cause movements, but, *unlike* the behaviors described above, are not regarded as active maintainers of no movement. Hence, these latter forms of immobility do not qualify as behavior. Though no movement occurs in either case, there is obviously an enormous difference between a balanced innervation of agonist and antagonist muscles and no innervation of these muscles at all. This contrast is the same as that we find in a machine with an automatic mechanism for temporarily shutting off its motors when they overheat. If the machine is never switched on, its motors don't run. Nothing happens. It doesn't do anything. If, on the other hand, nothing is happening *because* the motors overheated, because the motors were turned off *until* they cooled enough to resume operation, then the machine is properly described as doing something: *waiting* for its motors to cool.

There is another feature of behavior that I have so far neglected, one whose discussion should remove some of the artificiality that has so far characterized my treatment. Behavior, as we have seen, is the *production* of some effect by some internal cause. An effect, however, has many *aspects* or *facets*. A movement, for example, has a direction, a strength, an accuracy (in the case of aimed movements), and a speed. It occurs at a time and at a place. It starts here and ends there. If the movement has a cyclical pattern, as does the dance of a honeybee, we may be interested in its frequency, its amplitude, or its phase relationships to other movements. If the movement is a peck at a key, we may be interested in the force of the peck or its latency (how long it took the peck to occur after stimulus onset). If the movement is the movement of a goose's head (in rolling an egg back to its nest, for example), we may want to explain different components of this movement. These are what I shall call different *facets* of the behavior, but there is an important sense in which they are all really different behaviors. I say they are all really different behaviors because each facet can, and often does, have different internal causes. Hence, there is a *different* $C \rightarrow M$ process for each different facet of M. My tug on the steering wheel of my car, for instance, doesn't cause my car to move, much less to move at 63 mph. Rather, it causes the 63-mph movement to be in *that* direction. My heavy foot is responsible for the speed, the dirty carburetor for the intermittent pauses, and the potholes in the road for the teeth-jarring vertical component of the movement. It would be foolish to treat the movement of the car as a single entity in need of a single explanation. There are, or may be, as many explanations for the movement as there are distinguishable properties or facets of the movement.[17]

Since behavior is being identified with one thing's causing another, we have, potentially at least, a different behavior for each aspect of the internally produced effect. Or, if one doesn't like thinking of these different aspects of behavior as different behaviors, one must at least acknowledge, when the business at hand is explanation, that there may be a variety of different things to explain about any given piece of behavior. Breathing is one thing; breathing deeply, in a person's ear, and when the person asked you to stop, are all different things and may, accordingly, all have different explanations. A dog may scratch reflexively, but it scratches here, rather than there, with a purpose and for a reason.

A chimpanzee goes from here to there to fetch a banana. Even if there is an unobstructed path straight to the banana, young animals will often take a more devious route to reach the food. Like most vertebrates, they are cautious of open places and prefer a path that keeps them near vertical structures (Menzel 1978, p. 380). There may be an explanation for why the animal went from here to there and an explanation for why it took the particular path it did in getting there, but these will not be the same explanation. There is no reason they should be. These are different behaviors, or at least distinguishable aspects (what I am calling different

17. This is nicely illustrated in Lorenz and Tinbergen's (1938; cited in Lehrman 1953, p. 340) demonstration that, in the movements of a goose's head in rolling an egg back to the nest, the stimuli that guide and release the sagittal movements are not the same as those for the side-to-side movements. One movement is instinctive, the other a taxis (under the control of visual feedback).

facets) of the same behavior. Explaining why internal event C produced a movement with property A is not the same as explaining why C produced a movement with property B even if both C and the movement are the same.

For exactly this reason—i.e., that they may require quite different explanations—we want to distinguish between *when* birds start to migrate (this may be instinctive) and *when* (and therefore *where*) they stop migrating (this may, at least in the case of adult birds, be learned),[18] between (Grier 1984, p. 166) defecation *now* (involuntary) and defecation *here* (voluntary), and between (Rachelin 1976, p. 113) how *long* a rat licks (modifiable by learning) and how *fast* a rat licks (relatively fixed by genetic factors). This, too, is why we want to distinguish between talking and talking *loudly* (Goldman 1970).

For my purposes, it isn't particularly important whether we think of these different facets of behavior as merely different components of some single piece of behavior or as different behaviors. What is important is that we recognize that there are, potentially at least, *different* things to be explained. For unless one appreciates this fact, the role of *reasons* in the explanation of behavior, a role that I hope to make clearer in subsequent chapters, will remain obscure. Behavioral scientists are fond of pointing out that most, perhaps all, behavior is a mixture of many factors. The old nature-nurture dichotomy is too simple. Behavior is the product of a dynamic interaction between genetic and environmental influences. The innate and instinctive is inextricably intertwined with the learned and the acquired (Gould and Marler 1987), and this is sometimes so, as Mazur (1986, p. 36) notes, because many learned behaviors are derivatives, extensions, and variations of innate behaviors. Furthermore, experience is typically necessary to elicit, and sometimes to shape, genetically determined patterns of behavior. Even behavior that is under the control of a single gene (the cell-uncapping behavior of worker bees, for instance) is triggered—and hence partially determined—by the perception of cells containing diseased pupae (Rothenbuhler 1964). Hence, whether the behavior has a genetic explanation or a cognitive explanation depends on what *facet* of the behavior is being explained: *when* it is done, *where* it is done, or *how* it is done.

It may not always be easy (or possible) to tease apart these different facets of behavior (Sober 1987). Rats, for example, seem genetically disposed to a win-shift strategy in foraging for food (Olton 1978). If they find

---

18. See Gwinner 1986. For the same reason, we want to distinguish between flight in response to an alarm call, a fixed action pattern in many animals that herd or flock together, and the *direction* of the (instinctive) flight, something that is determined by cognitive factors (the perceived position of the predator).

food at one place, they will normally continue their search elsewhere. Rats trained on an eight-arm radial maze quickly learn to apply this strategy, but their application requires them to *remember* which arms of the maze they had already visited. A rat's selection of an arm to explore has, therefore, a peculiar mixture of phylogenetic and ontogenetic determinants. The shift to a different arm of the maze is explained partly by the innate strategy and partly by the cognitive factors that enable the rat to implement this strategy, to identify an arm of the maze as *different*. Rather than try to tease apart these different strands in the animal's behavior, it is sometimes tempting to throw up one's hands and admit that "every response is determined not only by the stimuli or stimulating objects, but also by the total environmental context, the status of anatomical structures and their functional capacities, the physiological (biochemical and biophysical) conditions, and the developmental history up to that stage" (Kuo 1970, p. 189).

There are, nonetheless, behaviors in which one or the other of these factors dominate. Or there are behaviors in which we can isolate, for separate attention, some single facet of a larger behavioral package. After all, reasons—what a creature knows and wants, if it knows and wants anything—will surely not explain every aspect of what it is doing. But why shouldn't they explain some aspects of what animals and humans do? When my cat runs from your dog, I see no reason why we shouldn't be able to explain some of this behavior in terms of what the cat knows about its surroundings. After all, the dog is here and the tree is there; surely the cat's knowledge of this fact is relevant to why it runs in a certain direction. Its genes and hormones won't help us explain this aspect of the cat's flight however much they help us to understand why cats are afraid of dogs or why they tend to run in such situations.

Chapter 2

Behavior as Process

Behavior has been identified with the production of external effects by internal causes. In typical cases, these external effects are either bodily movements or the causally more remote results of bodily movements. In either case, the behavior is neither the internal cause nor the external effect. It is the one producing the other—a process, not a product.

As a source of confusion, the process-product ambiguity is overrated. Most processes are easily distinguished from their corresponding products. Writing a book, baking a cake, and cleaning one's room are not likely to be confused with a book, a cake, and a clean room. Though the opportunities for confusion increase when the product is some event, state, or condition—especially when the same word (e.g., decay) is used for both process and product—the differences generally remain obvious enough. Learning Greek, a process, is clearly different from the product, one's consequent knowledge of Greek. Confusing your opponent is easily distinguished from your opponent's confusion (not to mention your confused opponent). But, as we saw in the preceding chapter, when the product is a bodily movement, the production of that movement (the *behavior*) is easily confused with its product (the *movement*).

In this chapter I hope to amplify this conception of behavior, to draw out the implications of viewing it as a process, in preparation for a later attempt to show how behavior, so conceived, is amenable to explanation by reasons.

2.1 Processes

Photosynthesis, digestion, pollination, mitosis, natural selection, and erosion are all processes having products, results, or outcomes whose production *is* the process in question. The process remains incomplete until the product is brought into being, just as a journey remains incomplete until the destination is reached. Until you *get* to Chicago, you haven't *gone* to Chicago. Digestion, for example, is a process in which food is brought into a certain chemical-mechanical state essential for its absorption by the body. The product of the digestive process is food in this assimilable state.

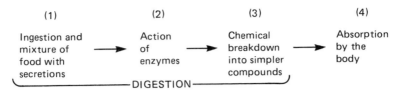

Figure 2.1

Digestion is not itself an event, state, or condition that *causes* food to be in this state. It is, rather, a process *in which* food is brought into this state, a thing which has this product as a *part*. Until this product is produced, until this part exists, *digestion* hasn't occurred. The sequence of events is something like that shown in figure 2.1.

Digestion itself is no single link in this causal chain. It comprises a segment of this causal chain: a process *in* which (3) is brought about—typically (in mammals, at least) by events like (1) and (2). Digestion, though it *begins* before the food is broken down into simpler compounds, isn't something that occurs *before* the food is brought into this state. It is a process that includes (3) as a part, something that cannot (logically) exist until this product exists. It is, therefore, not something that causes (3). The cause of (3) is (1) or (2).

What causes the food to be absorbed by the body is (3), its chemical breakdown into simpler compounds. Since (3) is the cause of (4), we can (and do) speak of the process having (3) as its product, digestion itself, as the cause of (4). Think of a process as a larger (temporal) entity having its product, in this case (3), as its leading edge or front surface. Just as we speak about an object's doing what its parts and surfaces do (changing color or reflecting light, for instance), we speak of processes doing and causing what their leading edges do and cause.

Erosion, for instance, causes whatever its product, barren or eroded soil, causes: spindly corn and poor harvests. For the same reason, we speak of photosynthesis as a process that enables plants to grow, because the products of this process, the sugars and starches, are necessary for plant growth.

A process, as I am now using the term, is not simply a temporally extended entity, a mere succession or sequence of events. Games are events composed of less global events: goals, passes, baskets, moves, fumbles, penalties, and so on. But games are not, in the present sense, processes. The same is true of wars, ceremonies, births, deaths, and plays. Even the simplest movements have temporally distinct phases—an infinite number of them, if Zeno was correct. Processes are something else. Or something *more*. A process is the bringing about, the causing, the production, of a terminal condition, state, or object—what I have so far called, and will continue to call, its product. The product is a *part* of the process, and therefore the process isn't complete until that product is produced. Refining steel is not something that *causes* impurities to be removed from pig iron. It is, rather, a process *in which* these impurities are removed. Until these impurities are removed, the steel hasn't been refined; the process hasn't occurred. The Bessemer Process (named for its inventor, Sir Henry Bessemer) is a particular *way* of refining steel. Impurities are removed by blowing compressed air through molten iron and then removing the oxidized impurities. The Bessemer Process is obviously not the refined steel. That is the product of this process. Neither is it the individual events (e.g., blowing compressed air through the molten iron) by means of which steel is produced. They are the steps *in* a process that has refined steel as its product. The Bessemer Process is, instead, a bringing about of this result *by* those particular steps.

A process stands in relation to the events that compose it in something like the way a marriage stands in relation to the married couple. Two people are married if and only if they stand in the appropriate marital relation to each other, but it would be a mistake to identify *a marriage* with the pair of people who stand in such a relation to each other. Marriages can be legally annulled; people, including people who are married, cannot. A marriage is a more complex entity than a pair of people *who* stand to each other in the marital relation. It is their *standing* to each other in this relation, their *being married*.

And so it is with a process. A process isn't a sequence of events *which* stand in certain causal relations to one another. It is their *standing* in these relations to one another—one event (or two or more events) producing or bringing about another. The causal relation is as much a part of a process, as much a part of what we are talking about when we talk about a process, as is the marital relation in a marriage.

Since behavior is a process, the things I have just said about processes can also be said, and in fact were said in chapter 1, about behavior. Special attention was paid to the distinction between the process and its product, to the difference between behavior and the movements, results, or conditions that partially constitute it. Thinking of behavior as a process is, I think, a helpful way of keeping these differences in mind, and this is why I have made a special point of it in this chapter.

There are, however, ways of talking about behavior that help to obscure this important contrast. The word *output* is a case in point. This word, a favorite among functionalists, invites confusion by making behavior sound like something that comes out of a system.

Think, for example, of the way one might be led to think about human and animal (not to mention plant) behavior if one starts to think about behavior in the way an engineer thinks about output—the output of, say, a power amplifier. Inevitably one begins thinking about behavior as something that is *emitted* or *produced* by a system, something that might come tumbling out of it like a gumball from a vending machine. Behavior, in the case of a computer, becomes more like the answer given than like the giving of it, more like the printout than like the printing. This is not to say that amplifiers don't do things. Of course they do. Among other things, they amplify electrical signals. But if one begins to think of what amplifiers do—of amplifier behavior—as what comes out of the amplifier, as what the amplifier *puts out*, (and what else could amplifier *output* be?), one will think of amplifier behavior as (what else?) the amplified signal. That, after all, is what comes out of the device. In testing and evaluating an amplifier, of course, a technician is naturally interested in this output, in the signal that comes out of the amplifier, since the condition of this signal is an index to whether the amplifier is working satisfactorily. If this signal is too low, then the amplifier isn't doing its job, it isn't amplifying (enough), and adjustments or changes have to be made. These adjustments and changes are a form of behavior modification; they are made *in* (or *to*) the amplifier to make it "behave" better and emit the desired output.

This way of conflating behavior and output does no great harm when one is thinking about amplifiers and their behavior; an engineer is typically interested only in an amplifier's output and in those conditions in the amplifier that are responsible for this output. But if one uses this model to think about human and animal behavior, great harm can be done. One can easily be misled into thinking that the cause of behavior is necessarily the cause of output. And once this confusion is in place, one will have no option but to identify causal explanations of why we *do* the things we do with causal explanations of why our body *moves* the way it does. One will, in other words, have succeeded in confusing psychological explanations of behavior with neurobiological explanations of motor activity. Reasons— our *thinking* this and *wanting* that—will have been robbed of an explanatory job to do. And with no explanatory job to do, reasons—and by this I mean the beliefs, desires, intentions, and purposes that common sense recognizes as reasons—will have been robbed of any scientifically reputable basis for existing.

As I hope to show in the next section, and more fully in later chapters, this is a mistake—a mistake that is made easier by a careless confusion of output with behavior. Thinking about behavior as a process, a process having output as its product, is, if nothing else, a useful way of avoiding this mistake.

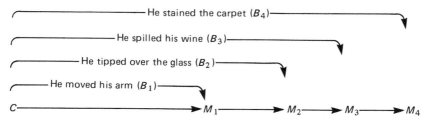

Figure 2.2

2.2 Causes and Effects of Behavior

Suppose Clyde accidentally knocks his wine glass over in reaching for the salt. The glass falls to the carpet, breaks, and leaves an ugly red stain. Clyde has done a number of things: moved his arm, knocked over the wine glass, broken it, spilled the wine, and ruined the carpet. He did all these things—the first intentionally, the others inadvertently. In speaking of these as things Clyde did, we locate the cause of these various events and conditions in Clyde. In each case the effect is different—arm movement, the glass toppling over, its breaking, the wine's spilling, and the carpet's being stained—and hence the behavior, the process having these different events or conditions as its product, is different. But the causal origin, some event or condition in Clyde, is the same.

Clyde moved his arm and he knocked over the glass. Since it was the movement of his arm that upended the glass, we say that he knocked over the glass *by* moving his arm. These facts, though they are facts, should not be misinterpreted. Clyde's moving his arm, this bit of behavior, does not *cause* his arm to move. Nor does this bit of behavior cause another bit of behavior, Clyde's knocking over the glass. Processes (moving your arm) do not cause their products (the movements of your arm), nor do they cause those larger processes (knocking over the glass) in which they are embedded.

To clarify these important points, consider figure 2.2, a diagram of a causal sequence beginning with an event, C, internal to Clyde, proceeding through M_1 (the movement of Clyde's arm) to M_2 (the glass's tipping over) and M_3 (the wine's spilling), and ending with M_4 (the carpet's being stained). Each piece of behavior is nested, Chinese-box-fashion, in its successor: B_1 in B_2, B_2 in B_3, and so on. B_1 (Clyde's moving his arm) doesn't cause B_2 (his knocking over the glass); instead, B_1 is, in a fairly literal sense, *in* B_2. Nor does Clyde's tipping over the glass (B_2) cause the glass to tip over (M_2). M_2 is *a part* of this behavior, not its effect. Killing a person doesn't cause the person to die. It is a causing, not a cause, of death. The poison (or whatever) is the cause of death.

Not only does the whole (the process) not cause its parts (the product); the parts don't cause the whole. As Thalberg (1977, p. 74) puts it, a whole action cannot result from one of its ingredient events. The internal event C (whether or not one thinks of this as some kind of *mental* event—a volition or intention, for instance—is irrelevant) is not the cause of the *behavior* ($C \rightarrow M_i$); it is the cause of that movement or result (M_i) that is the product of the behavior. This is not to deny that beliefs and desires figure in the explanation of behavior. Quite the contrary. As we shall see, it is *what* we believe and desire, the fact that we believe *this* and desire *that*, that explains our behavior by explaining, not why M_i occurs (for M_i isn't the behavior), but *why* C causes M_i.

What makes it true to say that Clyde tipped over the glass (B_2) is that C caused M_2 (the glass to tip over). What makes it true to say that Clyde did this *by* moving his arm (B_1) is that he moved his arm (C caused M_1) and M_1 caused M_2. Since M_1 caused M_2, we speak of the behavior having M_1 as its product—Clyde's moving his arm—as the cause of M_2. Hence, Clyde tipped over the glass *by* moving his arm.

Speaking of behavior is a way of carving out overlapping pieces of a causal chain—in this case, a chain extending from C to M_4. Saying *who* did it is a way of locating the origin of the process, the whereabouts of C. Saying *what* was done describes the nature of the product—what result or condition C managed to bring about. Saying that Clyde stained the carpet, for instance, is to say that some C internal to Clyde caused (by means that are left unspecified) a stained carpet. Saying *how* this was done is a way of identifying the intermediate links in this causal chain: he stained the carpet *by* tipping over his wine.

Philosophers, e.g. Goldman (1970), have long recognized that in saying that a person did one thing *by* doing another we are not giving expression to a causal relation between two bits of behavior. We are, instead, describing a causal relation between behavior and some further result, condition, or event. Clyde's knocking over his wine glass doesn't *cause* him to stain the carpet. Rather, it causes the carpet to be stained.[1] As figure 2.2 should make clear, Clyde's tipping over his wine glass is a part, not a cause, of his staining the carpet—just as his moving his arm (B_1) is a part, not a cause, of

---

1. As Goldman (1970) also notes, causality is not the only way of generating actions. If the circumstances (social, legal, etc.) are such that, in special circumstances, M qualifies as an X, then C's causing M "generates" (to use Goldman's language) the action C's causing X. In this case, neither C's causing M (the process) nor M (its product) causes X. For instance, given the legal arrangements in ancient Greece, and the fact that Xanthippe is married to Socrates, Xanthippe becomes a widow upon the death of Socrates. Hence, anyone who kills Socrates makes Xanthippe a widow and does so *by* killing Socrates. But in this case the "by" is not causal. Neither the behavior (killing Socrates) nor its product (the death of Socrates) *causes* Xanthippe to be a widow.

all the other behaviors (B_2, B_3, and B_4) described in this figure. What Clyde's moving his arm causes is the events, conditions, or results (M_2, M_3, and M_4) that are the *products* of these other behaviors.

In thinking about behavior as a process, as one thing's causing another, then, we can think about the behavior as causing whatever its product causes. If I move my arm, and the movement of my arm frightens a fly, then I frighten the fly *by* moving my arm. And if the movement of my arm causes the destruction of the universe, then I destroy the universe *by* moving my arm. This much seems obvious enough. But what about the causes of behavior? If behavior is a process wherein one thing causes another, the cause of behavior must be the cause of one thing's causing another. Does this make sense? Does it make sense, for instance, to say that something caused C to cause M_1 or caused C to cause M_3?

Although we don't often talk in an open, explicit way about the cause of one thing's causing another, we sometimes do. And we often speak, implicitly, about such causal arrangements. For instance, I arrange for one thing to cause another: I solder a wire here, rather than there, so that the flow of electric current (when it occurs) will cause one thing (a light to go on) rather than another (a bell to ring). I (or, if you prefer, my activities) seem to be the cause of one thing's causing another. One puts yeast in dough so that the bread will rise when put into the oven—so that the heat of the oven will cause the bread to rise. One puts oil on a bearing so that the torque generated by a mainspring will *turn* the wheel (i.e., cause it to move). In each of these cases, and in numerous others like them, an event of type C causes or brings about an event of type E *only in a certain restricted or special set of conditions*. Call these background conditions. If the right background conditions do not obtain, C will not cause E. You can push the button all you like; the bell won't ring unless the wires are connected. Once the wires are connected, pushing the button causes the bell to ring. Properly connected wires are, then, a background condition for one thing (pushing the button) to cause another (the bell to ring). And anything that causes these background conditions to exist—that causes the wires to be connected properly—will be the cause of one thing's causing another.

One can, of course, think of background conditions, as some philosophers like to think of them (see, e.g., Kim 1976), not as the cause of C's causing E but as *part* of the cause of E. On this way of looking at things, properly connected wires do not cause the button's being pushed to cause the bell to ring; rather, they, *together with* the button's being pushed, cause the bell to ring. The cause of E is $C + B$, where B now stands for *all* the background conditions necessary for E upon the occurrence of C.

I see little point in arguing about what the *real*—or, as philosophers used to put it, the *philosophical*—cause of an event is. This seems to be, at best, a terminological issue. We can divide things up as we please. The fact is that in ordinary affairs we seldom, if ever, regard the cause of an event as the *totality* of conditions relevant to the occurrence of the effect. Instead, we pick out some salient part of this totality and designate it as the cause. The remaining conditions are relegated to the background as conditions *in which* the cause produces the effect. These background conditions are typically conditions that have persisted, without change, for some time. Hence, the cause, being some *change*, appears as a figure against their (back)ground. Striking the backspace key on my computer keyboard *makes* the cursor move to the left. The cause of movement is pressure on the backspace key, *not* this event *and* the complete mechanical and electrical condition of the computer. Of course, *if* we change the wiring of the computer, pull the plug, change software, let contacts corrode, and so on, then striking the backspace key will no longer cause the cursor to move. True enough. However, what this shows is not that striking the backspace key *doesn't* cause the cursor to move, but that it doesn't *always* do so. It does so only in certain conditions, only when background conditions are right.

Given this way of understanding background conditions, we can say that either B itself, or certain salient parts of B, or whatever brings about these conditions *in which* C causes E is the cause of C's causing E. Since the heat of the oven won't cause the bread to rise unless there is yeast in the dough, we can say that yeast's being in the dough, or (if we are interested in more remote causes) my putting yeast in the dough, is the cause of the bread's rising when put in the oven. The designers and manufacturers of the computer and its associated software are (among) the causes of cursor movement's being controlled by the backspace key. They are the ones that saw to it that pressure on the backspace key would cause the cursor to move to the left.

If this is right, then the designers, manufacturers, and installers of a thermostat are (among) the causes of its turning the furnace on when it gets too cold in the room. They are the ones who, by proper arrangement of background conditions (wiring, calibration, electrical connection to the furnace, etc.) made the bimetallic strip into a *switch* for the furnace, thereby ensuring that movements of this strip in response to temperature variations in the room would *bring about*, would *cause*, furnace ignition. Since it is their activities that, in this sense, caused C (in the thermostat) to cause M (furnance ignition), it is their activities that caused the thermostat to behave the way it does.

Of course, as we all know, it is the present electrical-mechanical state of the thermostat—its *being* connected to the furnace, its *being* supplied with electricity, and so on—that constitutes the background conditions *in which* one thing (the movement of the bimetal strip) causes another (furnace ignition). These background conditions are, unlike the earlier activities of the manufacturers and installers, cotemporaneous with the causings for which they form the background. This being so, one could designate these conditions themselves, and not the earlier events that brought them about, as the cause of one thing's causing another—as the cause of thermostat behavior. The thermostat's *being* wired to the furnace, *being* supplied with electricity, and so on is *why* it turns the furnace on when the temperature drops. According to this way of looking at things, it is *B*, not the events that produced *B*, that is the cause of *C*'s causing *E*.

If *A* causes *B* and *B* causes *C*, there is no point in arguing about whether it is really *A* or *B* that causes *C*. They are both causes of *C*, and which one is selected as *the* cause of *C* will depend on one's explanatory interests. When background conditions are themselves unusual in some way, or if they are brought about for special purposes or in a special way, or if they have only recently come into being, then we typically look to *their cause* as the cause of *C*'s causing *E*. Not *B*, but the cause of *B*, becomes the cause of *C*'s causing *E*. If, for example, I wire my thermostat to the garage-door opener so that the thermostat opens the garage door whenever the room gets chilly, a mystified observer, told that my thermostat is doing this, can be excused for asking why my thermostat behaves in this unusual way. He will not be satisfied to be told that my thermostat is wired to the garage-door opener, supplied with electricity, and so on. He knows that—or should know it, if he knows anything about the way thermostats work. How else could it do it? No, what he wants to know is not details about the electrical wiring, not details about *current* background conditions, but who or what is responsible (to blame?) for the thermostat's being wired in this bizarre way. What caused current background conditions to be such that events occurring in the thermostat, events that normally bring about furnace ignition, now bring about the opening of the garage door? In asking this question—a question about *current* behavior, a question about why my thermostat *is* opening the garage door—my mystified guest is really asking a question about the past: what *happened*, perhaps yesterday, perhaps earlier, to change the way this thermal switch is wired to various (effector) mechanisms in the house. What past events brought about those present background conditions in which *C* (events occurring in the thermostat) cause M_1 (opening of garage door) instead of M_2 (furnace ignition)?

The thermostat example is meant to be suggestive. It echoes the kind of causal explanation we sometimes find appropriate for plants and animals: a causal explanation in terms of temporally remote factors, factors operating in the distant and sometimes the not-so-distant past. We explain instinctive behavior in terms of the evolutionary history of the species, for example, and we sometimes explain acquired behavior in terms of the earlier learning experiences of the individual. We advert to these earlier events in such explanations because these earlier events are thought to be relevant to *present* background conditions' being what they are, conditions *in which* one thing causes another. We shall take a longer look at some of these explanations in the next section, but for the moment I only point out that an appeal to the past, to the kind of events that enabled earlier plants and animals to flourish and more effectively distribute their seeds (adaptational accounts of instinctive behavior) or to the kind of experiences or learning that enabled an individual to more effectively satisfy his needs, is not a unique or unusual way of explaining behavior. We sometimes explain the behavior of artifacts in the same way.

Since a process has been identified with one thing's causing another, I have assumed up to this point that the cause of a process was either (1) the background conditions that enable the one thing to cause the other or (2) whatever earlier event or condition brought about these background conditions. What causes the thermostat to open the garage door (or turn the furnace on) is either the fact that it is wired to the garage-door opener (or the furnace) or the fact that I, or some electrician, wired it that way. But we sometimes speak of the cause of a process as the event that triggers the process. If we think of the process in question as C's causing M, the cause, in this second way of thinking about the cause, is whatever event causes C. So, for example, if a stimulus S produces C, and if C, in turn, causes M, then S, by triggering the sequence of events composing the process, causes the process to occur. In this second way of thinking about the cause, what caused the thermostat to open the garage door (or turn the furnace on) is the drop in room temperature. The drop in room temperature, by causing certain events to occur *in* the thermostat, events that (in turn) cause the garage door to open (the furnace to ignite), triggered a process (C's causing M) which *is* the thermostat's behavior—its opening the garage door (or turning on the furnace).

Each of these two different ways of thinking about the cause of a process is, in its own way, perfectly legitimate.[2] In looking for the cause of a process, we are sometimes looking for the triggering event: what caused the C *which* caused the M. At other times we are looking for the event or events that *shaped* or *structured* the process: what caused C *to* cause M rather than something else. The first type of cause, the triggering cause, causes the process to occur *now*. The second type of cause, the structuring cause, is responsible for its being *this process*, one having M as its product, that occurs now. This difference, a difference I have elsewhere (1972) described in contrastive terms, is familiar enough in explanatory contexts. There is a clear difference between explaining why, on the one hand, Clyde

---

2. I am indebted to Elliott Sober, Martin Barrett, and Ellery Eells for helpful criticism on this point.

stood up *then* and explaining, on the other hand, why what he did then was stand up (why he *stood up* then). He stood up *then* because that was when the queen entered, or when he saw the queen enter, the room. He *stood up* then as a gesture of respect. The difference between citing the triggering cause of a process (the cause of the C which causes M) and what I have been calling its structuring cause (the cause of C's causing M) reflects this difference.[3]

This difference helps to explain why one can know what caused each event constituting a process without knowing what caused the process. One can know what caused C (some triggering stimulus S), know what caused M (namely C), and still wonder about the cause of C's causing M. In this case, already knowing the triggering cause, one is clearly looking for the structuring cause of the process—what brought about those conditions *in which* C causes M (rather than something else).

Think of one animal's catching sight of another animal and running away. The approach of the second animal (let this be the stimulus S) causes certain events (C) to occur in the first animal's central nervous system: it *sees S*. Together with relevant motivational factors, these perceptual events in the animal bring about certain movements M: the animal *runs*. To oversimplify enormously, S causes C, and C in turn causes M. This much might be inferred from casual observation—the animal ran *when*, and presumably *because*, it saw the intruder. But why did sight of the intruder (C) cause flight (M)? Why did the animal run away? The intruder, after all, was not a predator. It was in no way dangerous. It was, in fact, a familiar neighbor. So why did C cause M? This question is a question about the structuring, not the triggering, cause of the process $C \rightarrow M$.

Consider a different case. A bell rings and a classically conditioned dog behaves the way it was conditioned to behave: it salivates. Perhaps, given the conditioning process, the dog cannot help salivating when it hears the bell. The behavior, though not voluntary, *is* behavior. And we can look for its causes. The bell rings (S), and this produces a certain auditory experience (C) in the dog. The dog *hears* the bell ring. These sensory events, *as a result of conditioning*, cause saliva to be secreted (M) in the dog's mouth. What, then, causes the dog to salivate? Well, in one sense, the ringing bell causes the dog to salivate. At least the bell, by causing the dog to have a certain auditory experience, triggers a process that results in saliva's being secreted into the dog's mouth. Yes, but that doesn't tell us why the dog is doing what it is doing—only why it is doing it *now*. What we want to know is why the dog is salivating. Why isn't it, say, jumping? Other (differently trained) dogs jump when they hear the bell. Some (not trained

---

3. I am grateful to Susan Feagin for calling my attention to this way of describing the difference between triggering and structuring causes.

at all) don't do much of anything. So what causes the dog to salivate? This, clearly, is a request, not for the triggering cause of the dog's behavior, but for the structuring cause. It is a request for the cause of one thing's causing another, the cause of the auditory experience causing salivary glands to secrete. And once again, it seems, the answer to this question lies in the past, in what learning theorists describe as the *contingencies* (correlations between the ringing bell and the arrival of food) to which the dog was exposed during training. If salivation is thought of as something the dog *does* (not simply as a glandular event occurring *to* the dog or *in* the dog)— if, in other words, it is thought of as *behavior*—then the causal explanation for it resides, not in the stimulus that elicits the behavior, but in facts about the dog's past experience.

On the other hand, it is easy enough to imagine the request for a cause, or a causal explanation, of the dog's behavior being a request for the *triggering* cause. One need only imagine a deaf laboratory assistant, someone completely familiar with the dog's training history, asking why the dog is salivating. This person needs to be told something about the triggering cause. He needs to be told that the bell is ringing, and that that is why the dog is salivating.

We shall return to this distinction between triggering and structuring causes. It obviously is an important distinction when one is thinking about the explanation of behavior. It is particularly important when one is thinking about the role of reasons in this explanatory enterprise. But before we turn out attention (finally!) to reasons, to the way beliefs and desires figure in the explanation of some of the behavior of some organisms, it may be worth illustrating some of the points that have emerged so far in connection with the simpler elements of plant and machine behavior. Though such behavior does not involve belief and desire, it nonetheless exhibits, in a particularly revealing way, some of the same distinctions that are operative in our explanations of the intentional behavior of animals.

2.3 Causes of Plant and Machine Behavior

Think, once again, of the difference between a tree's shedding its leaves in winter and its leaves falling off the tree in winter. The first is something the tree does, a piece of tree behavior. The second is the product of this process, an event or condition such that, until it occurs, the tree hasn't shed its leaves. A botanist might know all about the chemical processes occurring in certain broad-leaved trees each autumn, processes that weaken the mechanical bond between leaf and twig by the withdrawal of chlorophyll from the leaf. It may be obvious that such events, together with wind and gravity, cause leaves to fall. Were the botanist to know all this, he or she would then be able to tell us what *makes* the leaves fall at this time each year, what internal sequence of events leads to this autumnal output (M).

The chemical explanation of tree output (M), a description of those mechanisms whose operations *cause* the leaves to fall, is an explanation of *how* trees shed their leaves, not an explanation of *why* they shed their leaves. In specifying the internal cause of M, we do not give the cause, either triggering or structural, of C's causing M. Hence, though we know why M occurred (why the leaves fell), we may not know why C or $C \rightarrow M$ occurred (why the tree shed the leaves). Normally, the triggering cause of such behavior becomes obvious long before the structuring cause is known. The tree sheds its leaves because winter is approaching. We may be uncertain about the exact trigger. Is it an *external* cue, something like lower average temperature or shortened hours of daylight? Or is it instead some internal biological clock that signals seasonal change? Or is it some combination—perhaps an external cue calibrating an internal clock? Whatever it is, exactly, it must be something that is reasonably well correlated with the onset of winter and which, by causing certain internal chemical changes, initiates the leaf-shedding process, a process that culminates in M, the falling of the leaves. Since this is an annual process, we may, on simple inductive grounds, be fairly certain about the triggering cause without having a clear idea about the structuring cause: A prolonged period of cool weather obviously triggers a process having M as its product. But why do trees "respond" in this way to cold weather? After all, coniferous trees are equally sensitive to seasonal changes, but they don't respond to the arrival of winter in the same way. They behave differently. So, why do deciduous trees behave in this way? This, obviously, is a request for a structuring cause of a process that has leaf removal as its product.

There may not always be an explanation for this sort of botanical behavior, just as there isn't always an explanation for human or animal behavior. At least, there sometimes isn't an explanation of the *relevant* structural kind. Some behavior, after all, is merely a by-product of other behavior for which there is an acceptable explanation. Why did Clyde knock his glass over? No reason. No explanation. It was an accident, something he did *in* reaching for the salt. We may be able to explain why he moved his arm—to get the salt—without being able to explain, in terms of his reasons (his purposes and desires), why he knocked over the glass. This is not to say, of course, that we cannot explain why his glass tipped over.

Why do white-tailed deer lift their tails when disturbed by predators? One hypothesis (Alcock 1984, p. 320) is that this behavior has no anti-predator function; it may be merely an incidental effect of physiological changes that occur when an alarmed animal prepares itself for escape. Such behavior, that is, may be incidental to other behavior (flight) that *does* have an anti-predator function and therefore, in this sense, an evolutionary explanation. Although the behavior of a tree in shedding its leaves is probably not like this (having, in fact, a positive adaptive function), there may be other behavior associated with but incidental to leaf removal that cannot be explained in the same way as the tree's leaf-shedding behavior. Suppose, for instance, that a tree's autumnal change in color has no adaptive significance. Suppose, not implausibly, that it occurs as a by-product of leaf removal. The autumnal change in foliage color is then a piece of incidental behavior, incidental to the tree's shedding its leaves, in the way that a person's tipping over his wine glass is incidental to his reaching for the salt and in the way that a deer's raising its tail is (or might be) incidental to its flight. We can explain why Clyde reached for the salt in terms of Clyde's purposes, but we can't explain, in terms of his purposes, why he did what he did (knock over the glass) *in* reaching for the salt. We can explain why the tree is shedding its leaves in terms of the adaptive advantage to be gained by leaf removal, but we cannot explain, in terms of any adaptive advantage, why the tree does what it does (change color) *in* shedding its leaves. And we can perhaps explain why, in terms of adaptive function, deer run from predators without being able to explain, in terms of adaptive function, why they do what they do (raise their tails) *in* running from predators.

On the other hand, some changes in the color of plants have perfectly respectable explanations, the kind of explanation we can give for a tree's shedding its leaves. Some plants (the Scarlet Gilia, for example) change color as their flowering season progresses. Why do they do this? As in the case of leaf removal in maple trees, one must look to the adaptive value of this change in order to understand why the plant behaves this way. In the case of the Scarlet Gilia, at least according to the plausible speculations of Paige and Whitham (1985), the value lies in the plant's attraction of pollinators. Early in the flowering season, hummingbirds are the chief pollinators, and hummingbirds are more attracted to red blossoms. Later in the season the hummingbirds migrate and hawkmoths, preferring whiter blossoms, become the principal pollinator. The flower changes color "in order to" exploit this seasonal alteration in its circumstances. It sets more fruit by changing color, and this is why it does it. If we assume that this is, indeed, the explanation for the Scarlet Gilia's behavior, and if we assume that there is no corresponding explanation for the maple tree's change in color (it being, rather, an incidental accompaniment of the tree's shedding its leaves), we have the plant world's version of the difference between intentional and unintentional behavior in humans and animals—the difference between behavior (reaching) for which we have an explanation in terms of the agent's reasons (*intentionally* reaching for the salt) and behavior for which we have no such explanation (*accidentally* knocking over the wine glass).

Since trees, unlike people, do not have desires, fears, and beliefs, they do not shed their leaves for the sorts of reasons Clyde has for reaching for the salt or Maude has for writing a book. If there is an explanation for this behavior on the part of trees, the explanation will presumably come from evolutionary botany. Something in the history of the species will explain why such processes occur in today's plants. It will have something to do with the *adaptive value* of leaf removal during cold weather. Certain benefits having to do with moisture retention are conferred on trees that lose their leaves in cold, dry weather. *That* is why they shed them. This, of course, is not a causal explanation for why any particular tree sheds its leaves. The maple in my back yard doesn't shed its leaves with the purpose, hope, or intention of conserving moisture. Trees don't have purposes, hopes, and intentions, and therefore they don't do things *in order to* achieve beneficial effects. Instead, they shed their leaves because of the way they are chemically and mechanically constituted, and they are chemically and mechanically constituted the way they are (largely) because of the genes they inherited from the tree that supplied the seeds from which they sprang. That is, trees behave the way they do, not because of (prospective) benefits *they* might enjoy for behaving in this way, but because of the genes they received from ancestors who derived benefits for behaving in (inheritably) similar ways. The explanation of a tree's behavior is the same (in kind) as the explanation of an infant's behavior when it sucks on a nipple and blinks at puffs of air. As we shall see more fully later (chapter 4), evolutionary (or phylogenetic) explanations of behavior, whether the behavior of plants or animals, are best understood, not as supplying structural causes for the behavior of today's plants and animals, but as causal explanations for why there are, today, plants and animals that are structured to behave this way.

I do not mention these botanical examples and analogies (and, I assure the reader, they are intended *only* as analogies) in order to suggest that plants behave in any *psychologically* interesting way, or in order to suggest, by the mention of evolutionary explanations, that an understanding of human or animal behavior will always involve hereditary factors. Some of it doubtless will. Perhaps much of it will. Some ethologists, those behavioral scientists interested in the *biology* of behavior, seem to think *all* of it will. But this is an empirical issue to which I will return in later chapters. My present point is rather that the search for the causes of plant behavior, like the search for the causes of human and animal behavior, is typically a search for something quite different from the causes of output (M). We are, to be sure, sometimes interested in triggering causes, the external events or conditions that set the process in motion and, hence, help to bring about M, the product of that process. But we are more often interested in the structuring cause: what it is that accounts for the direction that process takes once it is set in motion; what it is that accounts for the production of M rather than something else. For the answer to questions of this kind, when the question *has* an answer, we must often look, in the cases of both plants and animals, to the evolutionary history of the species of which the plant or animal is a member. There, in the history of the species, will be found an explanation of why animals were favored in which a process occurred having M as its product.

A leaf falling from a tree is like a rat's paw movement. When a tree sheds its leaves, its leaves fall. When a rat moves its paw, its paw moves. The leaves can fall from the tree, as they sometimes do during a storm, without the tree's shedding them, just as a rat's paw can be moved without the rat's moving it. We can understand what makes the leaves fall from a tree (M), what causes this to happen, without understanding why the tree sheds them—*even when* they fall *because* the tree sheds them. And for the same reason we can understand why a rat's paw moves, what *causes* the paw to move, without understanding why the rat moves it—*even when* the paw moves *because* the rat moves it. We may know enough neurophysiology to know exactly what events occurring in the rat's central nervous system cause its paws to move without knowing what made these cerebral events have *this* effect rather than some other effect or, indeed, no effect (on motor output) at all.

Unlike plants, machines don't evolve. So we can't give phylogenetic explanations of their behavior. And unlike some animals (some of the time), machines don't have purposes for the things they do. So we can't give explanations in terms of their *reasons* for doing as they do. Nonetheless, machines do things, and the things they do, just as the things plants and animals do, must be distinguished from the output they produce in doing these things. Therefore, even in the case of machines, the search for the causes of behavior ($C \rightarrow M$) must be distinguished from the search for causes of output (M). We may know what causes the output without knowing what causes the behavior.

Machines are artifacts, things we design, build, and install with certain *purposes*. We solder the wire here, connect the driveshaft there, put a resistor in the output stage, adjust the bias, and supply electricity *so that* a machine will open the door when someone walks by, compensate for drift in the carrier frequency, or automatically downshift when the load increases. If, in the case of plants, natural selection sees to it that, when circumstances require, *some* internal process produces a needed external change, it is *we* who play this role with artifacts. If M is what is needed ($=$ what *we* need or want) in some special set of circumstances, then, if we are clever enough, *we* see to it that there is a C in some suitably positioned artifact to produce M when these circumstances obtain. In this sense, *we* are

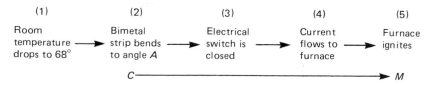

Figure 2.3

the explanation for why the machine does what it does. *We*, by the way we design, manufacture, and install it, cause the machine to do what we want it to do—i.e., *we* cause some C *in* the machine to bring about M in the desired circumstances.

There may seem to be exceptions to this general rule. Consider our example of the thermostat. It turns the furnace on when the temperature gets too low and turns it off again when the temperature reaches the desired (desired by *you*, not the thermostat) level. There isn't much else this device can do. Not a terribly interesting range of behavior, to be sure, but enough to make a point.

Suppose, then, that the room temperature drops to 68° and the thermostat responds, in its dull, predictable way, by turning the furnace on. Notice that by describing things in this way we imply that furnace ignition was caused by some state, condition, or event *in* (or possibly *of*) the thermostat. The thermostat turned the furnace on. This is something it did, and hence is to be classified as thermostat behavior, if some internal state or event C of the thermostat produces furnace ignition. When things are working normally, this is exactly the way things happen. A slowly falling temperature in the room causes a bimetal strip in the thermostat to bend slowly (the degree of curvature of this strip is, in fact, a reliable thermometer, an accurate representation of room temperature). When the bimetal strip bends to a point corresponding to 68°, then, given the initial (desired) temperature setting of 68°, it closes an electrical circuit. Current is sent to the furnace, and the furnace ignites. The causal sequence is illustrated in figure 2.3. Using symbols that should be familiar by now, I have designated (2) as the internal event whose production of M constitutes the thermostat's behavior, its turning the furnace on. This is somewhat arbitrary, of course; we could as easily let (3) = C. The point is that we are talking about thermostat behavior if *some* event, whether it be (2) or (3), in the thermostat causes M, the furnace to ignite.

According to this way of looking at things, the fall in room temperature is the cause of C, that internal event which, via (3) and (4), causes M. Given our earlier terminology, this means that the fall in room temperature is the *triggering cause* of the thermostat's behavior. We have this kind of cause in mind when we describe the thermostat as turning the furnace on *because* the room temperature drops below 68° (the desired setting). As we have seen, however, we are sometimes interested in the structuring cause of behavior, what caused C to produce furnace ignition rather than something else. And the answer to this causal question lies in the activities of those who installed and wired the device. *We* caused the thermostat to turn the furnace on (when it gets too cold) by wiring it to the furnace and supplying it with electricity. We are the ones who designed, manufactured, and installed the device so that (2) would produce (5) and not something else (or nothing at all). By wiring things differently, we could as easily have made the bending bimetal strip (2) cause the dishwasher to go on or the garage door to open. In that case the thermostat would behave differently when it got cold in the room. It would start the dishwasher or open the garage door. But we didn't wire the device in this way. That, obviously, wouldn't have served our purposes. We wanted automatic regulation of room temperature, so we made (2) cause (5). Once again, the answer to the structural question, and therefore an answer to a question about the cause of behavior, lies in the past, in the events or activities that are causally responsible, not for this behavior's occurring *now* rather than at some other time (the triggering cause is responsible for this), but for the fact that *this behavior*, rather than some other, occurs now.

To say that the thermostat turned the furnace on *because* the room temperature dropped to 68° is like saying that the duke stood up *because* the queen entered the room. To say that an object, whether it be a person like the duke or an instrument like a thermostat, did something because of some (cotemporaneous) fact about its external surroundings is to give the triggering cause of the behavior. In the duke's case, the queen's entry into the room caused in him a belief that the queen was entering the room—an internal state that, if things are working right, *represents* the queen's entry into the room. In the thermostat's case, the fall in room temperature brings about an internal condition—a condition that, if things are working right, *represents* the temperature in the room. In both cases this representation is harnessed to a motor control system. In the duke's case it brings him to his feet. In the instrument's case it switches on the furnace. And in both cases we can ask about the structuring cause of this behavior—why the internal representation has *this* effect rather than some other effect; why *this* process rather than some other process is triggered by the external stimulus. When we seek an explanation of behavior in terms of the agent's reasons, we are, I submit, always looking for a structuring cause.

Chapter 3

Representational Systems

Some behavior is the expression of intelligent thought and purpose. Clyde goes to the kitchen because he wants another beer and thinks there is one left in the refrigerator. Whether or not they are *causes* of behavior, Clyde's reasons—his desire for a beer and his belief that there is one in the fridge—are certainly thought to *explain* his behavior. They tell us *why* he made the trip to the kitchen.

This is our ordinary way of explaining behavior (at least, those behaviors we think of as purposeful). It is so familiar, so utterly common-place to all of us, that it is hard to see how there can be a problem with this type of explanation.

There is, nonetheless, a problem in understanding how this familiar pattern of explanation can take—or hold—its place alongside the emerging neuroscientific picture of living organisms. How do, how *can*, thoughts and purposes determine what we do when what we do, at least what our bodies do, seems so completely dependent on, and therefore determined by, those neuronal processes and mechanisms described, in increasingly rich detail, by neurophysiologists? If the neurophysiologists don't invoke thoughts, purposes, intentions, desires, hopes, and fears to explain the behavior of a person's body, what excuse (besides ignorance) do *we* have for appealing to such notions to explain the behavior of the person?

We have already taken the first step toward a better understanding of this apparent conflict. The first step is to understand the difference between a person's behavior and whatever bodily movements and changes constitute this behavior. An understanding of the difference between Clyde's going to the kitchen and the movements that get him to the kitchen is essential to an understanding of why an explanation of the one is not an explanation of the other. Knowing why Clyde went to the kitchen isn't the same as knowing why his legs moved so as to bring him into the kitchen; and knowing the causes of limb movement, at whatever level of biological detail, is not the same as knowing why he went to the kitchen. These are different explanatory games. Our familiar way of explaining purposive behavior in terms of an agent's intentions and beliefs does not *compete* with a neurobiological account of muscular activity and, hence, with a mechanistic account of motor output. It is, rather, an attempt to explain something altogether different: *behavior*, not output.

There is, however, a second step that must be taken. As yet we have no idea of how ordinary explanations, explanations couched in terms of an agent's *reasons*, explain. Since behavior has been identified with a process, with one thing's *causing* another, are reasons supposed to be the cause of one thing's causing another? If so, how is this supposed to work, and what is it about reasons that gives them this peculiar efficacy?

In order to answer these questions, in order to take this second step, it will be necessary to spend some time examining the idea of a representation. For beliefs, normally a prominent part of one's reasons for acting (desire being another prominent part), are special kinds of representations. Beliefs are those representations whose causal role in the production of output is determined by their meaning or content—by *the way* they represent what they represent. The general idea of a representational system is examined in this chapter. The special topic of belief is reserved for chapter 4.

3.1 Conventional Systems of Representation: Type I

By a representational system (RS) I shall mean any system whose function it is to indicate how things stand with respect to some other object, condition, or magnitude. If RS's function is to indicate whether O is in condition A or B, for instance, and the way RS performs this function (*when* it performs it) is by occupying one of two possible states, a (indicating that O is A) and b (indicating that O is B), then a and b are the expressive elements of RS and *what they represent* (about O) is *that* it is A (in the case of a) and *that* it is B (in the case of b).

Depending on the kind of function involved, and on the way a system manages to carry out this function (the way it manages to *indicate*), representational systems can be variously classified. What follows is one possible classification. My chief interest is in *natural* representations (systems of Type III), but the special properties of such systems are best understood by comparing and contrasting them with their conventional (to varying degrees) cousins. So I begin with conventional systems of representation.

Let this dime on the table be Oscar Robertson, let this nickle (heads uppermost) be Kareem Abdul-Jabbar, and let this nickle (tails uppermost) be the opposing center. These pieces of popcorn are the other players, and this glass is the basket. With this bit of stage setting I can now, by moving coins and popcorn around on the table, represent the positions and movements of these players. I can use these objects to describe a basketball play I once witnessed.

If memory fails me, I may end up misrepresenting things. I may move pieces of popcorn here when the players went there. The coins and the popcorn have been assigned a temporary function, the function of *indicating* (by *their* positions and movement) the relative positions and movements of certain players during a particular game. But these elements, the coins and the popcorn, obviously enjoy no intrinsic power to do what they have been assigned the function of doing—*indicating* the positions and the movements of various players in a game long since over. Whatever success they enjoy in the performance of their job obviously derives *from me*, from my memory of the game being represented and my skill in translating that knowledge into the chosen idiom. The popcorn and the coins indicate, and in this sense perform their assigned function, only insofar as *I* am a reliable conduit for information about the situation being represented and a reliable and well-intentioned manipulator of the expressive medium.

The coins and the popcorn do their job, then, only insofar as some *other* indicator system is functioning satisfactorily, only insofar as there is something in the manipulator of these symbols (in this case, something *in me*) that indicates how things stood on the basketball court at the time in question. If I am ignorant of what Oscar and Kareem did with the ball, the coins and the popcorn are unable to perform the function they have been assigned—unable to indicate, by their various positions and movements, what took place on the court that day. This is merely to acknowledge that these objects are, considered by themselves, representationally lifeless. They are merely my representational instruments.

The elements of Type I systems have no *intrinsic* powers of representation—no power that is not derived from us, their creators and users.[1] Both their function (what they, when suitably deployed, are *supposed* to indicate) and their power to perform that function (their success in indicating what it is their function to indicate) are derived from another source: human agents with communicative purposes. Many familiar RSs are like this: maps, diagrams, certain road signs (of the informational variety), prearranged signals, musical notation, gestures, codes, and (to some degree, at least) natural language. I call the representational elements of such systems *symbols*. Symbols are, either explicitly or implicitly, *assigned* indicator functions, functions that they have no intrinsic power to perform. *We*

---

1. That is, no intrinsic power to indicate *what it is their* (*assigned*) *function to indicate*. They may, of course, indicate something *else* in a way that is not dependent on us. For instance, the coins, being metal, indicate (by their volume) the temperature. They *could*, therefore, be used as crude thermometers. But, according to the story I am telling, this isn't their (assigned) function. If it was, then we would be talking about an RS of Type II.

give them their functions, and *we* (when it suits our purposes) see to it that they are *used* in accordance with this function. Such representational systems are, in this sense, *doubly* conventional: *we* give them a job to do, and then *we* do it for them.

3.2 *Natural Signs and Information*

In contrast with the relationship between popcorn and professional basketball players, we don't have to *let* tracks in the snow, bird songs, fingerprints, and cloud formations stand for the things we take them to indicate. There is a sense in which, whether we like it or not, these tracks, prints, songs, and formations indicate what they do quite independent of us, of how we exploit them for investigative purposes, and of whether we even recognize their significance at all. These are what are sometimes called *natural signs*: events and conditions that derive their indicative powers, not (as in the case of symbols) from us, from our *use* of them to indicate, but from the way they are objectively related to the conditions they signify.

To understand conventional systems of representation of Type II and the way they differ from RSs of Type I, it is important to understand the difference between symbols and signs. In systems of Type II, natural signs are *used* in a way that exploits their *natural* meaning, their *unconventional* powers of indication, for representational, and partly conventional, purposes. This makes systems of Type II a curious blend of the conventional and the natural. It is the purpose of this section to say something useful about signs and their meaning in preparation for the description of representational systems of Type II. This, in turn, will prepare the way for our discussion of the representational systems that are of real interest to this project: natural systems of representation.

Although a great deal of intelligent thought and purpose went into the design and manufacture of an ordinary bathroom scale, once the scale has been finished and placed into use there is nothing conventional, purposeful, or intelligent about its operation. This device indicates what it does without any cooperation or help from either its maker or its user. All you do is get *on* it. It then gives you the bad news. Somebody put the numbers on the dial, of course, and did so with certain intentions and purposes; but this is merely a convenience, something that (to use fashionable jargon) makes it user-friendly. It has nothing to do with what the instrument indicates. A clock doesn't stop keeping time if the numerals are removed from its face. The symbols on a clock or on a bathroom scale merely make it easier for us to *tell* what the pointer positions *mean*. They do not change what these pointer positions indicate.

The same is true of any measuring instrument. As long as an instrument is connected properly and functioning normally, it behaves in accordance with electrical and mechanical laws whose validity is quite independent of its creator's or its user's purposes or knowledge. Furthermore, these laws, by determining whether and (if so) how the pointer positions are correlated with weights, times, pressures, and speeds, determine what these pointer positions indicate about weights, times, pressures, and speeds.

Some people think that all indication is indication *for* or *to* someone. Gauge readings and naturally occurring signs (e.g., tracks in the snow) do not indicate anything if there is no one *to whom* or *for whom* they do this. Gauge readings are like trees falling in the forest: if no one is around to hear, there is no sound; if no one peeks at the scale, it doesn't indicate anything about anyone's weight. Tracks in the snow, fingerprints on a gun, and melting ice do not indicate anything about the animals in the woods, the person who touched the gun, or the temperature *unless* someone observes the tracks, the prints, or the melting ice and makes an appropriate inference. If no one knows that quail, and *only* quail, make tracks of *that* kind, then, despite this regularity, the tracks do not indicate that there are (or were) quail in the woods.

This view, I submit, is merely a special version of the more general and even more implausible idea that nothing is true unless it is true for someone, unless someone knows (or at least believes) it. I do not intend to quarrel about this matter. I shall simply assume that if one mistakes a perfectly reliable and properly functioning boiler-pressure gauge for something else, thinks it is broken, completely ignores it, or never even sees it—if, in other words, the registration of this gauge does not indicate what the boiler pressure is to *anyone*—it nonetheless still indicates what the boiler pressure is. It just doesn't indicate it *to* anyone. And, for the same reason, if, for superstitious reasons, everyone takes the color of the wooly caterpillar's fur as a indication or sign of a cold winter, everyone is simply wrong. That isn't what it means. Taking something to be so, taking it to be not so, or not taking it to be either does not make it so, does not make it not so, and does not make it neither. And this holds for what things indicate as well as for where things are and what they are doing.

I have occasionally used the verb "mean" as a synonym for "indicate." Let me explain. Paul Grice (1957) distinguished what he called a natural sense from a non-natural sense of the word "meaning." The natural sense of "meaning" is virtually identical to that of "indicate," and that is how I shall normally use the word. The 24 rings in a tree stump, the so-called growth rings, mean (indicate) that the tree is 24 years old. A ringing bell—a ringing *doorbell*—means (indicates) that someone is at the door. A scar on a twig, easily identified as a leaf scar, means, in this natural sense, that a leaf grew there. As Grice observes, nothing can mean that P in the *natural* sense of meaning if P is not the case. This distinguishes it from non-natural meaning, where something (e.g., a statement) can mean that P without P's being the case. A person can *say*, and *mean*, that a quail was here without a quail's having been here. But the tracks in the snow cannot mean (in this natural sense of "meaning") that a quail was here unless, in fact, a quail *was* here. If the tracks were left by a pheasant, then the tracks might, depending on how distinctive they are, mean that a pheasant was here. But they certainly do not mean that a quail was here, and the fact that a Boy Scout *takes* them to mean that cannot *make* them mean that.

Furthermore, even if *P* does obtain, the indicator or sign does not mean (indicate) that *P* is the case unless the requisite *dependency* exists between the sign and *P*. Even if the tracks in the snow *were* left by a quail, the tracks may not mean or indicate that this is so. If pheasants, also in the woods, leave the very same kind of tracks, then the tracks, though made by a quail, do not indicate that it was a quail that made them. A picture of a person, taken from the back at a great distance, does not indicate *who* the picture is a picture of if other people look the same from that angle and distance.

If a fuel gauge is broken (stuck, say, at "half full"), it *never* indicates anything about the gasoline in the tank. Even if the tank *is* half full, and even if the driver, unaware of the broken gauge, comes to believe (correctly, as it turns out) that the tank is half full, the reading is not a sign—does not mean or indicate—that the tank is half full. Broken clocks are *never* right, not even twice a day, if being right requires them to *indicate* the correct time of day.

When there is any chance of confusing this use of the word "meaning" with what Grice calls non-natural meaning—the kind of meaning associated with language, the kind of meaning that is (I shall later argue) closer to what it is the *function* of something to mean (naturally) or indicate—I shall either combine the word "meaning" with the word "natural" or use it together with its synonym "indicate." The word "represent" is sometimes used in a way that I am using "indicate" and "mean" (naturally). Since I wish to reserve the idea of representation for something that is closer to genuine meaning, the kind of meaning (Grice's non-natural meaning) in which something can mean that *P without P*'s being the case, I will *never* use the words "represent" and "indicate" interchangeably. As I am using these words, there can be no *misindication*, only misrepresentation.

The power of signs to mean or indicate something derives from the way they are related to what they indicate or mean. The red spots all over Tommy's face mean that he has the measles, not simply because he *has* the measles, but because people without the measles don't have spots of that kind. In most cases the underlying relations are causal or lawful in character. There is, then, a lawful dependency between the indica*tor* and the indica*ted*, a dependency that we normally express by conditionals in the subjunctive mood: if Tommy didn't have the measles, he wouldn't have those red spots all over his face. Sometimes, however, the dependency between a natural sign and its meaning derives, at least in part, from other sources. It is partly the fact, presumably not itself a physical law, that animals do not regularly depress doorbuttons while foraging for food that makes a ringing doorbell *mean* that some *person* is at the door. If squirrels changed their habits (because, say, doorbuttons were made out of nuts), then a ringing doorbell would no longer mean what it now does. But as things *now* stand, we can say that the bell would not be ringing unless someone was at the door. It therefore indicates or means that someone is at the door. But this subjunctively expressed dependency between the ringing bell and someone's presence at the door, though not a coincidence, is not grounded in natural law either. There are surely no laws of nature that prevent small animals from pressing, or randomly falling meteorites from hitting, doorbuttons. There certainly is nothing in the laws of physics that prevents an occasional short circuit in the electrical wiring, something that might cause the bell to ring when no one was at the door. Normally, though, these things don't happen. At least they have never happened to *me*. And this is no lucky coincidence, no freaky piece of good fortune. It isn't like getting a long run of heads while flipping a (fair) coin. Chance correlations between two variables, no matter how prolonged, are not enough. In order for one thing to indicate something about another, the dependencies must be genuine. There must actually be some condition, lawful or otherwise, that *explains* the persistence of the correlation. This is the difference between a lucky run of heads obtained with a fair coin and the not-at-all-lucky run of rings when someone has been at my door, a difference that enables my bell (but not coin flips) to indicate something about the correlated condition. This, of course, is a fact about *my* house, *my* neighborhood, and *my* doorbell wiring. If your house or neighborhood is different, maybe the ringing of *your* doorbell means something different.[2]

In many cases of biological interest, a sign—some internal indicator on which an animal relies to locate and identify, say, food—will only have this kind of local validity. It will, that is, be a reliable indicator only *in* the animal's natural habitat or in conditions that approximate that habitat. Flies,

---

2. Fodor (1987b) mentions an interesting illustration of this phenomenon discussed by David Marr and his associates: an algorithm (in the perceptual system) for computing three-dimensional form from two-dimensional rotation. The algorithm is not strictly valid, since there are worlds in which it reaches *false* three-dimensional conclusions from *true* two-dimensional premises—worlds in which spatial rotations are not rigid. Nevertheless, the algorithm is truth-preserving in the circumstances in which it is in fact employed—viz., *here*, in our world. Add to this the fact that the perceptual mechanisms that exploit this algorithm were evolved *here*, in *this* world, and we have a biological example of a uniformity—not lawful, but not fortuitous either—that enables sensory "premises" about two-dimensional rotations (that is, premises describing the two-dimensional transformations of the retinal image) to indicate something about the three-dimensional world we live in.

for instance, when given a choice between nutritionally worthless sugar fructose and some nutritive substance like sorbitrol, will invariably choose the nutritionally worthless substance and starve to death. Surprising? Not really. Under *natural* conditions (Grier 1984, p. 536) the substances that stimulate the receptors *are* nutritional. Under natural conditions, in a fly's normal habitat, then, receptor activity indicates a nutritional substance. Furthermore, the correlation between receptor activity and nutritional value of its activator is no accident. There is something that explains it. Flies would not have developed (or maintained without modification) such a receptor system in environments where such a correlation did not exist. The same is true of me and my doorbell. I would not keep a doorbell system that did not convey the desired information, that did not (because of pesky squirrels, say) indicate what it was installed to indicate. I would, as I assume the flies (over many generations) would, get a more discriminating detector.

I have elsewhere (1981, 1983), under the rubric *information*, tried to say something more systematic about the idea of an objective, mind-independent, indicator relation. Aside from the above brief remarks tracing the idea of natural meaning to the objective relations of dependency between a natural sign and its meaning, between the indicator and what it indicates, I will not here attempt to recapitulate that earlier analysis. Nor will I presuppose the details. Sufficient unto present purposes is the assumption—an altogether plausible assumption, I hope—that there is something *in* nature (not merely in the minds that struggle to comprehend nature), some objective, observer-independent fact or set of facts, that forms the basis of one thing's meaning or indicating something about another.[3] In what follows I shall occasionally, partly as a terminological convenience but also partly to exhibit the deep connections between representational systems and information-processing models of human cognition, advert to the idea of information. Talking about information is yet a third way of

---

3. This is not to say that descriptions of what something means or indicates are always free of subjective factors. We often describe what something means or indicates in a way that reflects what we already *know* about the possibilities. If there are only two switches controlling a light, the light indicates that one of the two switches is closed. Knowing, however, that *this switch* (one of the two) *isn't* closed, I take the light's being on as an indication that *the other switch* is closed. In this case, the light (is said) to indicate something that it would not indicate unless I, the speaker, *knew* something about other possibilities.

In this sense the meanings we ascribe to signs is relative. It is relative to what the speaker already knows about possible alternatives. This, however, doesn't mean that natural meaning is *subjective*. A person's weight isn't subjective just because it is relative, just because people weigh less on the moon than they do on earth. If nobody knew anything, things would still indicate other things. They just wouldn't indicate the specific sort of thing (e.g., the other switch is closed) we now describe them as indicating.

talking about the fundamentally important relation of indication or natural meaning. So, for example, if *S* (sign, signal), by being *a*, indicates or means that *O* is *A*, then *S* (or, more precisely, *S*'s being *a*) carries the information that *O* is *A*. What an event or condition (whether we think of it as a signal or not is irrelevant) indicates or means about another situation is the information it carries about that other situation.

3.3 Conventional Systems of Representation: Type II

In systems of Type II, natural signs take the place of symbols as the representational elements. A sign is given the job of doing what it (suitably deployed) can already do.

It should be remembered that what a system *represents* is *not* what its (expressive) elements indicate or mean. It is what these elements have the *function* of indicating or meaning. It is important to keep this point in mind, since the natural signs used in systems of Type II typically indicate a great many things. Normally, though, they are used to represent only *one* of these conditions—a condition which we, for whatever reason, take a special interest in and give the function of indicating. If a full tank of gas means (because of the weight of the gas) that there is a large downward force on the bolts holding the tank to the car's frame, then the fuel gauge indicates a large downward force on these bolts whenever it indicates a full tank of gas. In addition, electrically operated fuel gauges indicate not only the amount of fuel left in the tank but also the amount of electrical current flowing in the wires connecting the gauge to the tank, the amount of torque on the armature to which the pointer is affixed, and the magnitude of the magnetic field surrounding this armature. Given the way these gauges operate, they cannot indicate (i.e., have their behavior depend on) the amount of fuel in the tank without indicating (exhibiting at least the same degree of dependency on) these related conditions.

Nevertheless, we take one of these indicated conditions to be what the gauge *represents*, one of these correlated conditions to define what *kind* of gauge it is. It is, or so we say, a *fuel* gauge, not a galvanometer recording potential differences between points in the automobile's electrical wiring (though that, in a sense, is precisely what it is). Since we are interested in the amount of gasoline in the tank, not (except derivatively) in these correlated conditions, we *assign* the gauge the function of indicating the amount of gasoline in the tank. We *give* it the job of delivering *this* piece of information, calibrate and label it accordingly, and ignore the collateral pieces of information it necessarily supplies in the process. Since what an instrument or gauge represents is what it is *supposed* to indicate, what it has the *function* of indicating, and since *we* determine these functions, *we* determine what the gauge represents. If, by jacking up the fuel tank, I remove the force on the bolts securing the tank to the car frame, the fuel gauge, though still indicating the amount of fuel in the tank, no longer indicates the amount of force on these bolts. But, under these unusual conditions, the gauge does not *misrepresent* the force on these bolts the way it could, and the way gauges sometimes *do*, misrepresent the amount of fuel in the tank. The reason it doesn't is because the gauge, even when things are operating normally, does not *represent* (though it does *indicate*) the magnitude of this force. Its *representational* efforts—and therefore its representational failures, its *misrepresentations*—are limited to what it has the *function* of indicating. And since the gauge does not have the function of indicating the force on these bolts, it does not misrepresent this force when it fails to indicate it. Though it is hard to imagine why we would do this, we could *give* the gauge this function. Were we to do so, then, under the unusual conditions described above, when we removed the force on these bolts by jacking up the tank, the gauge would misrepresent the force on the bolts.

It is for this reason that what the gauge represents is *partly* conventional, *partly* a matter of what we say it represents. In contrast with the case of Type I systems, however, this dependence on us, our interests and purposes, is only partial. The reason it is only partial is because the indicator functions assigned an instrument are limited to what the instrument *can* indicate, to what its various states and conditions depend on. You can't assign a rectal thermometer the job of indicating the Dow-Jones Industrial Average.[4] The height of the mercury doesn't depend on these economic conditions. The mercury and the market fluctuate independently. Trying to use a thermometer in this way is like assigning a rock the job of washing dishes.[5] My son can be given this job (even if he never does it) because he, unlike the rock, *can* wash dishes. The functions we assign to instruments are similarly restricted to what the instruments *can* do, or, if Wright (1973) is correct, what (in the case of artifacts) we *think* they can do. This makes the functions of systems of Type II restricted in a way that those of Type I systems are not restricted. It is this fact, together with the fact that once a

4. Not, at least, as an RS of Type II. One could, however, use it as an RS of Type I. Just as I used coins and popcorn to represent basketball players, and the positions and movements of these elements the position and movements of the players, there is nothing preventing one from *using* a rectal thermometer in a similar fashion to represent the Dow-Jones average.

5. For those who want to quarrel about this issue, I could, I suppose, assign a rock the job of doing my dishes if I mistook it for my son, just as I could assign a thermometer the job of indicating fluctuations in the stock market if I mistook it for something else. I do not, however, think a rock could actually *have* this function. Nor do I think a simple instrument could *have* the function of indicating something it could not indicate. This is not to say that the thermometer could not be incorporated into a more complex system that *could* indicate, and therefore could have the function of indicating, something about the stock market. But, by the same token, I could also make the rock part of a machine (pulleys, etc.) that *could* do (and, therefore, could have the function of doing) my dishes.

device has been given such a functon it performs without any help from us, that makes such systems only *partly* conventional.

The conventional, interest-relative, and purpose-dependent character of systems of Type II is especially obvious when our interests and purposes change. An altimeter represents altitude until we remove it from the aircraft for testing on the ground. It then "becomes" an aneroid barometer, representing not altitude but air pressure—something it *always* indicated, of course, but something in which we weren't interested (except insofar as it depended on, and hence served as an accurate indicator of, altitude) when flying the plane. Calibration is a process in which one's interests and purposes undergo a temporary change. *Now*, during calibration, one uses the needle's position as an indicator, not of the quantity the instrument is usually used to measure, but of the instrument's own internal condition—whether, for example, its batteries are getting weak, or whether it needs adjustment, repair, or alignment. With RSs of Type II we can, and sometimes do, change the magnitude being represented (not merely the scale for measuring a given magnitude) merely by consulting a different set of numbers on the face of the instrument. A change in the way we *use* the instrument is enough to change its function and, hence, what it represents.

One way of thinking about the difference between Type I and Type II representational systems is that in systems of Type I the function, as it were, comes first. The representational elements are given a function and then, if things go right, are *used* in conformity with this function—*used* to indicate what, relative to this function, they are supposed to indicate. I first give the dime, *its* position and movements, the function of indicating the position and movements of Oscar Robertson. Then I manipulate the dime in accordance with this assigned function. I, in virtue of my knowledge and manipulative skills, see to it that it indicates what I have assigned it the function of indicating. Not only the coin's *job* but also its *performance* of that job derives, therefore, wholly from me, the creator and user of the representational system. RSs of Type I are, then, *manifestations* or *displays* of the representational talents of their users in much the same way that a TV monitor is a *display* of the information-processing capabilities of the machinery lying behind it. With systems of Type II, however, things are different. The power of their elements to indicate comes first; their function comes second. They acquire or are assigned the function of doing one of the things they are already doing or, if not *already* doing, already *capable* of doing once harnessed in the right way. Their ability to perform their function does *not*, as in the case of systems of Type I, depend on us, on a user-system already in possession of the required indicator skills. The status of these elements as indicators is therefore *intrinsic*. What is extrinsic, and therefore still conventional, still relative to the interests and purposes of its users, is the determination of which among the various things they can already do it is their function to do.

3.4 *Natural Systems of Representation*

A natural system of representation is not only one in which the elements, like the elements of Type II systems, have a power to indicate that is independent of the interests, purposes, and capacities of any other system, but also one in which, in contrast with systems of Type II, the functions determining what these signs *represent* are also independent of such extrinsic factors. Natural systems of representation, systems of Type III, are ones which have *their own* intrinsic indicator functions, functions that derive from the way the indicators are developed and used *by the system of which they are a part*. In contrast with systems of Type I and II, these functions are not assigned. They do not depend on the way *others* may use or regard the indicator elements.

Whatever one might think about the possibility of intrinsic functions, the type of functions that define Type III systems (a contentious point to which I will return in a moment), it is clear that what I have been calling natural signs—events, conditions, and structures that somehow indicate how things stand elsewhere in the world—are essential to every animal's biological heritage. Without such internal indicators, an organism has no way to negotiate its way through its environment, no way to avoid predators, find food, locate mates, and do the things it has to do to survive and propagate. This, indeed, is what sense perception is all about. An animal's senses (at least the so-called exteroceptors) are merely the diverse ways nature has devised for making what happens inside an animal depend, in some indicator-relevant way, on what happens outside. If the firing of a particular neuron in a female cricket's brain did not indicate the distinctive chirp of a conspecific male, there would be nothing to guide the female in its efforts to find a mate (Huber and Thorson 1985). The *place, misplace*, and *displace* neural units in the rat's brain (O'Keefe 1976), units that guide the animal in its movements through its environment, are merely internal indicators of place, of alterations in place, and of movement through a place. Such is the stuff of which cognitive maps are made, part of the normal endowment for even such lowly organisms as ants and wasps (Gallistel 1980).

The firing of neural cells in the visual cortex, by indicating the presence and orientation of a certain energy gradient on the surface of the photoreceptors, indicates the whereabouts and the orientation of "edges" in the optical input and therefore indicates something about the surfaces in the environment from which light is being reflected. The activity of these cells, not to mention comparable activity by other cells in a wide variety of sensory systems, is as much a natural sign or indicator as are the more familiar events we commonly think of as signs—the autumnal change in maple leaves, growth rings in a tree, and tracks in the snow.

We are accustomed to hearing about biological functions for various bodily organs. The heart, the kidneys, and the pituitary gland, we are told, have functions—things they are, in this sense, *supposed to do*. The fact that these organs are supposed to do these things, the fact that they have these functions, is quite independent of what *we* think they are supposed to do. Biologists *discovered* these functions, they didn't invent or assign them. We cannot, by agreeing among ourselves, *change* the functions of these organs in the way that I can change, merely by making an appropriate announcement, what the coins and the popcorn in my basketball game stand for. The same seems true for sensory systems, those organs by means of which highly sensitive and continuous dependencies are maintained between external, public events and internal, neural processes. Can there be a serious question about whether, in the same sense in which it is the heart's function to pump the blood, it is, say, the task or function of the noctuid moth's auditory system to detect the whereabouts and movements of its archenemy, the bat?

Some marine bacteria have internal magnets, magnetosomes, that function like compass needles, aligning themselves (and, as a result, the bacterium) parallel to the Earth's magnetic field (Blakemore and Frankel 1981). Since the magnetic lines incline downward (toward geomagnetic north) in the northern hemisphere, bacteria in the northern hemisphere, oriented by their internal magnetosomes, propel themselves toward geomagnetic north. Since these organisms are capable of living only in the absence of oxygen, and since movement toward geomagnetic north will take northern bacteria away from the oxygen-rich and therefore toxic surface water and toward the comparatively oxygen-free sediment at the bottom, it is not unreasonable to speculate, as Blakemore and Frankel do, that *the function* of this primitive sensory system is to indicate the whereabouts of benign (i.e., anaerobic) environments.[6]

Philosophers may disagree about how best to analyze the attribution of function to the organs, processes, and behaviors of animals and plants (see, for example, Nagel 1961, Wright 1973; Boorse 1976, and Cummins 1975, all conveniently collected in Sober 1984b), but that some of these things

6. There may be some disagreement about how best to describe the function of this primitive sensory system. Does it have the function of indicating the location, direction, or whereabouts of anaerobic conditions? Or does it, perhaps, have the function of indicating the Earth's magnetic polarity (which in turn indicates the direction of anaerobic conditions)? In Dretske 1986 I described this as an "indeterminacy" of function. As long as this indeterminacy exists, there is, of course, an associated indeterminacy in what the system represents. I return to this point later.

have functions—functions, like those of the bacterium's magnetic sense or the moth's auditory sense, to be *discovered* (not invented or assigned)— seems evident not only from a common-sense standpoint but also from the practice, if not the explicit avowals, of biologists and botanists.

This is, nevertheless, a controversial topic, at least among philosophers (see, e.g., Dennett 1987), and I do not wish to rest a case for a *philosophical* thesis on what seems evident to common sense or what is taken for granted by biologists. So for the moment I take the biological examples as more or less (depending on your point of view) plausible illustrations of intrinsic functions—plausible examples, therefore, of sensory systems that, by having such functions, qualify as *natural* systems of representation. As we shall see later (chapter 4), the case for representational systems of Type III will rest on quite different sorts of functions: those that are derived, not from the evolution of the species, but from the development of the individual. Nevertheless, it is useful to think, if only for illustrative purposes, about the way certain indicator systems developed, in the evolutionary history of a species, to serve the biological needs of its members. It should be understood, though, that my use of such examples is merely an expository convenience. The *argument* that there are functions of the kind required for Type III systems, hence an argument for the *existence* of Type III systems, systems with a natural power of representation, remains to be made.

3.5 Intentionality: Misrepresentation[7]

Philosophers have long regarded intentionality as a mark of the mental. One important dimension of intentionality is the capacity to misrepresent, the power (in the case of the so-called propositional attitudes) to *say* or *mean* that P when P is not the case. The purpose of this section is to describe how systems of representation, as these have now been characterized, possess this capacity and, hence, exhibit some marks of the mental. Two other important dimensions of intentionality will be discussed in the following section.

Before we begin, it is perhaps worth noting that, since systems of Types I and II derive their representational powers, including their power to misrepresent, from systems (typically humans) that already have the full range of intentional states and attitudes (knowledge, purpose, desire, etc.), *their* display of intentional characteristics is not surprising. As we shall see, the traces of intentionality exhibited by such systems are merely *reflections* of the minds, *our* minds, that assign them the properties, in particular the

---

7. The material in this section is based on Dretske 1986. That work, and in fact this entire chapter, was heavily influenced by the important work of Stampe (1975, 1977), Millikan (1984, 1986), Enc (1979, 1982), and Fodor (1984, 1987a). Also see Papineau (1984).

functions, from which they derive their status as representations. This is not so, however, for systems of Type III. If there are such systems, *their* intentionality will not be a thing of *our* making. They will have what Haugeland (1981b) calls *original* intentionality and Searle (1980) calls *intrinsic* intentionality.

The first aspect of intentionality to be described is the capacity some systems have to represent something as being so when it is not so—the power of *misrepresentation*. It may be thought odd to accent the negative in this way, odd to focus on a system's ability to get things wrong—on its vices, as it were, instead of its virtues. There is, though, nothing backward about this approach. The ability to correctly represent how things stand elsewhere in the world *is* the ability of primary value, of course, but this value adheres to representations only insofar as the representation in question is the sort of thing that *can* get things wrong. In the game of representation, the game of "saying" how things stand elsewhere in the world, telling the truth isn't a virtue if you *cannot* lie. I have already said that indication, as I am using this word, and as Grice used the idea of natural meaning, describes a relation that cannot fail to hold between an indicator and what it indicates. There can be no *misindication*. If the gas tank is empty, the gauge *cannot*, in this sense of the word, indicate that it is full. This is not to say that someone might not *take* the gauge as indicating a full tank. It is only to say that the gauge does not, in fact, indicate a full tank. Since indicators cannot, in this sense, fail to indicate, they do not possess the capacity of interest: the power to get things wrong. *They* don't get things wrong. *We* get things wrong by (sometimes) misreading the signs, by *taking* them to indicate something they don't. What we are after is the power of a system to say, mean, or represent (or, indeed, *take*) things as *P whether or not P is the case*. That is the power of words, of beliefs, of thought—the power that *minds* have—and that, therefore, is the power we are seeking in representational systems. Whatever *word* we use to describe the relation of interest (representation? meaning?), it is the power to misrepresent, the capacity to get things wrong, to say things that are not true, that helps *define* the relation of interest. *That* is why it is important to stress a system's capacity for misrepresentation. For only if a system has this capacity does it have, in its power to get things right, something approximating *meaning*. That is why the capacity to misrepresent is an important aspect of intentionality and why it figures so large in the philosophy of mind and the philosophy of language.

For this reason it is important to remember that not every indicator, not even those that occur *in* plants and animals, is a representation. It is essential that it be the indicator's *function*—natural (for systems of Type III) or otherwise (for systems of Type II)—to indicate what it indicates. The width of growth rings in trees growing in semi-arid regions is a sensitive rain gauge, an accurate indication of the amount of rainfall in the year corresponding to the ring. This does not mean, however, that these rings *represent* the amount of rainfall in each year. For that to be the case, it would be necessary that it be the function of these rings to indicate, by their width, the amount of rain in the year corresponding to each ring.[8] This, to say the least, is implausible—unless, of course, we start thinking of the rings as an RS of Type II. We, or botanists, might *use* these rings to learn about past climatic conditions. Should this happen in some regular, systematic way, the rings might take on some of the properties of an instrument or gauge (for the people who use them this way). Insofar as these rings start *functioning* in the information-gathering activities of botanists as a sign of past rainfall, they may, over time, and in the botanical community, acquire an indicator function and thereby assume a genuine representational (of Type II) status. At least they might do so *for* the botanists who use them this way. But this is clearly not an RS of Type III. Though there is something in the tree, the width of the fourteenth ring, that indicates the amount of rainfall fourteen years ago, it is implausible to suppose it is the ring's function to indicate this. The variable width of the rings is merely the effect of variable rainfall. The distension of an animal's stomach is, likewise, an indicator of the amount of food the animal has eaten and (for this reason, perhaps) an indicator of the amount of food available in its environment. But this is surely not the function of a distended stomach.

This point is important if we are to understand the way RSs manage to misrepresent things. The capacity for misreprentation is easy enough to understand in systems of Type I. For here the power of the elements to misrepresent depends on *our* willingness and skill in manipulating them in accordance with the (indicator) functions we have assigned them. Since I am responsible for what the coins and the popcorn in my basketball game stand for, since I assigned them their indicator function, and since I am responsible for manipulating them in accordance with this function, the arrangement of coins and popcorn can be made to misrepresent whatever *I*, deliberately or out of ignorance, make them misrepresent. Their misrepresentations are really *my* misrepresentations.

Misrepresentation in systems of Type II is not quite so simple an affair, but, once again, its occurrence ultimately traces to whoever or whatever assigns the functions that determine the system's representational efforts. Since there is no such thing as a *mis*indication, no such thing as a natural sign's meaning that something is so when it is not so, the only way a system of natural signs can misrepresent anything is if the signs that serve as its representational elements fail to indicate something they are *supposed*

8. Fodor (1984) makes this point against Stampe's (1977) idea that the rings in a tree *represent*, in the relevant sense, the tree's age. See Stampe 1986 for a reply.

to indicate. And what they are *supposed* to indicate is what *we*, for purposes of our own, and independent of a sign's success in carrying out its mission on particular occassions, *regard* them as having (or give them) the job of doing. Without *us* there are no standards for measuring failure, nothing the system fails to do that it is supposed to do. Although the actual failures aren't *our* failures, the standards (functions) that make them failures are our standards. Putting chilled alcohol in a glass cylinder doesn't generate a misrepresentation unless somebody calibrates the glass, hangs it on the wall, and calls it a thermometer.

Only when we reach RSs of Type III—only when the functions defining what a system is supposed to indicate are intrinsic functions—do we find a *source*, not merely a reflection, of intentionality. Only here do we have systems sufficiently self-contained in their representational efforts to serve, in this one respect at least, as models of thought, belief, and judgment.

A system could have acquired the *function* of indicating that something was F without, in the present circumstances, or any longer, or perhaps *ever*, being able to indicate that something is F. This is obvious in the case of a Type II RS, where, by careless assembly, a device can fail to do what it was designed to do. As we all know, some shiny new appliances don't work the way they are supposed to work. They *never* do what it is their function to do. When what they are supposed to do is indicate, such devices are doomed to a life of misrepresentation. Others leave the factory in good condition but later wear out and no longer retain the power to indicate what it is their function to indicate. Still others, thought they don't wear out, are used in circumstances that curtail their ability to indicate what they were designed to indicate. A compass is no good in a mineshaft, and a thermometer isn't much good in the sun. In order to do what they are supposed to do, care has to be taken that such instruments are used when and where they can do their job.

The same is true of RSs of Type III. Suppose a primitive sensory ability evolves in a species because of what it is capable of telling its possessors about some critical environmental condition F. Let us assume, for the sake of the example, that the manner in which this indicator developed, the way it was (because of its critical role in delivering needed information) favored by the forces of selection, allows us to say that this indicator has the function of indicating F. Through some reproductive accident, an individual member of this species (call him Inverto) inherits his F-detector in defective (let us suppose inverted) condition. Poor Inverto has an RS that always misrepresents his surroundings: it represents things as being F when they are not, and vice versa.[9] Unless he is fortunate enough to be preserved in

---

9. An artificial approximation of this situation occurred when R. W. Sperry (1956) and his associates rotated, by surgical means, the eyeball of a newt by 180°. The vision of the

some artificial way—unless, that is, he is removed from a habitat in which the detection of Fs is critical—Inverto will not long survive. He emerged defective from the factory and will soon be discarded. On the other hand, his cousins, though emerging from the factory in good condition, may simply wear out. As old age approaches, their RSs deteriorate, progressively losing their ability to indicate when and where there is an F. They retain their function, of course, but they lose the capacity to perform that function. Misrepresentation becomes more and more frequent until, inevitably, they share Inverto's fate.

And, finally, we have the analogue, in a Type III system, of an instrument used in disabling circumstances—the compass in a mineshaft, for instance. Consider a sensitive biological detector that, upon removal from the habitat in which it developed, flourished, and faithfully serviced its possessor's biological needs, is put into circumstances in which it is no longer capable of indicating what it is supposed to indicate. We earlier considered bacteria that relied on internal detectors (magnetosomes) of magnetic north in order to reach oxygen-free environments. Put a northern bacterium into the southern hemisphere and it will quickly destroy itself by swimming in the wrong direction. If we suppose (we needn't; see footnote 6) that it is the function of these internal detectors to indicate the whereabouts of anaerobic conditions, then misrepresentation occurs—in this case with fatal consequences.

Put a frog in a laboratory where carefully produced shadows simulate edible bugs. In these unnatural circumstances the frog's neural detectors—those that have, for good reason, been called "bug detectors"—will no longer indicate the presence or the location of bugs. They will no longer indicate this (even when they are, by chance, caused to fire by real edible bugs) because their activity no longer *depends* in the requisite way on the presence of edible bugs. Taking a frog into the laboratory is like taking a compass down a mineshaft: things no longer work the way they are

---

animal was permanently reversed. As Sperry describes it: "When a piece of bait was held above the newt's head it would begin digging into the pebbles and sand on the bottom of the aquarium. When the lure was presented in front of its head, it would turn around and start searching in the rear."

It should be noted that one doesn't disable an indicator *merely* by reversing the code—letting *b* (formerly indicating *B*) indicate *A* and *a* (formerly indicating *A*) indicate *B*. As long as this reversal is systematic, the change is merely a change in the way information is being coded, not a change in the information being coded. But though *A* and *B* are still being indicated (by *b* and *a* respectively), they are, after the inversion, no longer being accurately *represented* unless there is a corresponding change (inversion) in the way the representational elements (*a* and *b*) function in the rest of the system. This is what did not happen with the newt. It still got the information it needed, but as a result of the coding change it misrepresented the conditions in its environment.

supposed to work. Indicators stop indicating. If we suppose, then, that it is the function of the frog's neural detectors to indicate the presence of edible bugs, then, in the laboratory, shadows are misrepresented *as* edible bugs. The frog has an analogue of a false belief.[10] Occasionally, when an edible bug flies by, the frog will correctly represent it as an edible bug, but this is dumb luck. The frog has the analogue of a true belief, a *correct* representation, but no *knowledge*, no *reliable* representation. Taking a compass down a mineshaft will not change what it "says" (namely, that whichever way the needle points is geomagnetic north), but it will change the reliability, and (often enough) the truth, of what it says. Likewise, taking a frog into the laboratory will not change what it "thinks," but it will change the number of times it *truly* thinks what it thinks.

All this is conditional on assumptions about what it is the *function* of an indicator to indicate. Upon realizing that a typical fuel gauge in an automobile cannot distinguish between gasoline and water in the tank, one could insist that it is the gauge's function to register not how much gasoline is left in the tank but how much *liquid* is left in the tank. It is our job, the job of those who use the gauge, to see to it that the liquid is gasoline. If this is indeed how the function of the gauge is understood, then, of course, the gauge does *not* misrepresent anything when there is water in the tank. it correctly represents the tank as half full of liquid. And a similar possibility exists for the frog. If the function of the neural detectors on which the frog depends to find food is merely that of informing the frog of the whereabouts of small moving dark spots, then the frog is *not* misrepresenting its surroundings when, in the laboratory, it starves to death while flicking at shadows. For the internal representation triggering this response is perfectly accurate. It indicates what it is supposed to indicate: the presence and whereabouts of small, moving dark spots. The shadows *are* small moving dark spots, so nothing is being misrepresented.

Misrepresentation depends on two things: the *condition* of the world being represented and the *way* that world is represented. The latter, as we have seen, is determined, not by what a system indicates about the world, but by what it has the function of indicating about the world. And as long as there remains this indeterminacy of function, there is no clear sense in which misrepresentation occurs. Without a determinate function, one can, as it were, always exonerate an RS of error, and thus eliminate the occurrence of misrepresentation, by changing what it is *supposed* to be indicating, by changing what it is its *function* to indicate. It is this indeterminacy that

---

10. But not a real false belief, because, as we shall see in the next chapter, beliefs are *more* than internal representations. They are internal representations that help explain the behavior of the system of which they are a part.

Dennett (1987) dramatizes in his arguments against the idea of *original* or *intrinsic* intentionality.

What this shows is that the occurrence of misrepresentation depends on there being some principled, nonarbitrary way of saying what the indicator function of a system is. In systems of Types I and II there is no special problem because *we* are the source of the functions. We can, collectively as it were, eliminate this indeterminacy of function by agreeing among ourselves or by taking the designer's and the manufacturer's word as to what the device is supposed to do. If a watch is really a calendar watch, as advertised, then it is *supposed* to indicate the date. It "says" today is the fourth day of the month. It isn't. So it is misrepresenting the date. Case closed.

The case is not so easily closed in systems of Type III. It can only be successfully closed when internal indicators are harnessed to a control mechanism. Only by *using* an indicator in the production of movements whose successful outcome depends on *what is being indicated* can this functional indeterminacy be overcome, or so I shall argue in chapter 4.

3.6 Intentionality: Reference and Sense

If an RS has the function of indicating that *s* is *F*, then I shall refer to the proposition expressed by the sentence "*s* is *F*" as the *content* of the representation. There are always two questions that one can ask about representational contents. One can ask, first, about its reference—the object, person, or condition the representation is a representation *of*. Second, one can ask about the way what is represented is represented. What does the representation say or indicate (or, when failure occurs, what is it *supposed* to say or indicate) about what it represents? The second question is a question about what I shall call the sense or meaning of the representational content. Every representational content has both a sense and a reference, or, as I shall sometimes put it, a topic and a comment—what it says (the comment) and what it says it about (the topic). These two aspects of representational systems capture two additional strands of intentionality: the *aboutness* or *reference* of an intentional state and (when the intentional state has a propositional content) the *intensionality* spelled with an "s") of sentential expressions of that content.

Nelson Goodman (1976) distinguished between pictures *of* black horses and what he called black-horse pictures. This is basically my distinction between topic and comment. Black-horse pictures represent the black horses they are pictures of *as* black horses. Imagine a black horse photographed at a great distance in bad light with the camera slightly out of focus. The horse appears as a blurry spot in the distance. This *is* a picture of a black horse, but not what Goodman calls a black-horse picture. When invited to see pictures of your friend's black horse, you expect to see, not only pictures of a black horse, but black-horse pictures—pictures in which the denotation, topic, or reference of the picture is *identifiably* a black horse—or, if not a *black* horse, then at least a horse or an animal of some sort.

Not all representations are pictorial. Many representations are not expected, even under optimal conditions, to *resemble* the objects they represent. Language is a case in point, but even in the case of Type II RSs it is clear that ringing doorbells do not resemble depressed doorbuttons (or people at the door) and that fuel gauges (at least the old-fashioned kind) do not resemble tanks full of gasoline. And if, as seems likely, there is in a wolf's skull some neural representation of the wounded caribou it so relentlessly follows (ignoring the hundreds of healthy animals nearby), this representation of the caribou's condition, position, and movements does not actually resemble, in the way a photograph or a documentary film might resemble, a terrified caribou. A picture, though, is only one kind of representation, a representation in which information about the referent is carried by means of elements that visually resemble the items they represent. A nonpictorial representation, however, exhibits the same dimensions. It has a reference and a meaning, a topic and a comment. My fuel gauge is not only a representation *of* an empty gasoline tank; it is also (when things are working right) an empty-tank representation. That the tank is empty is what it indicates, the information it carries, the comment it makes, about that topic. My gas tank is also very rusty, but the gauge does not comment on this feature of its topic.

The wolf's internal representation of a sick caribou may or may not be a sick-and-fleeing-caribou representation, but it certainly is a representation *of* a sick, fleeing caribou. *How* the neural machinery represents *what* it represents is, to some degree, a matter of speculation, a matter of divining what the patterns of neural activity in the wolf's brain indicate about the caribou and (since we are talking about *representations*) what, if anything, it is the function of these sensory-cognitive elements to indicate about prey. Does the wolf really represent caribou *as* caribou? Sick and lame caribou *as* sick and lame? If it turns out (it doesn't) that the wolf cannot distinguish a caribou from a moose, the answer to the first question is surely No. Perhaps the wolf merely represents caribou as large animals of some sort. Or merely as food. But the point is that unless the wolf has some means of representing comparatively defenseless caribou—a way of commenting on these creatures that is, for practical wolfish purposes, extensionally equivalent to *good* being a (comparatively) defenseless caribou—its relentless and unerring pursuit of comparatively defenseless caribou is an absolute mystery, like the flawless performance of an automatic door opener that has nothing in it to signal (indicate) the approach of a person or an object. There has to be something in there that "tells" the door opener what it needs to know in order for it to do what it does—to open the door *when* someone approaches. The same is true of the wolf.

Our ordinary descriptions of what animals (including people) see, hear, smell, feel, know, believe, recognize, and remember reflect the distinction between a representation's topic and its comment. This, I think, lends support to the idea that a cognitive system *is* a representational system of some kind, presumably a system of Type III. We say, for example, that Clyde can see a black horse in the distance without (for various reasons having to do either with the great distance, the camouflage, the lighting, or the fact that Clyde forgot his glasses) its *looking like* a black horse to Clyde, without its presenting (as some philosophers like to put it) a *black-horse appearance.* Clyde doesn't know what it is, but he thinks it might be the brown cow he has been looking for. In talking this way, and it is a common way of talking, we describe what Clyde's representation is a representation *of* (a black horse) and say how he represents it (as a brown cow). In Goodman's language, Clyde has a brown-cow representation of a black horse. At other times perhaps all we can say about how Clyde represents the black horse is as *something* in the distance. This may be the only comment Clyde's representational system is making about that topic. This isn't much different from a cheap scale's representing a 3.17-pound roast as weighing somewhere between 3 and 4 pounds. It is a rough comment on a perfectly determinate topic.

Compare Clyde's perceptual relationship to the black horse with a fuel gauge's relation to a full tank of gasoline. When things are working properly, the gauge carries information about the tank: the information that it is full. Since it is the gauge's assigned function to deliver this information, it represents the tank as full. It does not, however, carry information about *which* tank is full. Normally, of course, an automobile comes equipped with only one gasoline tank. The gauge is connected to *it*. There is no reason to comment on which topic (which tank) the gauge is making a remark about, since there is only one topic on which to comment and everybody knows this. Suppose, however, there were several auxiliary tanks, with some mechanism letting the gauge systematically access different tanks. Or suppose we were to connect (by radio control, say) Clyde's gauge to *my* tank. In this case the representation would have a different referent, a different topic, but the *same* comment. The gauge would "say" not that Clyde's tank was full but that *my* tank was full. The fact that it was saying this, rather than something else, would not be evident from the representation itself, of course. But neither is it evident from Clyde's representation of the black horse that it is, indeed, a representation of a black horse. To know this one needs to know, just as in the case of the gauge, to what Clyde is connected in the appropriate way. Examining the representation itself won't tell you what condition in the world satisfies it, what condition would (were it to obtain) make the representation an accurate representation. For this one has to look at the wiring. In Clyde's case, there being no wires connecting him to the black horse, you have to look at the connections that *do* establish which topic his representation is a representation of. In the case of vision, that connection is pretty clearly, in most normal cases, whatever it is *from which* the light (entering Clyde's eyes) is reflected.[11]

The job of gauges and instruments is to carry information about the items (tanks, circuits, shafts, etc.) to which they are connected, not information about which item it is to which they are connected. So it is with pictures and most other forms of representation. Perceptual beliefs of a certain sort—what philosophers call *de re* beliefs (e.g., *that* is moving)—are often as silent as gauges about what it is they represent, about what topic it is on which they comment, about their *reference*. Clyde can see a black horse in the distance, thereby getting information about a black horse (say, that it is near a barn), without getting the information that it is a black horse— without, in other words, seeing *what* it is. Just as a gauge represents the gas level in my tank without representing it as the amount of gas in *my* tank, Clyde can have a belief about (a representation *of*) my horse without believing that it is (without representing it *as*) my (or even *a*) horse.

A great many representational contents are of this *de re* variety. There is a representation *of* the tank as being half full, *of* an animal as being lame or sick, *of* a doorbutton as being depressed, *of* a cat as being up a tree (or *of* a cat and *of* a tree as the one being up the other). These are called *de re* contents because the things (*re*) about which a comment is made is determined by nonrepresentational means, by means other than *how* that item is represented. That this is a picture, a photographic representation, *of* Sue Ellen, *not* her twin sister Ellen Sue, is not evident—indeed (given that they are identical twins) not discoverable—from the representation itself, from the *way* she is represented. One has to know who was standing in front of the camera to know who it is a picture of, and this fact cannot be learned (given the twin sister) from the picture itself. If causal theories are right (see, e.g., Stampe 1977), the reference of such representations will be determined by causal relations: that object, condition, or situation which is, as Sue Ellen was, causally responsible for the properties possessed by the representation (e.g., the color and distribution of pigment on the photographic paper).

Though most representations of Type II have a *de re* character, there are ready examples of comparatively simple systems having a *de dicto* content, a content whose reference is determined by *how* it is represented. Imagine a

---

11. Here I suppress difficult problems in the philosophy of perception, problems about the correct analysis of the perceptual object. Any responsible discussion of these topics would take me too far afield.

detector whose function it is to keep track of things as they pass it on an assembly line and to record each thing's color and ordinal position. At the time it is registering the color (red) and the position (fourth) of *delta*, it can be said that this mechanism provides a *de re* representation *of delta* as red and as the fourth item to pass by. The reference is *delta* because that is the item on the assembly line that the detector is currently monitoring (to which it is causally connected), and the meaning or sense is given by the expression "is red and number four" because that is what the detector indicates, and has the function of indicating, about the items it is presently scanning. At a later time, though, a time when the apparatus is no longer directly recording facts about delta, its representation of the fourth item as red changes its character. Its reference to delta, its representation *of* delta, now occurs via its description of delta as the fourth item. At this later time, *delta*'s color is relevant to the determination of the correctness of the representation *only insofar* as *delta* was the fourth item on the assembly line. If it wasn't, then even if *delta was* the item the detector registered (incorrectly) as the fourth item, *delta*'s color is irrelevant to the correctness of the representation. It is *the fourth item*, not *delta*, that has to be red in order for this (later) representation to be correct. Compare my belief, one day later, that the fourth person to enter the room was wearing a funny hat. If I retain in memory no other description capable of picking out who I believe to have been wearing a funny hat (as is the case with our imagined detector), then this later belief, unlike the original belief, is a belief about *whoever* was the fourth person to enter the room. I may never have seen, never have been causally connected to, the person who makes this belief true.

One can go further in this direction of separating the reference of a representation from the object that is causally responsible for the representation by equipping an RS with projectional resources, with some means of extrapolating or interpolating indicated patterns. Something like this would obviously be useful in a representation-driven control system that had a "need to act" in the absence of firm information. Imagine our detector, once again, given the function of simultaneously monitoring items on *several* assembly lines, recording the color and the ordinal value of each, and, on the basis of this information, making appropriate adjustments in some sorting mechanism. Think of it as an overworked device for weeding out rotten (nonred) apples. Since "attention" paid to one line requires ignoring the others, the device must "guess" about items it fails to "observe," or else a switching mechanism can be introduced that allows the detector to withdraw continuous attention from a line that exhibits a sufficiently long sequence of red apples. A "safe" line will be sampled intermittently, at a frequency of sampling determined by the line's past safety record. The detector "keeps an eye on" the lines that have poor performance records, and "infers" that the apples on good lines are OK. If things are working reasonably well, this device produces a printed record containing representations of apples it has never inspected. This device has the function of indicating something about objects to which it is *never* causally related.

It is not hard to imagine nature providing animals with similar cognitive resources. Donald Griffin (1984), drawing on the work of J. L. Gould (1979, 1982), describes the way honeybees perform a comparable piece of extrapolation. Honeybees were offered a dish of sugar water at the entrance of their hive. The dish was then moved a short distance away, and the bees managed to find it. This was continued until, when the feeder was more than 100 or 200 meters from the hive, the bees began waiting for the dish beyond the spot where it had last been left, at what would be the next logical stopping place (20 to 30 meters from the last location). The bees, Griffin observes, "seem to have realized that this splendid new food source moves and that to find it again they should fly farther out from home" (pp. 206–207). The benefits of such extrapolative mechanisms are obvious. Aside from the search technique of the bees, an animal without beliefs (whether we call them anticipations, expectations, or fears) about *the next A* will not survive long in an environment where the next *A* can be dangerous.

Much more can, and should, be said about the reference or topic of a representation. But it is time to turn to its sense or meaning, *how* it represents what it represents, the comment it makes on that topic. All systems of representation, whatever type they happen to be, are what I shall call *property specific*. By this I mean that a system can represent something (call it *s*) as having the property *F* without representing it as having the property *G* even though everything having the first property has the second, even though every *F is G*. Even if the predicate expressions "*F*" and "*G*" are *coextensional* (correctly apply to exactly the same things), this doesn't guarantee that an RS will represent *s* as *F* just because it represents *s* as *G* (or vice versa). These extensionally equivalent expressions give expression to quite different representational contents. This is a very important fact about representational systems. It gives their content a fine-grainedness that is characteristic of intentional systems. It makes verbal expressions of their content *intensional* rather than *extensional*. It is this feature, together with the system's capacity for misrepresentation and the reference or aboutness of its elements, that many philosophers regard as the essence of the mental.

Representational contents exhibit this peculiar fine-grainedness because even when properties *F* and *G* are so intimately related that nothing can indicate that something is *F* without indicating that it (or some related item) is *G*, it can be the device's *function* to indicate one without its being its function to indicate the other.[12] Nothing can indicate that *x* is red unless it thereby indicates that *x* is colored, but it can be a device's function to indicate the color of objects (e.g. that they are red) without its being its function to indicate that they are colored.

The specificity of functions to particular properties, even when these properties are related in ways (e.g., by logical or nomological relations) that prevent one's being indicated without the other's being indicated, is easy to illustrate with assigned functions, functions *we* give to instruments and detectors. For here the assignment of functions merely reflects *our* special interest in one property rather than the other. If we are, for whatever reason, interested in the number of angles in a polygon and not in the number of sides, then we can give a detector (or a *word*) the function of indicating the one without giving it the function of indicating the other even though the detector (or word) cannot successfully indicate that something is, say, a triangle without thereby indicating that it has three sides. We can make something into a voltmeter (something having the function of indicating voltage differences) without thereby giving it the function of indicating the amount of current flowing even if, because of constant resistance, these two quantities covary in some lawful way.

Though this phenomenon is easier to illustrate for Type I and Type II systems, it can easily occur, or can easily be imagined to occur, in systems of Type III. Dolphins, we are told, can recognize the shapes of objects placed in their pool from a distance of 50 feet. Apparently there is something in the dolphin, no doubt something involving its sensitive sonar apparatus, that indicates the *shapes* of objects in the water. But a dolphin that can infallibly identify, detect, recognize, or discriminate (use whatever cognitive verb you think appropriate here) cylinders from this distance should *not* be credited with the ability to identify, detect, recognize, or discriminate, say, *red* objects from this distance just because all (and only) the cylinders are red. If the fact that all (and only) the cylinders are red is a coincidence, of course, then something can indicate that *X* is a cylinder without indicating that *X* is red. This follows from the fact that an indicator could exhibit the requisite *dependence* on the shape of *X* without exhibiting any dependence on the color of *X*. But even if we suppose the connection between color and shape to be more intimate, we can, because of the different relevance of these properties to the well-being of an animal,

---

12. See Enc 1982 for further illustrations of this. Enc argues, convincingly to my mind, that we can distinguish between the representation of logically *equivalent* situations by appealing to (among other things) the functions of a system.

imagine a detector having the function of indicating the shape of things without having the function of indicating their color.[13]

3.7 Summary

The elements of a representational system, then, have a content or a meaning, a content or meaning defined by what it is their function to indicate. This meaning or content is a species of what Grice called non-natural meaning. These meanings display many of the intentional properties of genuine thought and belief. If, then, there are systems of Type III, and these are located in the heads of some animals, then there is, in the heads of some animals (1) something that is *about* various parts of this world, even those parts of the world with which the animal has never been in direct perceptual contact; (2) something capable of representing and, just as important, *misrepresenting* those parts of the world it is about; and (3) something that has, thereby, a *content* or *meaning* (not itself in the head, of course) that is individuated in something like the way we individuate thoughts and beliefs.

13. Taylor (1964, p. 150) notes that an experimenter can condition an animal to respond to red objects without conditioning it to respond to objects that differ in color from the experimenter's tie (which is green). He takes this to be a problem for how the property to which behavior is conditioned is selected. It should be clear that I think the answer to Taylor's problem lies, at least in part, in an adequate theory of representation, one that can distinguish between the representation of X as red and X as not green.

Chapter 4

The Explanatory Role of Belief

Armstrong (1973), following Ramsey (1931), has described beliefs as maps by means of which we steer. In the last chapter, we examined the maplike character of representations—the way they indicate, or have the function of indicating, the content and the nature of one's surroundings. But beliefs are not merely maps; they are maps *by means of which we steer*. And if this metaphor is to have any validity, as I think it does, then what makes the map a map—the fact that it supplies information about the terrain through which one moves—must, in one way or another, help to determine the direction in which one steers. If a structure's semantic character is unrelated to the job it does in shaping output, then this structure, though it may *be* a representation, is not a belief. A satisfactory model of belief should reveal the way in which *what we believe* helps to determine *what we do*.

The job of this chapter is to supply this account, to show that there are *some* representations whose role in the determination of output, and hence in the explanation of behavior, is shaped by the relations underlying its representational content or meaning. Such representations, I submit, are beliefs.

4.1 The Causal Role of Meaning

Something possessing content, or having meaning, can *be* a cause without its possessing that content or having that meaning being at all relevant to its causal powers. A soprano's upper-register supplications may shatter glass, but their meaning is irrelevant to their having this effect. Their effect on the glass would be the same if they meant nothing at all or something entirely different.

What is true of the soprano's acoustic output is true of reasons—those content-possessing mental states (belief, desire, fear, regret) we invoke to explain one another's behavior. We can, following Davidson (1963), say that reasons *are* causes, but the problem is to understand how their being reasons contributes to, or helps explain, their effects on motor output. It has been pointed out often enough that although reasons may cause us to behave in a certain way, they may not, *so described*, explain the behavior they cause (McGinn 1979; Mackie 1979; Honderich 1982; Robinson 1982; Sosa 1984; Skillen 1984; Follesdal 1985; Stoutland 1976, 1980; Tuomela 1977). McGinn (1979, p. 30) puts it this way: "To defend the thesis that citing reasons can be genuinely explanatory, we need to show that they can explain when described *as reasons*." The fact that they have a content, the fact that they have a *semantic* character, must be relevant to the kind of effects they produce. If brain structures possessing meaning affect motor output in the way the soprano's acoustic productions affect glass, then the meaning of these neural structures is causally inert. Even if it is there, it doesn't *do* anything. If having a mind is having *this* kind of meaning in the head, one may as well not have a mind.

Haugeland (1985, p. 40) notes that this problem is merely a reenactment within a materialistic framework of an old problem about mind-body interaction. Materialists think to escape this difficulty by claiming that a thought, like everything else, is merely a physical object—presumably (in the case of a thought) a neural state or structure. That may be so, of course, but what about the *meanings* of these physical structures? Are they, like the mass, charge, and velocity of objects, properties whose possession could make a difference, a *causal* difference, to the way these neural structures interact? If meaning, or something's *having* meaning, is to do the kind of work expected of it—if it is to help explain *why* we do what we do—it must, it seems, influence the operation of those electrical and chemical mechanisms that control muscles and glands. Just how is this supposed to work? This, obviously, is as much a mystery as the interaction between mind stuff and matter.

My task is to show how this embarrassment can be avoided within a materialist metaphysics. I will *not* try to show, of course, that meanings *themselves* are causes. Whatever else a meaning might be, it certainly is not, like an event, a spatio-temporal particular that could cause something to happen. It is, rather, an abstract entity, something more in the nature of a universal property such as redness or triangularity. Trying to exhibit the causal efficacy of meaning itself would be like trying to exhibit the causal efficacy of mankind, justice, or triangularity. No, in exploring the possibility of a causal role for meaning one is exploring the possibility, not of meaning itself being a cause, but of a *thing's having meaning* being a cause or of the *fact that something has meaning* being a causally relevant fact about the thing. In considering its effect on the glass, is the sound's having a meaning a causally relevant fact about the sound? Is it the sound's *having meaning* that explains, or helps explain, why it broke the glass?

We will see that there are *some* processes—those in which genuine cognitive structures are developed—in which an element's causal role in the overall operation of the system of which it is a part is determined by its indicator properties, by the fact that it carries information. The element does *this* because it indicates *that.* This connection between a structure's meaning and its causal role, though not direct, is, I shall argue, the connection that underlies the explanatory role of belief. Beliefs are representational structures that acquire their meaning, their maplike quality, by actually *using* the information it is their function to carry in steering the system of which they are a part.[1]

We are, remember, looking for an *explanatory* role for belief and, hence, an explanatory role for the semantic properties of a structure. If a symbol's meaning is correlated with the symbol's physical properties—if the semantics of symbols is faithfully reflected in their syntax, plus or minus a bit, as Fodor (1980) puts it—then meanings may turn out to be predictively useful without being explanatorily relevant. If I know that the high note is the only passage in the aria that has a certain meaning, I can predict that the glass will shatter when a passage with a certain meaning is sung. The fact that the words have this meaning, however, will not *explain* why the glass shattered. Rather, a sound's having a certain meaning will co-occur with something else (that sound's having a sufficient pitch and amplitude) that *does* explain this physical effect. It may even turn out, if the semantic features co-occur often enough with the right syntactic features, that useful generalizations (useful for *predictive* purposes) can be formulated in semantic terms. It may even be useful, perhaps even essential for methodological purposes, to catalog or index the causally relevant formal properties of our internal states in terms of their causally irrelevant meanings (see, e.g., Loar 1981; Pylyshyn 1984). But this, even if it turns out to be a fact, will not transform meaning into a relevant explanatory notion. If beliefs and desires explain behavior in this way, then *what* we believe and desire (the *content* of our beliefs and desires), however useful it might be for predicting what we are going to do, will not be a part of the explanation of what we do. What will then be relevant are the physical properties of the things that have these meanings, not the fact that they have these meanings. On this account of the explanatory role of meaning, meaning would be as relevant—i.e., wholly *irrelevant*—to explanations of human and animal behavior as it now is to explanations in the science of acoustics.

This, of course, is precisely why computer simulations of mental processes sometimes appear to be more than they are, why it sometimes

---

1. I will be developing a version of what Stich (1983) calls the *strong* Representational Theory of the Mind. His criticisms of this theory are often based on its uselessness to cognitive science in promoting generalizations about human behavior. Such criticisms of the strong RTM are irrelevant to my project. Ordinary belief (and desire) attribution—what Stich calls Folk Psychology—though it is in the business of *explaining* behavior, is *not* in the business (as is cognitive *science*) of looking for explanations of very general application.

I shall return in due course to other, more relevant, criticisms (e.g., the replacement argument) that Stich makes of representational theories.

appears that what a computer does with the symbols it manipulates depends on what these symbols mean. Though it can be disputed, let us agree that the symbols a computer manipulates *have* meanings. If, then, we devise a program for manipulating these symbols that preserves, in some relevant way, the semantic relations between their meanings, it will appear that what these symbols mean makes a difference to what happens to them. It will appear, in other words, that what the computer does—what it displays on the monitor, what it tells the printer to print, or, if we are dealing with a robot, what motors and solenoids it activates—is explicable in terms of the meanings of the elements on which it operates. It will appear, in other words, as though these symbols mean something *to the computer*. The robot went *there* because it *thought* this and *wanted* that. This, of course, is an illusion. It is an illusion that good programming is devoted to fostering. What *explains* why the device printed "Yes" in response to your question is not the fact that the computer knew this, thought that, had those facts in its data base, made these inferences, or indeed understood anything about what was happening. These semantic characterizations of the machine's internal operations may be predictively useful, but only because, by deliberate design, the meanings in question have been assigned to elements which, in virtue of possessing quite different (but appropriately correlated) properties, explain the machine's output. In Dennett's familiar terminology, the modern computer is a machine that is deliberately designed to make adoption of the intentional stance, a stance wherein we ascribe thoughts and desires, a *predictively* useful stance. The mistake lies in thinking that anything is *explained* by adopting this stance towards such machines.[2]

If this is the best that can be done for meaning—and a good many philosophers, for varying reasons and to varying degrees, have concluded that it is (see, e.g., Loar 1981 Fodor 1980, 1987a; Pylyshyn 1984; Stich 1983; Churchland 1981; Dretske 1981[3])—then the case for beliefs and desires as explanatory entities in psychology is exactly as strong as the case for the explanatory role of meaning in the science of acoustics.

2. Searle (1980) has dramatized this point in a useful and (I think) convincing way. Some of Block's (1978) examples make a similar point. Dennett's (1969) distinction between the (mere) storage of information and its intelligent storage makes, I think, basically the same point in a more oblique way. For more on the relevance of meaning to the explanation of machine behavior, see Dretske 1985, 1987; Haugeland 1985; Cummins 1987.

3. In Dretske 1981 I did not think that information, or (more carefully) a signal's carrying information, could itself be a *causally* relevant fact about a signal. I therefore defined the causal efficacy of information (or of a signal's carrying information) in terms of the causal efficacy of those properties of the signal in virtue of which it carried this information. For epistemological purposes (for purposes of defining knowledge) I think this characterization will do, but I no longer think it suffices for understanding the role of belief or meaning in the explanation of behavior. It makes meaning and information, and hence belief, epiphenomenal.

But something better can be done, and it is my purpose in this chapter to do it—to describe the way those relations that underlie an element's meaning, the relations that enable it to *say* something about another situation, figure in the explanation of the containing system's behavior. What we need is an account of the way reasons, in virtue of being reasons, in virtue of standing in semantically relevant relations to other situations, causally explain the behavior that they, in virtue of having this content, help to rationalize.

In pursuit of this end it is important that we avoid effects that are achieved through the mediation of intermediate cognitive processes or agents. So, for example, my automobile's gas tank gets filled with gasoline when I, at the right time and place, make sounds with a certain meaning, when I say "Fill it up, please." If I produce sounds with a substantially different meaning, the tank doesn't get filled. And if, at a different time and place, I produce completely different sounds with the same (or a similar) meaning (e.g., "Benzina, per favore"), the same result is achieved. So it looks like it is not the sounds I produce but their meaning that is having the desired effect. It is *what* I say, not *how* I say it, that explains, or helps to explain, why my gas tank gets filled.

I say we must avoid effects like this. The project is to understand how something's having meaning could itself have a physical effect—the kind of effect (e.g., muscular contraction) required for most forms of behavior—and to understand this *without* enlisting the aid of intelligent homunculi in the head, *without* appealing to hypothetical centers of cognitive activity who, like filling-station attendants, *understand the meaning* of incoming signals. Meaning itself, not some convenient but purely hypothetical understander-of-meaning, has to do the work. To introduce intermediaries who achieve *their* physical effects (on motor neurons, say) by understanding (= knowing the meaning of) the stimuli impinging on them is to interpolate into our solution the very mystery we are seeking to unravel. For to speak of an understander-of-meaning is to speak of something *on which* meaning, and differences in meaning, have an effect. An understander-of-meaning *is* the problem, not something we can use in a solution.

Earlier chapters have put us in a position to confront this problem with some realistic hopes for progress. The chief result of chapters 1 and 2 was that behavior, *what* we are trying to explain when we advert to such content-bearing entities as beliefs and desires, is *not* the physical movements or changes that are the normal *product* of behavior. What we are trying to explain, causally or otherwise, is not why our limbs move but why we move them.

So the explanandum, what is to be explained, is why some process occurred, why (in the case of a structuring cause) M (rather than some

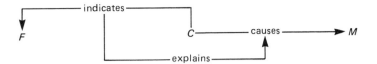

Figure 4.1

other result) is being produced by an internal C. Furthermore, given the results of chapter 3, this causal relationship between C and M, if it is going to be explained by something like the meaning of C, will have to be explained by the fact that C indicates, or has the function of indicating, how things stand elsewhere in the world. It will not be enough merely to have a C that indicates F cause M. We want the fact that it indicates F to be an explanatorily relevant fact about C—the fact about C that explains, or helps explain, *why* it causes M. What needs to be done, then, is to show how the existence of one relationship, the relationship underlying C's semantic character, can explain the existence of another relationship, the causal relationship (between C and M) comprising the behavior in question. With F standing for a condition that C indicates, what we need to show is illustrated in figure 4.1.

Once C is recruited as a cause of M—and recruited as a cause of M *because of what it indicates about F*—C acquires, thereby, the function of indicating F. Hence, C comes to *represent* F. C acquires its semantics, a genuine meaning, at the very moment when a component[4] of its natural meaning (the fact that it indicates F) acquires an explanatory relevance. This, indeed, is why beliefs are maps *by means of which we steer.* An indicator element (such as C) becomes a representation by having part of *what* it indicates (the fact that it indicates F) promoted to an explanatorily relevant fact about itself. A belief is merely an indicator whose natural meaning has been converted into a form of non-natural meaning by being given a job to do in the explanation of behavior. What you believe is relevant to what you do because beliefs are precisely those internal structures that have acquired control over output, and hence become relevant to the explanation of system behavior, in virtue of what they, when performing satisfactorily, indicate about external conditions.

What we must do, then, is show how the explanatory relationship depicted in figure 4.1, the relation between C's indicating F and C's causing

---

4. C will normally indicate a great many things other than F. Its indication of F is, therefore, only "one component" of its natural meaning. Nonetheless, it is this single component that is promoted to *representational* status, to a form of non-natural meaning, because it is C's indication of F, not its indication of (say) G or H, that explains its causing M. Hence, it becomes C's function to indicate F, not G or H.

M, can come about in some natural way. Once this is done, we will have a model of the way beliefs *might* figure in the explanation of behavior—and, hence, a model of the way reasons *could* help to determine what we do. The modesty (reflected in the qualifiers "might" and "could") is necessary because nothing has yet been said about the way *desire* and other motivational states fit into this explanatory picture. We pick up the phone not only because we *think* it is ringing but also because we *want* to answer it when it rings. This is a topic for the following chapter.

Aside from this gap, however, there will doubtless be deeper questions about the adequacy of our account of belief. Even if it can be shown that certain internal indicators can acquire an indicator function, hence a *meaning* or a *content*, in the process by means of which this content is made relevant to the explanation of behavior, it may be wondered whether such simple, almost mechanical, models of belief could ever provide a realistic portrait of the way reasons function in everyday action. Can one really suppose that our ordinary explanations of human behavior have this kind of tinkertoy, push-pull quality to them? Maybe for rats and pigeons it will do, but in explaining a person's weekly attendance at church, the sacrifices of a parent, or an act of revenge are we really talking about the operation of internal indicators? Indicators of what? Salvation? A divine being? An afterlife? Justice?

This challenge—a very serious and understandable challenge, even among those who are otherwise sympathetic to naturalistic accounts of the mind—will be confronted (with what success I leave for others to judge) in the final chapter. What we are after in the present chapter is something less ambitious: an account, however oversimplified and crude it might have to be, of the basic cognitive building blocks. What we are after in this chapter and the next are the elements out of which intentional systems, systems whose behavior can be explained by *reasons*, are constructed. How these basic elements might be combined to give a more realistic portrait of intelligent behavior I leave for later.

4.2 Why Machines Behave the Way They Do

To illustrate the structure of relations depicted in figure 4.1, it is useful to begin with simple artifacts. Though instruments and machines don't have beliefs and desires, much less do things *because* of what they believe and desire, they nevertheless *do* things. And *some* of this behavior is explicable, indirectly at least, in a way analogous to the way we explain the behavior of animals. Since these explanations make essential use of the purposes and beliefs of those who construct and use the device, nothing of deep philosophical interest—nothing that helps one understand the ultimate nature of purpose and belief—is revealed by the existence of such explanations.

Nonetheless, there are certain revealing similarities between these explanations and the ones that are of real interest, and it is to highlight these similarities that I begin with these artificial examples.

In an earlier chapter I described the behavior of a thermostat. A drop in room temperature causes a bimetallic strip in this instrument to bend. Depending on the position of an adjustable contact, the bending strip eventually closes an electrical circuit. Current flows to the furnace and ignition occurs. The thermostat's behavior, its turning the furnace on, *is* the bringing about of furnace ignition by events occurring in the thermostat—in this case (it may be different in other thermostats), the closure of a switch by the movement of a temperature-sensitive strip.

In asking why the device turned the furnace on, we are asking why these internal events—whatever, in detail, they happen to be—caused furnace ignition. As we saw in chapter 2, the drop in room temperature, though it caused the bimetallic strip to bend and, in this way, caused the furnace to ignite, and though it may therefore be identified as the *triggering* cause of this process (and, therefore, of the product of this process: furnace ignition), is not the *structuring* cause of this behavior. The drop in room temperature causes a C *which* (given the way things are wired) causes M. It, so to speak, initiates a process which has M as its outcome. But it does not cause C to cause M. It does not, therefore, help us to understand why the thermostat behaves this way—why it turns the furnace on rather than, say, opening the garage door or starting the dishwasher.

But if the drop in room temperature is not, in this sense, the cause (the *structuring* cause) of thermostat behavior, if it did not cause the thermostat to turn the furnace on, what did? *We* did. The movement of the bimetallic strip caused furnace ignition because that is the way it was designed, manufactured, and installed. *We* arranged things *so that* the movement of this temperature-sensitive component would, depending on the position of an adjustable setting, close an electrical circuit to the furnace, thereby causing furnace ignition. We wanted furnace ignition to depend on room temperature in some systematic way, so we introduced an appropriate causal intermediary: a switching device that was at the same time a thermometer, something that would cause furnace ignition depending on what it indicated about room temperature. If anyone or anything is responsible for C's causing M and, hence, for the thermostat's behaving the way it does, it is we, its creators.

So (referring to figure 4.1) *we* caused C to cause M. We did so, however, because of some fact about C. The bimetallic strip was made into a furnace switch, into a cause of M, because it has a special property: its shape varies systematically with, and therefore indicates something about, the temperature. The strip is given a causal role to play, assigned (as it were) control duties in the operation of this thermoregulatory system, because of what it indicates about a certain quantity. Ultimately, then, the strip causes what it does because it indicates what it does.[5]

The bimetallic strip is given a job to do, made part of an electrical switch for the furnace, *because* of what it indicates about room temperature. Since this is so, it thereby acquires the *function* of indicating what the temperature is. We have a representational system of Type II. An internal indicator (of temperature) acquires the function of indicating temperature by being incorporated into a control circuit whose satisfactory operation, turning the furnace on *when* the temperature drops too low, depends on the reliable performance of this component in indicating the temperature.[6] We can speak of (Type II) representation here, and therefore of misrepresentation, but only because the device's internal indicators have been assigned an appropriate *function*: the function of telling the instrument what it needs to know in order to do what it is supposed to do.

In a certain derived sense, then, it is the fact that *C* means what it does, the fact that it indicates the temperature, that explains (through us, as it were) its *causing* what it does. And its causing, or being made to cause, what it does *because* it means what it does is what gives the indicator the function of indicating what it does and confers on it, therefore, the status of a *representation*. An internal indicator acquires genuine (albeit derived) meaning—acquires a *representational* content of Type II—by having its natural meaning, the fact that it indicates *F*, determine its causal role in the production of output. In terms of figure 4.1, the situation looks something like figure 4.2. The indicator relation (between *C* and *F*) becomes the relation of representation insofar as it—the fact that *C* indicates *F*— explains the causal relation between *C* and *M*.

This account of the behavior of a thermostat is infected with intentional and teleological notions, and thus does not represent significant progress in our attempt to understand the causal efficacy of meaning. As figure 4.2 reveals, *C*'s causal efficacy is achieved through the mediation of agents (designers, builders, installers) who *give C* a causal role in the production of *M* because they *recognize C*'s dependence on *F* and *want M* to depend on *F*.

---

5. I am ignoring the fact that the bimetallic strip is only *part* of the furnace switch, the other part consisting of an adjustable contact point—adjustable to correspond to "desired" temperature (desired by *us*, of course, not the thermostat). In speaking of the cause of furnace ignition, then, there are really two separable factors to be considered: the configuration of the bimetallic strip (representing *actual* temperature) and the position of the adjustable contact point (corresponding to *desired* temperature). I ignore these complications now since I am, for the moment, interested only in developing a model for belief. I will return to this point later when considering the role of desire in the explanation of behavior.
6. See, e.g., Cummins 1975: "When a capacity of a containing system is appropriately explained by analyzing it into a number of other capacities whose programmed exercise yields a manifestation of the analyzed capacity, the analyzing capacities emerge as functions." (p. 407 in Sober 1984b)

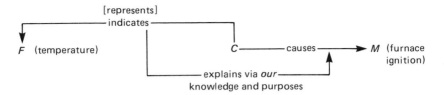

Figure 4.2

The intrusion of *our* purposes into this explanatory story is especially obvious if we consider circumstances in which the designers are confused—circumstances in which C, although it does not depend on F in the requisite way and therefore does not indicate anything about F, is nonetheless *thought* to depend on F. If this should occur, there is little question but that C would (or might) be given exactly the same causal role to play. In such a case, C would not indicate F; yet, because of our false beliefs, C would still (be made to) cause M.

Nevertheless, the case of the thermostat and those of various other control devices are suggestive. They suggest a way that the relations underlying genuine meaning, the indicator relations out of which Type II and Type III representations are fashioned, might figure in the explanation of a state's (C's) acquiring certain control duties and, hence, in the explanation of the behavior (C's causing M) of the containing system (the system of which C is a part).

It is these suggestive leads that I mean to develop in the rest of this chapter. The idea will be that during the normal development of an organism, certain internal structures *acquire* control over peripheral movements of the systems of which they are a part. Furthermore, the explanation, or part of the explanation, for this assumption of control duties is not (as in the case of artifacts) what anyone *thinks* these structures mean or indicate but what, in fact, they *do* mean or indicate about the external circumstances *in which* these movements occur and *on which* their success depends. In the process of acquiring control over peripheral movements (in virtue of what they indicate), such structures acquire an indicator function and, hence, the capacity for misrepresenting how things stand. This, then, is the origin of genuine meaning and, at the same time, an account of the respect in which this meaning is made relevant to behavior.

We can come a bit closer to getting what we want—getting *us* (intentional agents) out of the explanatory picture—by looking at the way detector mechanisms are developed for control purposes in plants and animals. In some of these cases natural selection plays a role similar to that which *we* play with artifacts. The chief difference is that natural selection does not literally *design* a system. There is nothing comparable to a human agent's installing components and assigning control functions because of what things are capable (or what the designer *thinks* they are capable) of doing. For this reason the evolutionary development of control mechanisms, because it gets along without the assistance of any intentional agent, promises to come much closer to our ultimate objective: a completely naturalized account of the explanatory relation illustrated in figure 4.1. It will turn out that this is *still* not quite what we need, but the respects in which it falls short are illuminating.

4.3 *Explaining Instinctive Behavior*

It seems plausible to suppose that certain patterns of behavior—those commonly thought of as instinctive, innate, or genetically determined—involve internal triggering mechanisms that were developed over many generations because of the adaptive advantage of reacting quickly, reliably, and in a stereotypical way to recurring situations. If M is always, or almost always, beneficial in conditions F, why not hard-wire the system to produce M when F occurs?

We have already spoken of plant behavior. Some of this behavior depends on the operation of internal indicators. As was noted in chapter 2, it is important that certain trees shed their leaves at the approach of cold, dry weather. In order that this be done in a timely way, it is essential that whatever it is *in* the tree (C) that initiates the chemical activity leading to leaf removal (M) itself be (or be coupled to) a mechanism sensitive to seasonal changes: perhaps a biological clock of some sort; perhaps a thermal sensor responsive to the gradual temperature gradients characteristic of seasonal change; perhaps a photoreceptor signaling the shortening of days as winter approaches. This is the only way that such activities as dormancy, leaf abscission, and flowering can be synchronized with the external conditions in which these behaviors are beneficial to the plant.

It is interesting in this connection to listen to the biologists Raven, Evert, and Curtis (1981, p. 529) describe a plant's informational needs:

> After periods of ordinary rest, growth resumes when the temperature becomes milder or when water or any other limiting factor becomes available again. A dormant bud or embryo, however, can be "activated" only by certain, often quite precise, environmental cues. This adaptation is of great survival importance to the plant. For example, the buds of plants expand, flowers are formed, and seeds germinate in the spring—*but how do they recognize spring* [my italics—F.D.]? If warm weather alone were enough, in many years all the plants would flower and all the seedlings would start to grow during Indian summer, only to be destroyed by the winter frost. The same could be said

for any one of the warm spells that often punctuate the winter season. The dormant seed or bud does not respond to these apparently favorable conditions because of endogenous inhibitors which must first be removed or neutralized before the period of dormancy can be terminated.

In such cases it seems reasonable to suppose that whatever it is in the plant that causes the buds to expand, the flowers to form, and the seeds to germinate in the spring is something that was selected for this job *because* it tended to occur at the right time, *when* the plant profited from the kind of activity (growth, germination, etc.) that it brought about. In other words, the chemical trigger for growth, germination, flowering and leaf removal was selected for its job, over many generations, because of its more or less reliable[7] correlation with the time of year in which this activity was most beneficial to the plant. Here again we find a structure's causal role in the production of output explained, in part at least, by its indicator properties.

We earlier saw how predaceous fungi capture, kill, and consume (eat?) small insects and worms. The mechanisms these plants use to trap their prey embody sensitive indicators (C) of movement (F). These indicators, once activated by movement, cause a rapid swelling (M) of a ring that "grasps" or "holds" the prey. More sophisticated plants have more dis-criminating sensors. The Venus flytrap, for instance, comes equipped with sensitive hairs on each half-leaf. When an insect walks on the leaf, it brushes against these hairs, triggering a traplike closing of the leaves. The leaf halves squeeze shut, pressing the insect against the digestive glands on the inner surfaces of the leaves. This trapping mechanism is so specialized that it can distinguish between living prey and inanimate objects, such as pebbles and small sticks, that fall on the leaf by chance. Once again, leaf movement (M) is caused by an internal state (C) that signals the occurrence of a particular kind of movement, the kind of movement that is normally produced by some digestible prey. And there is every reason to think that this internal trigger was selected for its job *because* of what it indicated, because it "told" the plant what it needed to know (i.e., *when* to close its leaves) in order to more effectively capture prey.

---

7. Elliott Sober has pointed out to me that for selection to take place all that is needed is for the triggering state to be *better* correlated with the appropriate season than are the corre-sponding states in competing plants. A state need not be reliably correlated with spring—hence, need not indicate the arrival of spring—in order to be correlated sufficiently well with the arrival of spring to confer on its possessor a competitive advantage. In cases where the correlation (with spring) is not of a sort to support the claim that there is an indication of spring, there will always be an indication of something (e.g., an interval of mild weather) which will (via its past correlation with the arrival of spring) explain its selection. The indicator properties are still relevant to the thing's selection, just not its indication of *spring*. I return to this point in section 4.4.

Explaining a plant's behavior (its closing its leaves, trapping an insect, or strangling a nematode) by describing the event that, by activating the internal indicator, brings about leaf movement, enclosure of insect, or strangulation of nematode, is merely a way of describing the triggering cause of the plant's behavior: the condition (F) the internal indication of which (by C) led (presumably by natural selection) to C's causing M. But though the movement of an insect on the plant's leaves triggers a process that culminates in closure of the leaves (M), it does not explain why the process has this, rather than another, outcome. If we want a *structuring* cause of plant behavior, an explanation of why the plant did *this* then, rather than an explanation of why it did this *then*, we have to look for the cause, not of C, not of M, but of C's causing M. And here, just as in the case of the thermostat, we find the explanation coming back to some fact about C. It is a fact about C's status as an indicator—the fact that it registers the occurrence of a certain kind of movement, the kind of movement that is usually (or often, or often *enough*) made by a digestible insect—that explains why, over many generations, C was selected, installed, or made into a cause of M. Because M is beneficial to the plant when it occurs in conditions F (but not generally otherwise), some indicator of F was given the job of producing M. It is this fact about C that explains, via natural selection, its current role in controlling leaf movement in the same way a corresponding fact about the bimetallic strip in a thermostat explains, via the purposes of its designers, its causal role in regulating a furnace.

As with plants, so with animals. The noctuid moth's auditory system is obviously designed with its chief predator, the bat, in mind. The moth's ear does not relay information about a host of acoustical stimuli that are audible to other animals. Prolonged steady sounds, for example, elicit no response in the receptor. The bat emits *bursts* of high-frequency sound, which are what the moth's receptors are "designed" to pick up and respond to. The moth's ear has one task of paramount and overriding importance (Alcock 1984, p. 133): the detection of cues associated with its nocturnal enemy. And its behavioral repertoire is equally constrained and simple: it turns away from low-intensity ultrasound (the bat at a distance) and dives, flips, or spirals erratically to high-intensity ultrasound (the bat closing in).

Why did the moth's nervous system develop in this way? Why did it inherit neural wiring of this sort, wiring that automatically adjusts the moth's orientation (relative to the incoming sound) and, hence, its direction of movement so as effectively to avoid contact with the source of that sound? The answer, obviously, is to enable moths to avoid bats. Inspection of the comparatively simple wiring diagram of the moth's central nervous system reveals that the motor neurons that adjust orientation, and hence the moth's direction of movement (M), are controlled, through a network of interneurons, by structures that indicate the *location* (distance and direction) of the sound source (*F*). What the theory of evolution has to tell us about these cases (and these cases are typical of motor control systems throughout the animal kingdom) is that *C*'s production of *M* is, at least in part, the result of its indication of *F*. *M* is produced by an indicator of *F* because such an arrangement confers a competitive advantage on its possessor. If you want *M* to occur in conditions *F* but not generally otherwise, and if *F*, left to its own devices, won't produce *M*, then the best strategy (indeed the only strategy) is to make an indicator of *F* into a cause of *M*. If the organism already has an indicator of *F*, *make it* into a cause of *M*. If it doesn't have such an indicator, *give it* one. This is the course that engineers follow in designing control systems such as the thermostat. It is also the course that nature takes, in its own nonpurposeful way, in the design of plants and animals.

Though the evolutionary development of control systems for the instinctive or innate behavior of animals does not, like figure 4.2, involve an interpolated *agent*, it nonetheless fails to meet the explanatory requirements of figure 4.1 for another reason. As Cummins (1975) notes, natural selection (assuming this is the chief pressure for evolutionary change) does not explain why organisms *have* the properties for which they are selected any more than Clyde's preference for redheads explains why Doris, his current favorite, has red hair. It is, if anything, the other way around: her having red hair explains why Clyde selected her. The neural circuitry in a particular moth, the connections in virtue of which an internal sign of an approaching bat causes evasive wing movements, is, like other phenotypical structures, to be causally explained by the genes the moth inherited from its ancestors. This isn't to suggest that there is a sharp distinction between nature and nurture, between genetic and environmental determinants of behavior, but it is to suggest that the explanation for the control circuitry in *this* moth— the explanation for why *this C* is causing *this M*, why the moth is now executing evasive maneuvers—has nothing to do with what *this C* indicates about this moth's surroundings. The explanation lies in the moth's genes. They (given anything like normal conditions for development) determine that *C*, *whatever* it in fact happens to indicate about the moth's surroundings, will produce *M*.

Elliott Sober (1984a, pp. 147–152), applying a distinction of Richard Lewontin (1983), contrasts selectional explanations with developmental explanations. In explaining why all the children in a room read at the third-grade level (Sober's example), one explains it developmentally by explaining why each and every child in the room reads at this level. Or one can explain it selectionally by saying that *only* children reading at the third-grade level were allowed in the room (selected for admission into the room). The latter explanation does not tell us why Sam, Aaron, Marisa, et

but you never get that; this C is a particular!

al. read at the third-grade level. In effect, it tells us why all of them read at the third-grade level without telling us why any one of them reads at that level. Sober correctly diagnoses this difference in explanatory effect by pointing out that the difference between a selectional and a developmental explanation of why all the children in the room read at the third-grade level is a *contrastive phenomenon* (Dretske 1973; Garfinkel 1981). It is, in effect, the difference between explaining why (all) my friends imbibe martinis, an explanation that requires my telling you something about them, and explaining why I have (only) martini imbibers as friends, an explanation that requires my telling you something about me.

The moth has the kind of nervous system it has, the kind in which an internal representation of an approaching bat causes evasive movements, because it developed from a fertilized egg which contained genetic instructions for this kind of neural circuitry, circuitry *in which* the occurrence of C will cause M. This is a developmental explanation, a causal explanation of why, in today's moths, tokens of type C produce movements of type M. These genetically coded instructions regulated the way in which development occurred, channeling the proliferation and specialization of cells along pathways that produced a nervous system with these special features. Even if through a recent freak of nature (recent enough so that selectional pressures had no time to operate) the occurrence of C in contemporary moths were to signal not the approach of a hungry bat but the arrival of a receptive mate, C would still produce M—would still produce the same evasive flight manuevers. What C indicates in *today's* moths has nothing to do with the explanation of what movements it helps to produce. And the fact that tokens of C indicated in remote ancestors the approach of hungry bats does not explain—at least not causally (developmentally)—why *this* (or indeed, why *any*) C produces M. Rather, it explains (selectionally) why there are, today, predominantly moths in which C causes M.

The moth's behavior is, like so much of the behavior of simple organisms, tropistic. Tropisms are simple mechanical or chemical feedback processes or combinations of such processes that have the interesting property of looking like organized motivated behavior. According to Jacques Loeb (1918), who first described tropisms in plants and simple animals, the working of all tropisms can be explained with two principles: symmetry and sensitivity. Caterpillars emerge from their cocoons in the spring, climb to the tips of tree branches, and eat the new buds. This apparently purposeful behavior has a simple explanation in terms of Loeb's two principles. Rachlin (1976, pp. 125−126) describes it thus:

> The caterpillars are sensitive to light and have two eyes, symmetrically placed one on each side of the head. When the same amount of light comes into the two eyes, the caterpillars move straight ahead;

but when one of the eyes gets more light, the legs on that side move more slowly. The result is that the caterpillars tend to orient toward the light—which in nature invariably is strongest at the tops of trees. Thus, whenever they move, they move toward the tops of the trees, ending up at the tip of a branch. When, in his experiments, Loeb put lights at the bottom of the trees, the caterpillars went down, not up, and would starve to death rather than reverse direction. When the caterpillars were blinded in one eye, they traveled in a circle like a mechanical toy with one wheel broken.

A symmetrical placement of light-sensitive indicators, each indicator harnessed to an appropriate set of effectors, is capable of explaining most of this behavior. Though a plant doesn't have a nervous system, similar mechanisms help explain the climbing behavior of some plants. And they are equally at work in guiding the moth away from the bat.

Such tropistic behavior has a rather simple mechanical basis. And the blueprint for the processes underlying this behavior is genetically coded. The behavior is instinctive—i.e., not modifiable by learning. But it is not the simplicity of its explanation that disqualifies such behavior from being the behavior of interest in this study. *Reasons* are irrelevant to the explanation of this behavior, not because there is an underlying chemical and mechanical explanation for the movements in question (there is, presumably, some underlying chemical and mechanical explanation for the movements associated with all behavior), but because, although indicators are involved in the production of this movement, *what they indicate*—the fact that they indicate thus and so—is (and was) irrelevant to what movements they produce. If we suppose that, through selection, an internal indicator acquired (over many generations) a biological function, the function to indicate something about the animal's surroundings, then we can say that this internal structure *represents* (or *misrepresents*, as the case may be) external affairs. This is, in fact, a representation of Type III. But it is *not* a belief. For to qualify as a belief it is not enough to *be* an internal representation (a map) that is among the causes of output, something that helps us steer. *The fact that it is a map*, the fact that it *says* something about external conditions, must be relevantly engaged in the way it steers us through these conditions. What is required, in addition, and in accordance with figure 4.1, is that the structure's indicator properties figure in the explanation of its causal properties, that what it *says* (about external affairs) helps to explain what it *does* (in the production of output). That is what is missing in the case of reflexes, tropisms, and other instinctive behaviors. Meaning, though it is there, is not relevantly *engaged* in the production of output. The system doesn't do what it does, C doesn't cause M, *because* of what C (or anything else) means or indicates about external conditions. Though C has meaning of the relevant kind, this is not a meaning it has *to* or *for* the animal in which it occurs. That, basically, is why genetically determined behaviors are not explicable in terms of the actor's reasons. That is why they are not *actions*. What (if anything) one wants, believes, and intends is irrelevant to what one does.

The distinction between developmental and selectional explanations is not, therefore, merely the difference in what behaviorial biologists call *proximate* factors and *ultimate* factors (Alcock 1984, p. 3; Grier 1984, p. 21). What they mean by ultimate factors (the selectional explanations one finds in sociobiological "explanations" of behavior, for instance) are not factors that figure in the causal explanation, proximate *or* remote, of the behavior of any individual. In such cases an internal state, C, which means (indicates) that a hungry bat is approaching and which even (let us say) has the *function* of indicating this (in virtue, let us suppose, of its evolutionary development in this *kind* of moth), *does*, to be sure, cause orientation and wing movements of an appropriate (evasive) sort. C (something that indicates the approach of a bat) causes M (bat-avoidance movements). Nevertheless, it is not C's meaning what it does (F) that explains why it causes this (M). In this case the internal state *has* a semantics—something it is (given its evolutionary development) *supposed* to indicate—but the fact that it indicates this, or is supposed to indicate this, is irrelevant to an understanding of why it actually does what it does. A selectional explanation of behavior is no more an explanation of an individual organism's behavior—why *this* (or indeed *any*) moth takes a nosedive when a bat is closing in—than is a selectional account of the antisocial behavior of prison inmates an explanation of why Lefty forges checks, Harry robs banks, and Moe steals cars. The fact that we imprison people who forge checks, steal cars, and rob banks does not explain why the people in prison do these things.

False

4.4 *Putting Information to Work: Learning*

To find a genuine case where an element's semantic character helps to determine its causal role in the production of output—a case where what the (internal) map *says* helps explain what kind of (external) effects the map has—one must look to systems whose control structures are actually shaped by the kind of dependency relations that exist between internal and external conditions. The places to look for these cases are places where individual learning is occurring, places where internal states *acquire* control duties or *change* their effect on motor output as a result of their relation to the circumstances on which the success of this output depends.

There are many forms of learning, or what generally passes as learning, that have little or nothing to do with the meaning, if any, of internal states.

If learning is understood, as it sometimes is, as *any* change in behavior (or, perhaps, any *useful* change of behavior) brought about by experience, then habituation and sensitization may qualify as elementary forms of learning. Roughly speaking, habituation is a decrease, and sensitization an increase, in response to a repetitive stimulus. Such changes are often mediated by relatively peripheral mechanisms. For example, the change in movements produced by a certain stimulus may be due entirely to receptor (or muscle) fatigue. It seems fairly clear that if there are internal maps that help us steer, one isn't likely to find them playing a significant role in explaining the behavior resulting from changes of this kind.[8]

It is only when we get to a form of learning whose success depends on the deployment and the use of internal indicators that it becomes plausible to think that the causal processes constitutive of behavior may actually be explained by facts about what these indicators indicate. And this means that we must look to kinds of learning in which the *correlations* (*contingencies*, as they are sometimes called) underlying the indicator relationship play a prominent role. We must look, in other words, to certain forms of associative learning if we are to find the kind of explanatory relationship depicted in figure 4.1. Only (but, as it turns out, not always) in this kind of learning do we find internal states assuming control functions *because* of what they indicate about the conditions in which behavior occurs. Only here do we find *information*, and not merely the structures that carry or embody information, being put to work in the production and the control of behavior.

Consider the following common problem, whose general form I shall call The Design Problem: We want a system that will do *M* when, but only when, conditions *F* exist.[9] How do we build it? Or, if we are talking about an already existing system, how do we get it to behave in this way?

In very general terms, the solution to The Design Problem is always the

---

8. Staddon (1983, p. 2) sees no hard and fast line separating learning from other kinds of behavioral change: "... we do not really know what learning is." Experience can change behavior in many ways that manifestly do not involve learning: "... a change brought about by physical injury or restraint, by fatigue or by illness doesn't count. Short-term changes, such as those termed *habituation, adaptation,* or *sensitization,* are also excluded—the change wrought must be relatively permanent. *Forgetting* has an ambiguous status: The change is usually permanent and does not fall into any of the forbidden categories, yet it is paradoxical to call forgetting an example of learning. Evidently it is not just *any* quasi-permanent change that qualifies. *Learning* is a category defined largely by exclusion." (ibid., pp. 395–396)

9. In order to minimize the use of symbols I will hereafter (in this and later chapters) let "*M*" do double duty. I shall, as before, let it stand for some external movement; but I shall also let it stand for behavior, the process of producing movement. It will, I hope, always be clear which is intended. When I speak of behavior *M*, or of someone's *doing M*, I should be understood as referring to *the production of M* (by some internal state *C*).

same. Whether it is the deliberate creation of an engineer, the product of evolutionary development, or the outcome of individual learning, the system S must embody, and if it doesn't already embody it must be supplied with, some kind of internal mechanism that is selectively sensitive to the presence or absence of condition F. It must be equipped with something that will indicate or register the presence of those conditions with which behavior is to be coordinated. We have already taken note of the way this works with artifacts: If you want a device that will turn the furnace on when the temperature gets too low, (a particular instance of The Design Problem), this device must be supplied with a temperature indicator. We have also noted how it works with instinctive behavior: If you want young animals to stop or change direction when they encounter cliffs, they must, sooner or later, be supplied with a mechanism sensitive to steep (downward) depth gradients—a "cliff" indicator. If you want chickens to hide from hawks (another instance of The Design Problem), you have to give them an internal hawk indicator, or at least an indicator of something (e.g., a certain silhouette in the sky) that is sufficiently well correlated with the approach of a hawk to make concealment a beneficial response when there is a positive indication. The same is true of learning. If you want a rat to press a bar when and only when a certain tone is heard, a pigeon to peck a target when and only when a light is red, or a child to say "Mommy" to and only to Mommy, then the rat needs a tone indicator, the bird a color indicator, and the child a Mommy indicator. Only if such indicators exist is it possible to solve The Design Problem. You can't get a system to do M in conditions F unless there is something in it to indicate when these conditions exist.

In the case of learning, this is merely to say that you must begin with a system that has the appropriate sensory capacities. The system must have a way of getting the information that condition F obtains if it is going to learn to do M in conditions F. The rat must be able to hear, able to distinguish one tone from another, if it is to learn to respond in some distinctive way to a particular tone. The pigeon must be able to *see*, to distinguish visually, one color from another if it is to learn to peck when the light is red. The child must be able to see Mommy, or at least sense her presence in some way, before she can be taught to say "Mommy" when Mommy is present. If Mommy has a twin sister who regularly babysits for the child, this learning is going to be impaired or, depending on the degree of resemblance, impossible. It will be slower because the infant's Mommy detector has been neutralized by the presence of the twin. If the child's powers of discrimination are such that she cannot tell the difference between Mommy and Auntie, the child *cannot* learn to say "Mommy" in the prescribed way (i.e., only to Mommy), for she no longer has a Mommy indicator. It would be like trying to teach a tone-deaf rat to respond to middle C or a color-blind bird to peck at red targets.

So the first requirement for a solution to The Design Problem is that the system be equipped with an F indicator. Once this requirement is satisfied, all that remains to be done is to harness this indicator to effector mechanisms in such a way that appropriate movements (M) are produced when and only when the indicator positively registers the presence of condition F. This is something the engineer accomplishes by soldering wires in the right places. This is something nature accomplishes in the case of instinctive behavior by selecting systems whose wires are already secured, if not soldered, in the right place (or, if not in the right place, at least in a place that is more nearly right—a place that confers on its possessor a competitive advantage). And, finally, this is something that is accomplished in certain forms of learning by the kind of *consequences* attending the production of M.

By the timely reinforcement of certain output—by rewarding this output *when*, and generally *only when*, it occurs in certain conditions—internal indicators of these conditions are recruited as causes of this output.[10] Just *how* they are recruited by this process may be (and to me is) a complete mystery. The parallel distributed processing (PDP) networks, networks of interconnected nodes in which the strength of connections between nodes is continually reweighted (during "learning") so that, eventually, given inputs will yield desired outputs, provide intriguing and suggestive models for this recruitment process (Hinton and Anderson 1981; McClelland and Rumelhart 1985). In these models, the internal indicators would be patterns of activation of the network's input nodes, and recruitment would proceed by selection (by appropriate reweighting between nodes) of the desired input (i.e., an F indicator) for an appropriate activation of effector mechanisms (M). But no matter how the nervous system manages to accomplish this trick, the fact that it does accomplish it, for many animals and for a variety of different behaviors, is obvious. Learning cannot take place *unless* internal indicators of F are harnessed to effector mechanisms in some appropriate way. Since this learning *does* occur, the recruitment *must* take place. These internal indicators are assigned a job to do in the production of bodily movement—they get their hands on the steering wheel (so to

10. It sounds a little odd to say that the indicators are *recruited* for this job if they are, for whatever reason, *already* serving as causes of the appropriate movements. Though this seems improbable for *learned* behaviors, the behaviors we are presently concerned with, the possibility figures in some philosophical thought experiments—e.g., Stich's (1983) Replacement Argument and Davidson's (1987) Swampman. If, however, the *continued* service of an indicator (as a cause of a movement) depends on the occurrence of reinforcement, I shall, for purposes of brevity, speak of this as recruitment. I am grateful to Dugald Owen for discussion on this point.

how is this guided?

speak)—in virtue of what they "say" (indicate or mean) about the conditions in which these movements have beneficial or desirable consequences. Since these indicators are recruited for control duties *because* of the information they supply, supplying this information becomes part of their job description—part of what they, once recruited, are *supposed to do*.

Just as our incorporation of a bimetallic strip into a furnace switch *because* of what it indicates about temperature gives this element the function (Type II) of indicating what the temperature is, the reorganization of control circuits occurring during learning, by converting internal elements into "movement switches" in virtue of what they indicate about environmental conditions, confers on these elements the function (Type III) of indicating whatever it is that brought about their conversion to switches. As a result, learning of this sort accomplishes two things: it reorganizes control circuits so as to incorporate indicators into the chain of command, and it does so *because* these indicators indicate what they do. Learning of this sort mobilizes information-carrying structures for control duties *in virtue of the information they carry*. In bringing about this transformation, learning not only confers a function on these indicators, and thereby a *meaning*, but also shapes their causal role, and hence the behavior of the system of which they are a part, in terms of *what they mean*—in terms of the information they now have the function of providing. Such learning *creates* maps at the same time it gives these maps, *qua* maps, a job to do in steering the vehicle.

The kind of learning we are talking about is a special form of *operant* or *instrumental* learning, a kind of learning sometimes called *discrimination* learning. One learns to identify F, or at least to distinguish (discriminate) F from other conditions, by having particular responses to F (or particular responses *in* condition F) rewarded[11] in some special way. The literature on instrumental conditioning, not to mention that on learning theory in general, is enormous. Fortunately, not all this material is relevant to the present point. We need only two facts, both of which are (as facts go in this area) relatively unproblematic.

First, there is Thorndike's Law of Effect, which tells us that successful behavior tends to be repeated (Rachlin 1976, pp. 228–235). More technically, a reward (alternatively, a positive reinforcement) increases the probability that the response that generates it (or with which it co-occurs) will occur again in the same circumstances.

It isn't particularly important for my purposes (though it certainly may be for other purposes) whether we think of rewards as stimuli (e.g., food)

---

11. Learning theorists typically distinguish between rewards (e.g., the delivery of food) and reinforcement (and effect of the reward on the organism). Unless these differences are important to the point I am making, I shall ignore them and use these terms interchangeably.

or as responses (e.g., *eating* the food). One can even think of them as the *pleasures* (need or tension reduction) that certain stimuli (or responses) bring to an organism.

Neither is it important that we get clear about the exact status of this law. There have been deep (and often legitimate) suspicions about the empirical significance of this law (see, e.g., Postman 1947; Meehl 1950). Unless there is available some *independent* specification of what a reward or reinforcer is—independent, that is, of its effect on the probability of a response—the law seems devoid of empirical content. It becomes a mere tautology: results that tend to increase the probability of behavior tend to increase the probability of that behavior. There is also disagreement about exactly how the reward must be related to the response it strengthens (temporal contiguity? mere correlation?) and about the "associability" of some response-reinforcement pairs (Garcia and Koelling 1966). The latter issue raises questions about the scope of this law—whether, indeed, it is applicable in every situation. Even if cookies reinforce some behavior, they surely will not be equally effective for all behavior. A child might eat her vegetables to get a cookie but refuse to walk on hot coals for the same reward. Finally, Premack (1959, 1965) has argued persuasively for the relative nature of the concept of reinforcement, i.e., that reward and punishment are determined by relations between events in a "value" hierarchy. Any event in this hierarchy (as long as there is a lower event) can be a reward, and any event (as long as their is a higher one) can be a punisher. The critical relationship is the contingency of one event on the other. When a higher event is contingent on the occurrence of a lower event, the higher event serves as a reward and the lower event becomes reinforced. When a lower event is contingent on a higher event, the lower event serves as a punisher and the higher event is punished.

Serious and important as some of these issues are, they are not directly relevant to the way I propose to use this law. What is important is that *something* (call it what you will), *when* it occurs in the right relationship (whatever, exactly, that might be) to behavior performed in certain stimulus conditions, tends (for *some* behavior and *some* stimulus conditions) to increase the chances that that behavior will be repeated in those conditions. There are *some* consequences of *some* behaviors of *some* organisms that are causally relevant to the likelihood that such behaviors will be repeated in similar circumstances.[12]

12. It is especially important to understand that what is changing during learning of this sort is *behavior* (a bringing about of some result or condition), *not* some particular *way* of producing that result (e.g., some particular bodily movement). So, for instance, if going to (or avoiding) place *P* is the behavior reinforced, what is reinforced is (roughly speaking) a process having *occupation* (or *non-occupation*) *of place P* as its product. Since (see chapters 1 and 2) *any* process having this product is the *same* behavior, this behavior can be realized in

Second, we need the fact that such learning requires, on the part of the learner, a sensitivity to specific conditions F. Rewards tend to increase the probability that M will be produced *in conditions F*. Whether the rewards are administered by a teacher or by nature, making the rewards dependent (in some way) on the existence of special conditions increases the probability of the response in those special conditions. Hence, if learning is to occur, there must be something *in* the animal to "tell" it when conditions F exist.

Given these two facts, it follows that when learning of this simple kind occurs, those results (bodily movements or the more remote effects of bodily movements) that are constitutive of the reinforced behavior are gradually brought under the control of internal indicators (C), which indicate *when* stimulus conditions are right (F) for the production of those results. Making reinforcement of M contingent on the presence of F is a way of solving The Design Problem. It solves The Design Problem (for those creatures capable of this kind of learning) by promoting C, an internal indicator of F, into a cause of M. C is recruited as a cause of M *because* of what it indicates about F, the conditions on which the success of M depends. Learning of this sort is a way of shaping a structure's causal properties in accordance with its indicator properties. C is, so to speak, *selected* as a cause of M because of what it indicates about F. Unless this is done, The Design Problem cannot be solved. Learning cannot take place. An animal cannot learn to behave in the prescribed way—it cannot learn to coordinate its output (M) with condition F—unless an internal indicator of F is made into a cause of, a switch for, M. This is why learning of this sort must recruit indicators of F as causes of M.

During this process, C becomes a cause of M. It gets its hand on the steering wheel (if not for the first time, at least in a new way[13]) *because* of what it indicates about F. C thereby becomes a representation of F. After learning of this sort, the bird pecks the target because it *thinks* (whether

---

many different bodily movements (e.g., in the case of avoidance learning, flight *from* place P during learning or *avoidance of place P* after learning).

I think it was Taylor's (1964) failure to appreciate this point about the structure of behavior, about *what* was being reinforced, that led him to criticize (pp. 250ff.) the possibility of avoidance behavior as an operantly conditioned response. I shall return to this important point, and to a fuller discussion of the plasticity of behavior, in chapter 5.

13. I postpone until the last chapter (section 6.4) a discussion of the possibly multiple indicator functions an element might acquire in learning. That is, an element originally recruited to do one thing because of what it indicated about F might be recruited to do other things because of this same fact, or recruited to do other things because of what it indicated about some associated conditions G. Such developments require at least a preliminary understanding of the way motivational factors contribute to the explanation of behavior, a matter to be discussed in chapter 5.

rightly or not) that the light is red. Or, if one is skittish about giving beliefs to birds, if one thinks that the word "belief" should be reserved for the elements in larger representational networks, the bird pecks the target because it *represents* (whether rightly or not) there being a red light. This explanatory relation, the fact that the bird's behavior is explained (in part at least) by the way it represents the stimulus, derives from the role this internal indicator, and *what* it indicates, played in structuring the process $(C \rightarrow M)$ which *is* the behavior. C now causes M; but what explains why it causes M, and therefore explains why the bird *behaves* the way it does, is the fact that C indicated F—the fact that C did what it now has the function of doing. If, before learning, C happened to cause M, or if M was merely produced when C happened to be registering positive, then the bird pecked the target *when* the light was red, but it did not peck the target *because* the light was red. The fact that the light was red does not explain the earlier (prior to learning) behavior of the bird because, prior to learning, even if C happened to cause M, the fact that C indicated that the light was red did not *explain why* it caused M. This was, rather, a chance or random connection between C and M. The bird was just poking around. It is only after learning takes place that facts about the color of the light figure in the explanation of the bird's behavior, and this is so because, after learning, an internal element produces M precisely *because* it indicates something about the light's color.

If we have a system that lacks an internal indicator for condition F, a temporary solution to The Design Problem can nonetheless be reached *if* there is an internal indicator of some condition which, through coincidence, temporary arrangement (by an experimenter, say), or circumstances of habitat, is correlated with F. Suppose, for instance, that the animal has no detector for F (the condition on which the arrival of food is actually dependent) but does have a detector for G. If the animal is placed in circumstances in which all, most, or many G's are F, then the internal indicator of G will naturally be recruited as a cause of M (the movements that are rewarded by food in condition F). The animal will learn to produce M when it senses G. Its G indicator will be converted into a cause of M, and the explanation of this conversion will be the fact that it indicates G (and, of course, the fact that, for whatever reason, G is temporarily correlated with F). An internal representation of G develops because the internal indicator of G is given its job in the production of output because of what it indicates about external affairs. Depending on the degree of correlation between F and G, this will be a more or less effective solution to The Design Problem. The better the correlation, the more successful the animal will be in producing M in conditions F (and, therefore, in getting whatever reward it is that promotes that response).

If the correlation (however temporary) between F and G is perfect, this solution to The Design Problem will (for however long the correlation persists) be indistinguishable from the original solution, the solution by a system that has an *F* indicator. But the explanation of the resultant behavior of these two systems will be different. Using the intentional idiom to describe this case, we say that the second animal produces *M* in conditions *F*, not because it thinks that *F* exists, but because it thinks *G* exists (and, of course, thinks that doing *M* in conditions *G* will get it food—more of this in chapter 5). The second animal has a set of beliefs that are temporarily effective in securing food, but whose effectiveness depends on the continuation of an external correlation between *F* and *G*, a correlation which the animal itself (having no way of representing *F*) has no way of representing. This is the situation of rats and pigeons subjected to experiments in discrimination learning. Their internal indicators for rather simple stimuli— the patterns of color and sound they are being taught to discriminate—are enlisted as causes of movement because of a temporary contingency, instituted and maintained by the investigator, between these discriminable stimuli and rewards. Once the training is over, the correlations are suspended (or reversed) and the animal's "expectations" (that doing *M* in conditions *G* will get it food) are disappointed.

If the correlations between *F* and *G* are reasonably secure, as they often are in an animal's natural habitat, it may be more economical to solve The Design Problem by exploiting a simpler and less costly *G* indicator than to waste resources on a more complicated *F* indicator. Engineers do it in their design of machines, nature does it in the design of sensory systems and instinctive patterns of behavior, and individuals do it in developing, through learning, the cognitive rules of thumb for negotiating their way through complex situations. In the case of nature, we know from Tinbergen's (1952) studies that stickleback rely on what Tinbergen calls "sign stimuli." The fish exploit rather crude indicators (a bright red underside, for instance) to recognize one another. Males use the bright red underside to recognize male intruders, and females use it to identify interested males. The fish react similarly to a variety of objects of similar coloration: painted pieces of wood elicit aggressive behavior in the males and sexual interest in the females. But in the fish's natural habitat the correlation is good enough. By and large, *only* stickleback have this coloration. So why develop more expensive receptor hardware for representing conspecifics *as* conspecifics (i.e., as stickleback) when representing them *as* objects with a red underside works well enough? The same economy of effort is evident, as it should be, in individual learning. The Design Problem is solved with whatever resources are available for its solution. If there is no *F* indicator to convert into a cause of *M*, there are less optimal solutions. A *G* indicator will be enlisted *if G* exhibits *enough* correlation with *F* to make it a useful switch for

M. How much is "enough" depends on the energy required to produce M and the consequences of producing M when F does not exist.

Some animals exhibit a plasticity, a susceptibility, a disposition to have their control processes reconfigured by their experience of the world. As we move up the phylogenetic scale, we find that the behavior of an animal is shaped, not primarily by its genes, but, in larger and larger measure, by the contingencies that dominate the environment in which it lives. Staddon (1983, p. 395) writes:

> Most animals are small and do not live long; flies, fleas, bugs, nematodes, and similar modest creatures comprise most of the fauna of the planet. A small, brief animal has little reason to evolve much learning ability. Because it is small, it can have little of the complex neural apparatus needed; because it is short-lived, it has little time to *exploit* what it learns. Life is a tradeoff between spending time and energy learning new things, and exploiting things already known. The longer an animal's life span, and the more varied its niche, the more worthwhile it is to spend time learning.... It is no surpise, therefore, that learning plays a rather small part in the lives of most animals.... Learning is interesting for other reasons: It is involved in most behavior we would call intelligent, and it is central to the behavior of people.

The reason learning is so central to *intelligent* behavior, to the behavior of *people*, is that learning is the process in which internal indicators (and also, as we shall see in the next chapter, various motivational factors) are harnessed to output and thus become relevant—as representations, as *reasons*—to the explanation of the behavior of which they are a part. It is in the learning process that information-carrying elements get a job to do *because* of the information they carry and hence acquire, by means of their *content*, a role in the explanation of behavior.

It should be apparent that C, the internal indicator that is recruited as a cause of M during this kind of learning, could have any shape, form, or physical realization. As long as it is the sort of structure that *could* affect M (and hence could be recruited as a cause of M), what is important about it is not its neurophysiological character, its *form* or *shape*, but the fact that it stands in certain *relations* to those external affairs (F) on which the beneficial consequences of M depend. It is *what* information C carries, not *how* it carries it, that explains its newly acquired causal powers and, hence, the altered behavior of the system of which it is a part. This system's control circuits were reconfigured—C was given command duties (or at least given access to those mechanisms having command functions)—*because* it *told* the system what it needed to know. In the business of espionage, informants are recruited because of what they know or are capable of finding out. As long as the way they talk, look, or dress doesn't interfere with their information-gathering and communication functions, details about *how* they do their job are irrelevant. The same is true of an animal's behavior-guidance systems. It is the *semantic*, not the syntactic properties of these internal elements that explain their impact on behavior, and it is for basically this reason that a syntactic theory of the mind (Stich 1983) is unsatisfactory.[14]

As we shall see more fully in chapter 5, it would be wrong to say that, as a result of this kind of learning, C's function is to produce M, or even to produce M *when* F obtains. What this kind of learning confers on C is an indicator function: the function of indicating when F exists. C's function is not to produce M. The production of M depends not only on C, not only on a certain positive *cognitive* state, but also on the right *motivational* or *conative* conditions. The animal must have a *desire* for whatever reward or reinforcement promoted C into a cause of M. If a rat isn't hungry, it isn't going to behave in the way it was trained to behave on the appearance of the discriminative stimulus. If it isn't hungry, C won't cause M. The rat won't press the bar. So the function of C is not to cause M, but to indicate the presence of those conditions that, if the right motivational state is present, will lead, other things being equal, to M. In this respect the function of C can be usefully compared to the function of the bimetallic strip in a thermostat. The function of this strip is *not* to turn the furnace on. Whether the furnace is turned on depends on *two* factors: the temperature (which the curvature of the strip supplies information about) *and* the position of the adjustable contact (representing what we desire the temperature to be). That is why the strip is only *part* of the furnace switch. Its duties are purely cognitive.

But even this is too strong. The effects of C do not depend simply on what I am here calling the motivational state of the organism. The thermostat is too simple an analogy to capture the way C may interact with *other* cognitive structures. Even if we suppose that the drive or desire is the same as that existing during learning, once C has acquired an indicator function it may produce quite different effects on motor output (quite different, that is,

---

14. It should also be clear why I reject Stich's autonomy principle and his replacement argument (1983, p. 165) against the relevance of intentional explanations of behavior. A physical duplicate of an intentional agent, though it behaves the same, does not *yet* (not until it acquires sufficient experience to give the internal indicators the requisite functions) behave that way for the same reasons. Although physically indistinguishable systems will behave the same way (C will cause M in both), there is no reason to suppose—and if they have had different *histories* every reason *not* to suppose—that the explanation of *why* C causes M, of *why* they behave that way, will be the same for both. The only reason one might think the explanations must be the same is if one mistakenly identifies the bodily movements, M, with the behavior, C's causing M, of which they are a part.

from those it had during learning), depending on what other indicator states are registering positive and depending on what other sorts of associative learning may have taken place between C and these other structures. A consistent pairing of conditions F and G (and, hence, a consistent pairing of the internal indicators of F and G), for instance, or a change in the kind of consequences (from rewarding to punishing) associated with M, may cause a change in the sort of movements (or nonmovements) that C (the internal indicator of F) produces. What the original learning situation did was to give C, not the job of producing M, but instead the job of supplying intelligence relevant to the production of M and whatever other movements might secure results of the kind that happens to be desired at the time. C retains this information-supplying job even when the *use* to which that intelligence is put changes as C becomes integrated into a larger and more complex control system.

I do not greatly care whether, in the case of very simple creatures, one chooses to call the products of this learning process—the representational structures described above—*beliefs*. Perhaps this is premature. Perhaps, as was suggested above and as some philosophers have argued (see, e.g., C. Wright 1986; Davidson 1987; Evans 1981), the ascription of belief requires a *system* of beliefs—a representational *manifold* in which the elements not only interact with one another to produce (via inference) new beliefs, but also interact with desires, emotions, intentions and attitudes to yield novel forms of behavior. If sea snails are capable of the kind of associative learning described here (and it seems they are capable of a rather primitive version of it[15]), then surely, some will say, this type of learning is too humble to be the source of genuine beliefs. Snails don't have minds. Their behavior isn't to be explained by what they *believe* and *desire*. Dogs, cats, and chimps may have reasons for some of the things they do, but not bugs and snails.

We will explore the way simple representations interact to generate more complex representational structures in chapter 6, and we will explore the way desires figure in this explanatory scheme in chapter 5. If it turns out that one feels more comfortable in reserving the intentionalistic

---

15. *Hermissenda crassicornis*, a marine snail, can be conditioned by pairing stimuli (light and turbulence) to which the snail is sensitive. Daniel Alkon and his associates (1983) have not only taught these snails something; they have also traced, at the neuroanatomical and the chemical level, the level *at which* one can trace the *change* in the efficacy of internal indicators (of light and turbulence) on the motor control system.

Though this type of learning is naturally thought of as a form of classical (Pavlovian) conditioning, the learning can also be regarded as a form of operant conditioning. The snail has its response to light (forward movement) punished by turbulence and thereby changes the way it responds to light. I am grateful fo Ruth Saunders, Naomi Reshotko, and Rob Cummins for helpful discussions on this point.

idiom—the language of *desire, belief, knowledge,* and *intention*—for creatures exhibiting a certain minimum level of organization, a certain critical mass of representational complexity, well and good. I have, as I say, no great interest in what seems to me to be a terminological boundary dispute of negligible philosophical interest. The important fact, or so it seems to me, is that even at this simple level we can find organisms that not only have a system of internal indicators on which they depend to guide them through their environment (this itself is nothing very special; it occurs at almost every biological level) but also have internal representations that acquire their status and function *as guides* (thereby getting their hands on the steering wheel) *because* of what they *tell* the organism about the environment in which guidance is necessary. Even at this level, then, we have internal structures whose relevance to the explanation of behavior resides in *what* they say (mean, indicate) about the conditions on which the success of behavior depends. Even at this level, then, we have internal structures that not only mean something but also mean something *to* the organism in which they occur.

If such behavior to which these structures give rise is still too simple and stereotyped to qualify as intelligent, and if, therefore, the internal determinants of such behavior are not to be classified as *reasons*, then some other name must be found. Perhaps we can think of these simple and comparatively isolated representations as proto-beliefs, and of the behavior they give rise to as (in some way) goal-directed but not goal-*intended* (for more on this distinction, see chapter 5). Proto-beliefs may then *become* beliefs by becoming integrated into a larger constellation of representational elements or by acquiring whatever other external trappings may be required of genuine belief. Whatever we choose to call them, though, the individual elements described here exhibit the essential properties of genuine beliefs: they *have* a propositional content, and their possession of this content helps explain why the system in which they occur behaves the way it does.

Chapter 5

Motivation and Desire

Nothing has yet been said about the role of desire, purpose, drive, or motivation in the explanation of behavior—that part of one's primary reason for acting that Davidson (1963) calls the pro attitude. The rat presses the bar not just because it can see that the light is on, but because it is hungry. It *wants* food. Well-fed but otherwise knowledgeable rats behave differently. Clyde goes to the refrigerator not *just* because he knows the beer is there, but because he *wants* a beer. His wife, knowing what Clyde knows and equally thirsty, doesn't go to the refrigerator; she prefers the lemonade that is within her reach.

Until we have an idea of how such conative factors—drives, desires, motives, preferences, purposes, and incentives—figure in the explanation of behavior, we will not have a complete account of the role of reasons in this explanatory scheme. For although there is generally more at work in the determination of voluntary behavior than a simple belief and a simple desire, *both* belief (or some cognitive variant thereof) and desire (or some conative variant thereof) are operative in everything we do that is explicable by means of an agent's reasons. Without an account of desire, then, our analysis of the way reasons explain behavior is at best only half finished.

5.1 Goal-Directed Behavior

In developing a model for belief in chapter 4, I found it necessary to distinguish the internal cause of movement, C, from those facts about it that *explained* its causing those movements. C is *inside* the system, directing traffic, but what it is about C that explains, or helps explain, why it directs traffic the way it does is the fact that it indicates external affairs to be one way rather than another. This is a matter of how C is related to things outside the system, and C's relationship to external affairs is not, of course, inside the system.

Since we are now embarked on the project of describing the contribution of desire and other motivational states to the explanation of behavior, it will be necessary to resolve, so to speak, the internal cause of movement, C, into its separate parts—into its cognitive and conative components. We can change our beliefs without changing our desires, and vice versa. These factors vary more or less independently. So we need at least two distinguishable elements inside the system operating together as causes of M. One of these elements—we shall now call it B, to suggest belief—has already been described in the last chapter. B is, in effect, that *part* of C, the internal cause of movement, that represents the current state of external affairs. B is only a *partial* cause of the movements (M) involved in the system's behavior. What must now be described are the other parts of this internal cause. We shall be primarily interested in the conative or motivational part of this internal cause, a component we shall label D to suggest desire. But we shall also say something about the network of other beliefs that play a role in this enterprise.

In developing the account of the explanatory role of meaning in chapter 4, I ignored an important part of the account. I said that the timely administration of rewards tends to increase the probability of movements' being caused by internal indicators. This, though true enough, ignores an important qualification, a qualification having to do with the *receptivity* of the organism. Rewards tend to encourage reproduction of rewarded events *only when* the organism is in a certain internal condition. Feeding a *hungry* rat when it performs satisfactorily is one thing; feeding a rat that has just eaten is quite another. Food tends to increase the probability of movements' being caused by internal indicators only when the rat is hungry, and the hungrier the better. Likewise, a promotion tends to encourage the kind of behavior for which it is a reward only when the employee in question *wants* a promotion, and the more he wants it the better. Promoting someone who wants something else can have quite the opposite effect. The same is true of most of the consequences of behavior. Their effectiveness in modifying behavior depends, critically, on the receptiveness of the system relative to the consequences in question. The more receptive the system, the more effective the rewards are in modifying behavior.

I shall use the letter D to stand for the receptivity of an organism relative to outcome R. When necessary I shall use the symbol $D[R]$ to distinguish this receptive state from others, to indicate that it is specifically a receptivity *for* R and not for some other outcome, S. The effectiveness of R (food, say) as a reinforcer, its effectiveness in modifying behavior, depends on the organism's occupying state D . Without D, the occurrence of R does not tend to increase the probability of those behaviors that result in R.

The use of the letter D, suggesting desire, to designate these receptive states is deliberate. Such states function as *motivational* states.[1] They are

---

1. Compare Catania's (1984, p. 217) description of the study of motivation as the study of the conditions that determine the effectiveness of contingent stimuli as reinforcers or as punishers.

what I shall call *pure* desires, and they are desires *for* whatever condition or outcome they make the organism receptive to. There are as many different (pure) desires as there are distinguishable states of receptivity (i.e., states of receptivity for different things).[2] Other desires—what I shall call (cognitively) *derived* desires—are generated by beliefs about what will secure the objects of *pure* (and other derived) desires. Without pure desires, though, there would be no desire at all, and hence no motivation, no purpose, no behavior explicable in terms of an agent's *reasons*. I shall return to the topic of derived desires in the final chapter. The project here, in this chapter, is to show how pure desires, and what they are desires for, figure in the explanation of behavior.

For convenience I will continue assuming that *R*, the effect or consequence of movement, is some positively reinforcing event, an event that *raises* the probability of the behavior that produced it. It should be remembered, however, that as long as *R changes* the probabilities, the fact that *M* results in it will be relevant to the explanation of behavior. Negative reinforcement (sometimes called escape conditioning or avoidance learning) increases the probability of an animal's doing something *else*. Punishment—decreasing the probability of the animal's repeating the same behavior by making *R* noxious, aversive, or punishing—is also a possibility. Larvae of monarch butterfly feed on milkweed and store the toxins they ingest. Bluejays that eat these butterflies become violently sick and thereafter refuse to eat them. They even avoid other butterflies—such as the viceroy—that mimic the appearance of the monarch. In this case, the jay's *avoidance* of monarch-like butterflies (the production of not-*M*, if you like) is a piece of behavior that has the fact that *M* results or resulted in *R* (violent sickness) as part of its explanation.

Let us say, following Taylor (1964) and Wright (1973, 1976), that goal-directed behavior is not only behavior that tends to have a certain result but behavior that occurs *because* it tends to have this result.[3] My dialing

---

2. The number of different pure desires will vary depending on how one identifies the reinforcing result. If one identifies *R* with external stimuli (e.g., food, water, warmth, sex) of the kinds that, as we like to say, bring pleasure, then one will have a different pure desire for each such result. If, however, one identifies *R* with the internal state (pleasure? need reduction?) that such different stimuli produce, one will presumably have fewer pure desires—perhaps, even, *one* pure desire: the desire for pleasure (need reduction, equilibrium, or whatever). See Papineau 1984, pp. 562ff., on this "concertina" effect in the specification of the object of desire.

I have no interest in legislating about this issue. It is enough (for my purposes) if there is at least *one* pure desire—as indeed there must be if learning of the sort now in question is to occur.

3. This isn't quite right, but it will do for the moment. The condition is actually only sufficient, not also necessary, for goal-directed behavior. As we will see, behavior that does not (and never did) result in *R* may still be done *in order* to get *R*, with the purpose or desire

your telephone number is goal-directed (the goal being to talk to you) if I do it *because* it normally results in my talking to you on the telephone. If we take this as a working definition, or at least (see footnote 3) a sufficient condition for goal-directedness, then, if certain movements tend to result in R and if a system produces these movements because they result in R, the system's production of these movements is goal-directed and the goal *to which* the production is directed is R. Alternative ways of describing such behavior are to say that these movements are produced in order to get R, for the sake of R, and with the purpose of obtaining R.

Think of an organism learning to do something in a specific set of conditions: it learns to produce M in conditions F by having the rewards R for producing M contingent on M's production *in F*.[4] As we saw in the preceding chapter, such a process will result in the recruitment of an F-indicator as an internal cause of M. We have relabeled this internal indicator B. So, if learning is successful, B is enlisted as a partial cause of M. Since D is the internal state on which R's effectiveness as a reinforcer depends, successful learning also requires the animal to occupy state D when movements M are produced. R will not be effective in promoting the production of M unless the organism is in *both* state B and state D. Since M doesn't lead to R except in F, and since R isn't reinforcing unless D, learning requires that *both* F and D exist for the production of M. Since this is so, R will recruit, as a cause of M, both B and D. Or, if you please, the occurrence

---

to get R, and thus be goal-directed (toward R). If one mistakenly thinks that doing M will get one R and (wanting R) does M in order to get R, the behavior is goal-directed without the behavior's tending to result in R. I leave aside such cases for the moment. I return to them later.

I also set aside, for the moment, complications having to do with the ambiguity in "tends to produce a certain result." For example, must the behavior *now* tend to produce these results, or is it enough if it tend*ed* to produce them? For discussion of these points see Ringen 1985, Porpora 1980, and Woodfield 1976.

4. It isn't, of course, necessary that behavior be rewarded *every* time. There are reinforcement schedules (as they are called) that are intermittent and irregular but still effective in learning. I look in the cookie jar, not because there have *always* been cookies there, but because there are *sometimes* cookies there.

Also, what I am here calling the *result* of M, namely R, needn't actually be the result of M in order to be effective in reinforcing behavior. It is well known that behavior can be shaped by the regular occurrence of some event (e.g., arrival of food) that is unrelated to what the animal is doing—unrelated, that is, to the occurrence of M. See Rachlin 1976, pp. 240–245, for a discussion of (1) lack of discrimination, (2) superstition, and (3) pseudoconditioning, processes that change an animal's response probabilities but do not qualify as instrumental (operant) learning because there is no instrumental relationship, no real dependency, between the animal's movements M and the occurrence of R. The animal, as it were, mistakenly thinks it is bringing about R by producing M, and, wanting R, produces M again in order to get it. This is a case of goal-directed behavior that is not explained by the behavior's tendency to produce some result.

of R will recruit B as a cause of M only if B is accompanied by D. The only way to arrange things so that M is produced when both B and D exist, but (in the interest of economy of effort) not otherwise (i.e., when either B or D exists alone), is to make B and D necessary parts of a sufficient condition for M.[5] Hence, this kind of learning results in the recruitment of B and D as *partial* or *contributory* causes of M.

We have just seen that if D is an internal state on which the reinforcing character of R depends, then behavior that is reinforced by R will be behavior in which D is recruited as an internal cause of whatever movements the behavior requires. D becomes a cause of M *because* M results in R. Given our earlier description of goal-directed behavior, though, this implies that M's production by D and B is goal-directed, that the behavior has R as its goal. It implies, in other words, that such behavior can be *explained* by facts about B and D—the facts, namely, that B indicates or means that condition F exists (that is why *it* was recruited as a partial cause of M) and the fact that D is *for* R (that is why *it* was enlisted as a partial cause of M). The animal behaves that way because it believes that F exists and wants R.

The argument that such behavior is goal-directed, and that it is to be explained (in part, at least) by the fact that the animal occupies an internal state that is *for* R (has R as its goal), is quite straightforward. We have introduced D as an internal state on whose presence the reinforcing quality of R depends. Given this, part of the explanation of why D causes M is surely that M tends to produce R. It is the fact that M leads to the sort of result that D renders an effective reinforcer that explains why D was selected as a cause of M. If M did not lead to R, then either M would not be reinforced—in which case D would not be established as a cause of M—or, if it was (by some reward other than R) then, since the reinforcing quality of this other reward would not depend on D, D would not, once again, be established as a cause of M. So D's role as a (partial) cause of M depends critically on the fact that M has R—what D is *for*—as its result. Since it is the fact that M leads to R that explains why D was enlisted as a cause of M, the behavior—$(D + B)$ causing M—is explained, in part at least, by the animal's occupation of an internal state (D) that has R as its goal.

---

5. In saying that B and D are necessary parts of a sufficient condition (for M), I do not, of course, mean that they are necessary for M, that M cannot occur without them. M may be produced, on other occasions, for other reasons, and sometimes perhaps for no reasons at all. Animals kill, not just when they are hungry, but also (it seems) for the sport of it. And we can certainly imagine an animal trained to perform the same movements for different reasons—under two different stimulus conditions for quite different rewards. So neither B (the internal indication of the appropriate stimulus conditions) or D (hunger) is a necessary condition for M. They are, however, supposed to be parts—necessary parts—of *a* (causally) sufficient condition.

Normally we think of behavior that is successful in reaching its goal as *satisfying* the desire in question. Since the desire is satisfied, the behavior it inspired ceases. Reaching the goal is *consummatory*. This means that, normally, when M results in R, R will eliminate, extinguish, or remove D (something we describe by saying the desire has been satisfied), and the goal-directed behavior will therefore cease. Though this may be the normal sequence of events, it is by no means necessary. R may *not* extinguish D, and even if it does the behavior may persist for other reasons. If R does not extinguish D, the behavior will persist, and it will persist as long as D remains. I will *keep* eating until I'm full, until R (in this case the ingestion of food) extinguishes D. And for some reinforcing experiences (direct electrical stimulation of the brain, for instance) there is an apparent lack of satiation (Stellar and Stellar 1985, p. 83).

It isn't, of course, necessary for a system to reach its goal in order for that goal (or an internal state having that as its goal) to be explanatorily relevant to the behavior undertaken to reach that goal. A rat doesn't actually have to be given food when it presses a bar in order for food to be the goal that "directs" the rat's behavior. And even if it is given food, *that* (future) event could never explain, at least not causally, why the rat *pressed* the bar. Causes do not come *after* their effects. No, what makes food explanatorily relevant to the rat's behavior is not the fact that food *will* arrive, and not even the fact that it will *probably* arrive. For, as we all know, food may *not* arrive. Its arrival may not even be probable; the mechanism for delivering it may be broken, or the experimenter may have decided to extinguish bar-pressing behavior by no longer rewarding it. Rather, what makes it true to say that the rat presses the bar *in order to get food*, that getting food was the rat's *purpose* or *reason* for pressing the bar, that the rat pressed the bar because it *wanted* food, is that the rat's movements (M) are being caused, in part at least, by an internal state, D, having food as its goal; and the explanation of *why* D is causing M, and hence an explanation of the behavior, is the fact that D has this goal, the fact that D is, specifically, a receptivity *to food*. It is this fact that explains D's recruitment as a cause of M and, thus, helps explain the rat's current behavior.

The fact that a hungry rat, furiously pressing a bar in order to get food, occupies state D, a state that was recruited as a cause of bar-pressing movements because, *in the past*, these movements led to food does not, obviously, explain why D *now* exists, why the rat is *now* hungry. Nor does it explain why M is now occurring. D's having R as its goal, its being *for* R, is not a triggering cause of behavior. It is a *structuring* cause. It helps explain, not why D or M is occurring now, but why, now, D is causing M (rather than something else). Failure to appreciate the difference between bodily movements (or external changes) and the behavior having those movements and changes as a product—hence, failure to appreciate the difference between a triggering and a structuring cause of behavior—is, I suspect, partly responsible for the mistaken idea that whatever triggers the behavior, whatever causes the beliefs (*B*) and desires (*D*) that (by causing *M*) constitute the behavior, must be the ultimate (causal) explanation of that behavior.

It may appear mildly paradoxical that desire—normally thought of as a future-oriented attitude, something that moves us toward the attainment of a yet-to-be-secured goal—is, on this account of things, a reflection of things past. The paradox is only apparent. In pressing the bar because it is hungry, the rat wants food; it does *not*, to be sure, want food it has *already* eaten. The desire, *D*, exists *now*, of course, and if it is causally effective in securing its own satisfaction, it will do so by bringing about some *future* condition. But what makes the present internal state a desire for food, and not, say, a desire for water or sex, is the fact that it is receptivity *to food*, the fact that it makes *getting food* a result that will encourage the reproduction of movements yielding food. And what makes this internal state explanatorily relevant to current behavior is the fact that its being *for* food is what explains why movements (*M*) constitutive of this behavior are now being produced.

It is, of course, quite possible to have two identically trained rats that, on particular occasions, behave quite differently. Reggie eagerly presses the bar when he sees the light; Ronnie, his littermate, remains indifferent when he observes the same stimulus. Why the difference? Reggie is hungry; Ronnie isn't. A visual stimulus that will evoke a motor-cortex discharge in a properly motivated animal will evoke no discharge at all in one that is satiated (Evarts 1980, p. 229). The difference between these rats is obviously a difference in their internal conditions, a difference in their motivational states. Though both Ronnie and Reggie have *B* (they both see the light), and though they have both had the same training (both have been "restructured" so that *B* and *D* will produce *M*), only Reggie has *D*. In explaining Ronnie's failure to press the bar (despite his training) when the light comes on by saying that he isn't hungry, we are merely identifying one factor in the cause of movement—the motivational factor—that distinguishes him from Reggie. An essential part of the sufficient condition (for *M*) is missing.

5.2 Goal-Intended Behavior

Something, it seems, has been left out. Suppose an animal learns to produce *M* in conditions *F* in order to get *R*. A rat learns to press the bar when the light is red in order to get food. If we keep things simple, and suppose there are no countervailing motivational states or interfering beliefs, then such learning will generate internal conditions (*B* + *D*) that are, given normal conditions, sufficient for M. Henceforth, when the animal wants R (is in state D) and believes F (is in state B), M will be produced. The rat will press the bar. Furthermore, it will press the bar *because* it wants R and believes F. The behavior is both goal-directed and cognitively guided.

But is this the correct, or the *complete*, explanation of the rat's behavior? Consider an untrained rat, or this (trained) rat *before* it was trained. Or think about a rat that learned to do something *else* when the light was red in order to get food. Such rats might want food, know that stimulus conditions are F, and *not* press the bar. So, it seems, wanting food (D) and knowing the light is red (B) are *not* sufficient to produce bar-pressing movements. Therefore, something else is needed to complete the explanation of the first rat's behavior. In describing him as wanting food and thinking the light is red, we have not distinguished him from his cousins who know and want the same things but behave quite differently. It seems we need something in the way of a background belief about the *way* to achieve one's ends, some belief to the effect that producing M in conditions F will bring about R. The first rat, as a result of training, must know, or at least believe, that pressing the bar when the light is red will bring it food. The other rats don't know this. So the complete, or at least a *more* complete, explanation of the first rat's behavior is that he knows the light is red, wants food, and thinks that by pressing the bar when the light is red he will get food.

This objection raises an important point about the way background beliefs, beliefs about the efficacy of means for bringing about ends, figure in the explanation of goal-directed behavior. To explain someone's performance it isn't enough to point out that, in the conditions he believes to obtain, his behavior leads to results he desires. One also wants to know whether the agent *knows* (or at least believes) that his behavior *will* lead to results he desires. Was his getting a desired result a mere fluke, or did he do what he did *in order* to achieve that result—with the belief that such action would, or would likely, get him what he wanted? We can imagine a hungry but untrained rat pressing the bar at random, in play, out of curiosity, or accidentally when it observes a red light come on. Though this rat *is* hungry and believes the red light is on, the explanation of its pressing the bar is *not* that it wanted food and saw the light come on. It *was* hungry and it *did* see the light come on, but that isn't *why* it pressed the bar. This isn't goal-directed, purposeful behavior, although it may later *become* so if the consequences are appropriate.

Any animal that has been trained to do something in a certain set of conditions in order to secure a certain result has what we might call *procedural knowledge*—a knowledge of *how* to achieve those results, a knowledge of *what* to do, and *when* to do it. This is a form of knowledge that is a unique mixture of the practical and the theoretical. it isn't *just* a piece of know-how, like knowing how to swim or to wiggle one's ears. It is a *skill*, if you will, but not just a motor skill. Even untrained rats, we may suppose, know *how* to press the bar. They often do it in play. It is, rather, a cognitive skill: knowing *when* to press the bar. This practical knowledge, this cognitive skill, is an inevitable accompaniment of instrumental learning: you can't, by appropriate rewards and punishments, shape an animal's responses to stimuli without also teaching it, at some level, *that* those responses lead, in these conditions, to those rewards and punishments.

The fact that, even in the simplest cases of instrumental learning, what is developed is not just a pattern of behavior, but a genuine cognitive skill, something more like knowing-*that*, a piece of factual knowledge, rather than just a knowing-*how*, becomes apparent when this procedural knowledge is applied in abnormal or simply changed circumstances, thus failing to yield the usual result. We then speak of *beliefs*. Reggie, we say , knows *when* to press the bar. At least he *did* know this. Now that he is no longer being rewarded for pressing the bar when the light is red, how do we explain his bar-pressing behavior? Well, during learning Reggie acquired a piece of procedural knowledge: the knowledge that pressing the bar would bring food. Since it is now *false* that pressing the bar will bring food, we can no longer call this knowledge. But we can, and regularly do, call it belief. The rat presses the bar, not because he *knows* he will get food in that way, but because he still *thinks* he can get food that way. He may, after a sufficient number of disappointments, stop thinking this, but that, surely, is part of the explanation of why he behaves that way the first few times after rewards are discontinued.

It is perhaps best at this juncture to distinguish between *explicit* and *implicit* representations, beliefs, and knowledge (Cummins 1983, 1986). Procedural knowledge (or belief) of the type developed during instrumental learning may only be implicit. An implicit belief or representation is something like what Ryle (1949) called a single-track disposition, but in this case it is a single-track disposition, acquired during learning, to do or believe something *given* certain other beliefs and desires. If, for example, the disposition in question is a disposition to believe Q when one believes that P, we can speak (see Armstrong 1973; Ramsey 1931) of the (implicit) belief that *if P, then Q* (or, depending on the strength of the dispositions, probably Q). If the disposition is to produce M when one believes that F and wants R, we can speak of the belief that producing M will (or probably will, or might) secure R in conditions F. In the latter case, when the disposition in question is one connecting certain beliefs and desires with certain *outputs* the implicit belief resembles what computer scientists call a *production*—a rule specifying which actions are to occur under what conditions (Haugeland 1985, pp. 157–164).

An implicit belief or a production, then, is not just any disposition. My disposition to perspire when it gets hot and my car's disposition to start when I turn the ignition key are not implicit beliefs. Rather, an implicit belief is a disposition or rule that describes the relationship among entities that are already intentionally characterized (beliefs and desires, for instance) or among such intentionally characterized entities and movements. A rule or disposition that says, simply, "Produce movement M when conditions F and D obtain" is *not* an implicit belief. It is, at best, merely a regularity of some kind. My car "follows" the rule "Start the engine when the key is turned on, the battery is charged, and there is gas in the tank." But this is not a belief. In order to qualify as a *belief*, the disposition or rule must be defined over intentional elements (beliefs and desires) *qua* intentional elements. So, for example, the rule that says "Produce movement M when you believe (or represent things as) F and when you want R" gives rise to the implicit belief that M will yield R in conditions F. Unlike the first rule, the one that merely gave expression to a regularity, this rule can be applied whether or not condition F exists (it need only be believed to exist) and whether or not D exists (as long as there is some internal state that has R as its goal).

An implicit belief, then, derives its content from a rule or disposition defined over intentionally specified elements. This being so, implicit beliefs have a content with a very narrow range of application. Such beliefs are perhaps better thought of as ways a system has of manipulating information than as part of the information they manipulate. They are, as it were, part of the program, not part of the data on which this program operates. Alternatively, it may be useful to think of implicit beliefs as "distributed" associations constructed during learning in a connectionist network by the continual reweighting of the excitatory and inhibitory connections between nodes. The content of such beliefs is not available, as it is with explicit beliefs, for other jobs. Depending on a system's motivational state, explicit beliefs can enter into combination with other beliefs to generate a wide range of different actions. They are potentially limitless in their application. An *implicit* belief that doing M in conditions F will yield R, on the other hand, can be applied only in circumstances where one believes F and wants R. And the way it is applied is by generating movement M. It has this narrow range of application because the belief is, basically, the disposition to *do M* when one believes F and wants R. An *explicit* belief with the same content, however, has a much wider range of application. It can be applied whether or not one believes F or wants R. It can be used, for instance, to infer that F is *not* the case when R does not result from M, or to infer that *someone else's* production of M in conditions F will yield R.

Since learning is a way of recruiting representations and motivational states *qua* representations and motivations as causes of M, learning is a way of installing a new rule, a new production, in the system's command center: produce M when you think F and want R. Since learning does not occur unless this recruitment is to some degree successful, learning does not occur unless there is, to the same degree, the development of a representation, either implicit or explicit, to the effect that M will yield R in conditions F. Hence, even when the learning in question occurs at this simple level, even when we are talking about conditioning a rat to press a bar, the learning process brings with it, if only at the *implicit* level, the kind of background belief that is required to make the behavior goal-directed. The trained rat presses the the bar because it thinks the light is red, wants food, and thinks (implicitly) that pressing the bar when the light is red will get it food.

With more advanced systems (human beings, for instance), the representation of the relation between environmental conditions, behavior, and results may be, and often is, explicit. In fact, the representation of this relationship between outcomes and the movements and conditions in which it can be obtained may come *before* the animal does anything to secure this outcome—*before*, in fact, the animal desires this outcome. Such learning, (sometimes called latent or observational learning) is a way of developing, without trial-and-error practice, without the kind of conditioning regimen we have so far been concerned with, explicit representations of environmental relationships that one can later exploit, if the appropriate desires develop, to achieve one's ends. I can, for instance, learn to get a cola from the machine, not by having the appropriate maneuvers rewarded by obtaining a cola, but by watching someone else's activities rewarded in this way. Then, when (if ever) I want a cola, I know what to do to get one. I have developed *explicit* representations that, when desires and beliefs (about currently prevailing conditions) change, I can exploit for my own purposes. Rats and pigeons, it turns out, are capable of the same kind of learning. So are monkeys. Monkey see, monkey do. In chapter 6 we shall look at the way this capacity for explicitly representing the relationships between variables—some of which (i.e., M) the animal itself can produce, some of which (i.e., R) it may need or desire, and others of which (i.e., F) may be required in order for M to yield R—greatly enlarges the animal's capacity for satisfying needs and desires. In very simple animals, though, the rules of action (what we are here calling *implicit* representations) may be the only way the animal has of representing the relationships in question (Staddon 1983, p. 424).

It may be that one finds the conditioned behavior of simple creatures, such as rats and pigeons, too simple, too rigid, and too nonadaptive to qualify as goal-directed or purposeful, and hence too simple to be explained in terms of *reasons* (what the animal believes and desires). Although in *some* sense the rat is pressing the bar *in order to get food*, this isn't the kind of deliberate, intentional, intelligent behavior that we humans exhibit in our quest to satisfy our desires and realize our purposes. Even if one agrees that such simple creatures have something like desires (internal states that are, in a sense, directed toward food, water, sex, warmth, shelter, and comfort), even if one agrees that they also have the capacity to register (and in this sense represent) the environmental conditions on which the satisfaction of those desires depends, and even if one agrees that, through certain kinds of learning, these representational and motivational states become, in virtue of what they *mean* and what they are *for*, explanatorily relevant to acquired behavior, one can still insist that these forms of life lack sufficient plasticity, creativity, or intelligence in their pursuit of goals to exhibit real purposiveness in their selection of means to serve their needs.

The feeling that the rat's behavior, however goal-directed it might appear, is not genuinely purposeful, not really to be explained in terms of desires and beliefs, may spring from a simple dislike of rats. Some people tolerate—indeed insist on—such explanations for their pets' behavior, but are unwilling to accept their application to the behavior of less cuddly creatures. Aside from simple prejudice, though, this feeling may have a perfectly legitimate source in the felt distinction between behavior that is generated in part by implicit beliefs and behavior whose cognitive background is fully explicit. One may feel, for instance, that behavior having as part of its explanation what we have been calling implicit beliefs is not genuinely goal-directed, or that, if (for whatever reasons) such behavior is to be classified as goal-directed, only goal-*intended* behavior (Braithwaite 1953: Woodfield 1976)—goal-directed behavior (in the present sense) whose cognitive origin is fully explicit—should be regarded as genuinely purposive and, hence, as explicable in terms of reasons.

Crispin Wright (1986), summarizing the views of G. Evans (1981), puts the case against isolated and single-purpose (and, hence, implicit) beliefs quite effectively. When a rat acquires a disposition to avoid a kind of foodstuff that is poisonous and has caused it sickness in the past, we might, to explain its behavior, assign it a belief that the food is poisonous. But this belief, which I am calling an implicit belief, is quite different from *our* belief that the food is poisonous. Our belief that the food is poisonous has achieved *explicit* status and is, therefore, available for a variety of jobs and applications:

> ... my belief that a certain substance is poisonous may manifest itself in a literally indefinite variety of ways. I may, like the rat, avoid the substance. But I may also take steps to ensure my family avoid it, or take steps to ensure they don't! ... I may take a large quantity if I wish to commit suicide, and a smaller one if I wish to incapacitate myself so as to avoid an obligation. My belief that the substance is poisonous is thus, as Evans puts it, at the service of indefinitely many potential

projects corresponding to indefinitely many transformations in my other beliefs and desires. With the rat, in contrast, concepts like the desire for suicide, or malign intent, can get no grip.... its 'belief' that the substance is poisonous has consequently no other expression than in shunning it. (Wright 1986, pp. 33–34)

This may simply show that we should not say that the rat believes the food is *poisonous*. Perhaps that is the wrong way to describe the way the rat represents the food. Perhaps we should say that the rat represents the food as tasting awful, or as the sort of stuff that makes it (the rat) feel sick or whatever.

Aside, though, from the question of how best to express the rat's way of representing the food (and I don't see why there must be, in our language, a convenient way of expressing what the rat believes), the deflationary (of rats) sentiments expressed in the above passage will surely appeal to many readers. The narrow dispositions to which implicit beliefs give expression may be too narrow for the purpose of capturing our common and familiar idea of purposive, intentional, goal-directed behavior. If this is so, then we must reserve these labels for behavior that is not only goal-directed in the present sense but is also goal-*intended*— behavior that is the expression of fully explicit internal representations, and hence internal structures that have, in virtue of their content, a more versatile role in the production of output. According to this classificatory decision, then, genuine purposive behavior will be constituted by movements, M, that have as their cause, not only a B (of conditions F) and a D (for result R), but an *explicit* representation (some internal structure having the function of indicating) that M tends to yield R in conditions F.

I shall return to this topic in the final chapter, where I will try to say something more systematic about the way beliefs and desires, or what I am here *calling* beliefs and desires, interact to generate more complex cognitive and motivational structures. I shall, in particular, try to say something about the way desires for things one has never had can help to explain behavior that one has never (yet) performed. I do not think it of great importance that precise boundaries be drawn, that we try to say exactly when and where on the biological continuum (a continuum of increasing representational and motivational complexity) it becomes true to say that organisms do things because of what they believe and desire. It is enough, perhaps, to see (1) the way internal structures having some of the intentional properties of human belief and desire appear fairly early on this scene—as soon, in fact, as the requisite forms of learning are possible; (2) how, during learning, the intentional properties of these structures become relevant to the explanation of the acquired behavior; and (3) how such representational and motivational atoms can be combined, in more developed systems, into cognitive and conative molecules that exhibit some of the organizational and explanatory complexity of *our* reasons for acting.

5.3 *Drives and Desires*

When psychologists and physiologists speak of *drives*, they are usually thinking of the internal determinants of a certain species of motivated behavior. They are not necessarily thinking of behavior that is explicable in terms of an agent's reasons and purposes. *Homeostatic drives*, for example, are processes that function automatically to keep internal states near certain "set" levels (Groves and Schlesinger 1979, p.351). Body temperature, blood pH, and the concentrations of sodium, sugar, and many other substances in the body are regulated by the autonomic nervous system. Usually, the animal in which these activities occur is quite unaware of their occurrence. There is certainly nothing purposive about them, if we think of the purpose in question as the purpose of the animal in which they occur. Nevertheless, these processes exhibit some aspects of goal-directedness. Certain events seem to occur *because* of the beneficial consequences they have for the animal in which they occur, and this, as I have suggested, is the essence of goal directedness.

If we regard these homeostatic activities as behaviors at all, we tend to think of them as the behaviors of certain organs and glands—of *parts* of the animal—rather than as behaviors of the animal. However, a variety of instinctive behaviors that are equally automatic, equally involuntary, and equally the product of the organism's genetic inheritance clearly qualify as behaviors of the animal. The reflexes and Fixed Action Patterns (FAPs) mentioned above are cases in point. The tropistic maneuvering of the moth to escape the bat, the instinctive flight of birds at the sight of short-necked (i.e., hawklike) profiles, the nut-burying activities of the European red squirrel, and the "hill climbing" (up and down chemical gradients) of bacteria— all such behaviors, though not learned, normally have beneficial results. There is, furthermore, reason to think that these behaviors were favored by natural selection, were established and flourished in the species, *because* they had these beneficial consequences. Hence, such behaviors appear to be goal-directed. The animal does M because, under normal conditions, doing M tends to result in something, R, that is beneficial to the organism. Hence, the animal does M in order to get R.

As we know, however, such behavior will occur *whether or not* it has satisfactory consequences. The moth will take a nosedive whether or not this behavior helps it to avoid the bat. Even if the maneuver repeatedly ends in disaster (as long as the disaster doesn't prevent it from executing these maneuvers again), the moth will behave the same way. And, as was noted above, squirrels will execute the scratching, digging, pushing, covering, and tamping-down motions used in burying nuts whether or not these movements have their normal (nut-burying) results. They will do so, with little or no effect, on a hardwood floor. The following description of Dethier's (1976) experiments with blowflies is illustrative:

> Blowflies, the organisms that Dethier used in these experiments, live on pure sugar solutions. If they have not eaten for some time they will consume such solutions when they find them, and how much they consume depends on their state of deprivation. Eating, in these animals, consists of a series of stereotyped, reflexive acts. If a fly happens to step on a drop of sugar water, chemical taste receptors located on the legs are stimulated. The next response depends on the state of the organism, its drive. If it has not eaten for some time, the fly will automatically extend a tonguelike proboscis and suck in the fluid. If the fly has eaten recently this response will not occur. Proboscis extension depends entirely on the state of sensory adaptation of the chemical receptors located on the animal's legs and on the neural signals originating in the foregut of the animal and transmitted to the brain via the so-called recurrent nerve. If this recurrent nerve is cut, proboscis extension can no longer be inhibited and the fly will continue to eat until it quite literally bursts. The behavior of the animal, proboscis extension, depends on the biological deficit created when the animal has not eaten for some time. (Groves and Schlesinger 1979, pp. 349–350)

Assuming that proboscis extension is a piece or innate behavior the mechanisms for which are genetically coded, and that this behavior evolved because of its beneficial consequences for the fly (in securing nourishment), this behavior, though not goal-*intended* (see section 5.2), does seem to be goal-directed (section 5.1). If we let the biological deficit (created when the fly has not eaten for some time) be D and activity in the fly's chemical receptors (indicating the presence of sugar water) be B, then $B + D$ appear to be causing M (proboscis extension), and the explanation for this behavior seems to come back to what B represents and what D is for.

But can this be right? Leaving aside for the moment the intentional acts of purposeful human beings, do we really want to classify the *reflexive* behavior of the blowfly with the kind of *acquired* behavior an animal (such as a trained rat) exhibits when it presses a bar (in the only way I can think to describe it) *in order* to get food? Do blowflies even have desires? Needs, yes, but desires?

One can concede that the blowfly occupies a motivational state of *some* kind without admitting that the fly has a desire *for* anything. After all, a (pure) desire *for* R was defined as a state of the organism that made R reinforcing. If, then, the blowfly's behavior is not modifiable by the receipt of sugar water—if it is incapable of *learning* of the kind described earlier—then, whatever it is *in* the blowfly that (together with the registration of sugar water) causes proboscis extension, it is *not* a desire for sugar water (or for anything else). Unlike a desire, it cannot explain the fly's behavior in terms of what it is for. Though it may produce movements that normally have R as their result, it is not *for R*.

Nevertheless, though this internal state (call it *d*) lacks the intentional properties of a desire, it is , like a desire, a variable *motivational* state that operates in tandem with various indicators to generate output. Let us, therefore, borrow a term from recent motivational psychology and call it a *drive*.[6] As I shall use the term, a drive is, like a desire, a cause of movement; however, unlike a desire, it is not *for* anything (not even the sort of beneficial thing it normally brings about as the result of the movements it causes), nor is it (therefore) recruited as a cause of movement because of what it is *for*. As we shall see more fully in a moment, we cannot explain behavior by appeal to drives in the way we can explain behavior by appeal to desires.

If a drive produces movements M that typically yield a beneficial result R, and the behavior (*d*'s causing M) was selected for because it tended to yield R, then we can say that *d* is a drive *toward R*. But just as one can drive *toward* Chicago while having no intention or desire to go *to* Chicago, so a drive toward R lacks the intentional properties of a desire. A drive toward R is merely one that typically causes movements that result in R and which, because R is beneficial, may have been selected for this job because of this fact. But the fact that *d* was selected for this job (producing M) by evolutionary processes does not mean that the behavior is goal-directed . Behavior in which drives rather than desires figure may exhibit some of the external marks of goal-direction, but it is, at best, behavior directed *toward* a goal, not *by* a goal.

To understand why this is so, one need only recall the discussion in section 4.3 of the difference between selectional and developmental explanations. It was argued there that in order for meaning to be explanatorily relevant to behavior it is not enough for some internal state to have meaning and for it (the state) to participate in the causation of movement. More is needed: the fact that this state has this meaning must *explain* why it causes what it does. And for this further condition to be satisfied it is not enough that there be some evolutionary or *selectional* explanation for the

---

6. The concept of a drive was the successor of the idea of an instinct in modern psychology. Hull (1943) suggested that physiological deficits, or needs, instigate an organism to undertake behaviors that result in the offsetting of those needs. "Drives, therefore, are a motivational characteristic or property of need states. They result from physiological disequilibrium and instigate behaviors that return the organism to a state of equilibrium." (Weiner 1985, p. 92)

role of the internal indicator in the production of movement, for such explanations make it quite clear that it is not the meaning (if any) of *this indicator* that explains its causal role in the production of movement. Quite the contrary. It is, presumably, the performance of ancestral indicators, together with the genetic transmission of genes coding for the behavioral processes to which these indicators contributed, that explains why this indicator is now functioning the way it is. Selectional explanations of why this B is causing M make the meaning of *this B* quite irrelevant to the explanation of why it is causing M. This B would cause M no matter what it meant, or even if it meant nothing at all.

And so it is in the case of selectional explanations of the role of d in the production of M. In order for d to be involved in goal-directed behavior, behavior having R as its goal, d's causal contribution to the production of those movements that have R as their result must be explained by the tendency of these movements to produce R. A selectional explanation does not supply this. Quite the contrary. This animal inherits genes that program d to cause M *whether or not M* tends to yield R. The explanation for the fact that the animal inherited these genes may reside in the fact that productions of M by ancestors of this animal tended to yield R. But what happened to ancestors of this animals says nothing about what the production of M in this animal *did* or *will* yield. *This* animal may be in a completely different enviroment, one in which tokens of M no longer lead to R. Still, given the genetic programming, d will *still* produce M. As long as the behavior is not modifiable by learning[7], nothing will change. If the blowfly's consumption of sugar water is indeed instinctive, embodying what I am calling *drives* and not *desires*, then if *today*'s sugar water (unlike the stuff that existed when this behavior developed in the species) makes the fly sick, the animal is going to get sick. It will get sick again and again—whenever it finds sugar water to consume.[8] As I am using the terms, this is the basic difference between a drive and a desire. Behavior whose internal source is a drive toward sugar water cannot be explained by an internal state that is *for* sugar water. Hence, when we have an evolutionary (and, in particular, a selectional) explanation of why d produces M, the fact that M tends to result in R, even if we suppose that M *does* (still) result in R, is quite irrelevant to *explaining* why d produces M. Behavior that is not the result of learning, whether it be the rigidly programmed behavior

---

7. If it is modifiable by learning, then of course we are back to the present model of goal-directed behavior. That is, d will now be a desire *for R* (since d will be an internal state on which the reinforcing quality of R depends), and the explanation of behavior (acquired by reinforcing certain movements by R) will be explicable in terms of the fact that d is for R.

8. Stellar and Stellar (1985, p. 41) remark that to date it has not been found that the blowfly can learn to modify its responses on the basis of food rewards. If this is so, then the blowfly's behavior is explicable in terms of drives (*toward* goals), not desires *for* goals.

of regulative bodily subsystems or the instinctive behavior of the animal itself, is *not* goal-directed behavior. Whatever drive or motive, *d*, we suppose is operating inside the animal to produce the movements resulting in *R* does not qualify as a desire *for* the condition it drives the animal toward. This internal state, though it drives the animal *toward R*, does not have *R* as its goal, because reaching this goal does not explain why the animal is driven toward it.

What I have said about drives, and about the way they operate in the instinctive behavior of animals, can also be said, but for slightly different reasons, about the apparent goal-directedness of artifacts. A heat-seeking missile may be driven *toward* a goal by certain cybernetic mechanisms, but it is not goal-*directed*. At best, it is directed by the goals, purposes, and intentions of those who designed and manufactured it. The reason is much the same as that for denying a role to the meaning of a machine's internal states in the explanation of its behavior (section 4.2). Even supposing that there are internal states with meaning, the fact that these states have this meaning is not, except in the most indirect way (through its designers and manufacturers), relevant to explaining why these internal states exercise the control functions they do. The thing is there, doing what it is doing, because I put it there. The reason I did this is because *I wanted* a certain result and *I thought* (possibly incorrectly) that by arranging things this way I could achieve that result. The tendency of the process to achieve that result (if, indeed, it has this tendency) is only indirectly, through me as it were, responsible for things' being wired the way they are. At best, we can give such artifacts a kind of borrowed goal-directedness—the same kind of intentional loan that words on a page have with meaning. If the missile reaches its target, it does so not because *it* occupies an internal state having the target as its goal but because I occupy an internal state that has the missile's reaching the target as *its* goal.

There is, of course, no point in arguing about words. If someone thinks that the behavior of some machines—behavior that persists, in varying circumstances, toward some final result—is goal-directed (the goal in question being the final result that the machine overcomes various obstacles to achieve), so be it. I do not own the term, and others can (and will) use it as they please. The same can be said for the activities of various homeostatic and regulatory mechanisms in animals, and for the innate, rigidly programmed, and (in general) need-satisfying behavior of animals themselves. These activities do, admittedly, exhibit some of the interesting properties of genuinely purposive behavior—the kind of behavior I am calling goal-directed, the kind of behavior that is *explained* by its tendency to achieve a certain goal. We can say, if we like, that such behavior has a *function*: to achieve those results that (in the case of biological mechanisms and processes) led to their selection and preservation or (in the case of artifacts) that was our purpose in constructing them. The important point is not what word we use to describe the phenomena that I am using the word "goal-directed" to describe, but the fact that the behaviors I am calling goal-directed are beyond the self-regulating, "goal"-achieving, or "goal"-maintaining behavior of artifacts and bodily organs and are quite different from the unlearned, instinctive, and (in general) need-satisfying behavior of animals, the kind of behavior that is driven (by internal motivational states) *toward* a goal. Goal-directed behavior (not to mention goal-*intended* behavior) is not only behavior that tends to produce certain beneficial results but behavior that is undertaken precisely because *it* (not some ancestral replica) tends (or tended) to produce that result. It is this fact—a fact about what the system's having this goal helps explain—that justified calling this special class of behaviors goal-*directed* behaviors.

5.4 The Intentionality of Desire

Desires, though they are not representational states[9], do have an object, something they are a desire *for*, that gives them a special status. This special status is often acknowledged by saying that desires, like beliefs, are intentional states or attitudes. It is the purpose of this section to describe the intentional aspect of desire and to show how the current account of desire captures this aspect.

Note first that ascriptions of desire are, like ascriptions of belief, referentially opaque. The belief that s is F is not the same as a belief that t is G, although $s = t$ and although the predicate expressions, "F" and "G", are co-extensional (are true of, or refer to, exactly the same things). The same is true of desire. Oedipus wants to marry Jocasta, but does not want to marry his mother (and perhaps even wants *not* to marry his mother), despite the fact that Jocasta *is* his mother.

Some desires inherit their referential opacity from the beliefs and *other* ? desires from which they are derived. For example: I want to speak to the manager. I think the well-dressed woman standing on the far side of the room is the manager, so I want to speak to her. Given my desire to speak to the manager, my desire to speak to *her* is derived from my belief that she is the manager. If she happens to be, not the manager, but a clerk with no authority to help me, this (as long as I don't know it) makes no difference to what I want. I still want to talk to her. But I do not, of course, want to talk to a clerk who can't help me. So my desire to talk to a person who, as things stand, is a person who cannot help me is entirely a function of my beliefs about the person (and my desire to talk to the manager).

9. Not, at least, on the face of it. However, Stampe (1987) describes desires as something like perceptions (and hence representations) of needs.

But we are not now concerned with such cognitively derived desires, with desires generated by beliefs and more basic, or less derived, desires. We will return to them later. For the moment let us think about a simpler kind of goal-directed behavior. My friend has a pet rabbit named PJ. There is a bottle attached to PJ's cage with water in it. A spout leads from the bottle into cage, and when PJ is thirsty all he has to do is lick the spout. He learned to do this very quickly. When PJ now licks the spout, it seems natural enough to say that he does so because he is thirsty, because he wants some water. That is his motive, his purpose, his reason for licking the spout. According to the present account of desire, this is not only a natural thing to say, it is the *correct* thing to say if PJ's behavior is the result, in the way described above, of his past experience with the spout.

As we have already noted, PJ may not actually get what he wants. If the water bottle is empty, he licks the spout in order to get water, but this goal—getting water—is never reached. This doesn't prevent it from *being* PJ's purpose in licking the spout. It doesn't prevent *water*, or *getting water*, from being the goal of that internal state (D) that is now active in producing licking movements. For what makes *water* the goal of this state is not what *will* satisfy it (perhaps nothing ever will satisfy it) but the fact that it makes water reinforcing, makes water the sort of result that tends to promote the behavior that leads to it. And what makes this state, and the fact that it is, in this sense, *for* water, explanatorily relevant to PJ's current licking behavior is the fact D was recruited as a (partial) cause of licking movements because these movements *resulted* in water.

So an unsatisfied desire—perhaps even a currently unsatisf*iable* desire—can, like a false belief, help explain behavior. This is an important intentional property of desire. A desire can take nonexistent things—at least, things that do not now exist and never will—as its object *without* sacrificing its explanatory relevance to current behavior.[10]

It is, by the way, quite clear from examples like this that, if we are going to explain an animal's behavior in terms of what it wants or desires, the *object* of that motivational state—what the desire is a desire *for*—is determined, not by what the behavior *will* produce, not by what it *now* tends to

10. When we are dealing with simple desires, those that are *not* cognitively derived, there must *have been* past tokens of R in order for the present desire for R to explain behavior. PJ may never get water, but if he licks at the spout because he wants water he must, sometime in the past, have received water for behaving in this way. If PJ never received water, then the receipt of water could not possibly explain D's (an internal state that makes water reinforcing) recruitment as a cause of M—could not possibly explain, therefore, current behavior (D's causing M).

I will return to cognitively derived motivational states (those that, by having their object determined by an associated belief, can take as their object things and conditions that never did and never will exist—things, in fact, that are are impossible).

produce, but by the sort or results it *tended* to produce in the animal's past experience. If we now, after learning, put beer in PJ's water bottle, the fact that licking the spout will now give the rabbit beer, the fact that such behavior now tends to produce nothing but beer, is irrelevant to understanding why PJ licks the spout. He licks it because he wants water even if licking no longer tends to give him water. And even if PJ likes the beer he gets, even if it quenches the thirst that motivated him to lick, he still licked because he wanted *water*. The rabbit may, *hereafter*, lick in order to get beer. He may, that is, develop *new*, more discriminating, desires. But until that happens, the desire that explains the behavior is a desire *for* whatever past result figured as a structuring cause of the the behavior.[11]

Suppose we put nothing but Perrier water in PJ's water bottle the first few weeks. Does this means that, once PJ learns his lessons, he licks at the spout in order to obtain Perrier water? Has our rabbit developed fancy tastes—desiring, thereafter, nothing but mineral water bottled in France?

Possibly yes, possibly no. It depends on PJ. Nothing in the present analysis of desire forces us to either conclusion. Let us suppose, however, that PJ can't tell the difference between ordinary tap water and spring water bottled in France. If this is so, then we cannot suppose that what it was about the water we used in PJ's bottle that made it reinforcing was its being *Perrier* water. It was merely the fact that it was water. Since this is so, we must say that D is a desire, not for Perrier water, but simply for water. The fact that Perrier water is water, and not the fact that it was bottled in France, is what explains why PJ's receipt of it during learning enlisted D as a cause of licking motions. Hence, what PJ has a desire *for* is water. It is an internal state having that goal or object that explains PJ's current behavior at the spout. Despite the fact that PJ received only Perrier during learning, it is an internal state that is for *water*—a desire for water, not for Perrier water—that is currently active in the production of those movements constituting behavior. It is the fact that PJ wants water, not that he wants Perrier water, that explains why he is licking the spout.[12]

Not every property of a reinforcing event is relevant to its efficacy as a reinforcer. Though PJ was always rewarded with water bottled in France, *that* property of the reward is not relevant to the effects this water had on PJ. It doesn't figure in the *explanation* of PJ's altered pattern of behavior. It does not, therefore, become a motivationally relevant object—something

11. Ringen (1985) effectively makes this point against Porpora's (1980) criticism of Wright (1973).
12. This assumes that it *is* the fact that it was water that explains the change in PJ's behavior. It may not be. It may simply be the fact that by licking at the spout he received a cool liquid that explains the change in PJ's behavior (cool beer would have had the same effect). If this is so, then PJ has a desire for a cool liquid, and *that* is why he licks the spout.

we can appeal to as a goal, objective, or purpose—in explaining PJ's present behavior. The fact that the water was bottled in France did not help to *structure* this behavior.

Even if all R's are S, so that one cannot get R without getting S, one can still want R without wanting S, for all R's can be S (and vice versa) without the property R being the same as the property S. As long as these properties are different, the fact that something is R and the fact that something is S will be explanatorily different. Even if we imagined that all (and only) water was bottled in France, this wouldn't make the fact that something is water and the fact that it came from France explanatorily equivalent. Being bottled in France has nothing to do with extinguishing fires. Fires can't tell the difference between regular tap water and Perrier water. Neither can PJ. That is why the fact that he received Perrier water during learning doesn't help explain anything about why he now, as a result of learning, licks the spout. If you can't tell the difference between Bordeaux and Burgundy wines, you cannot develop a genuine taste, desire, *for* Bordeaux. An affectation, perhaps; a cognitively *derived* desire, maybe; but not a pure desire.

To summarize, then: Our account of cognitively pure desires, those that do not inherit their intentional properties from the beliefs and desires from which they are derived, leaves them with the following properties.

> 1. A desire for R may be misdirected in the sense that behavior having R as its goal or objective—behavior that is explained, in part at least, by the desire *for R*—may fail to produce R. The rabbit may lick the spout because it is thirsty even when there is no liquid to be obtained in that way.
> 2. A desire that is satisfied *by S* may nonetheless not be a desire *for S*. PJ may be satisfied with beer, but that doesn't mean he licked the spout out of a desire for beer.
> 3. A desire for R must be distinguished from a desire for S even when nothing is, perhaps nothing *can be*, R without being S. Even if all water contains hydrogen atoms, this doesn't mean that we should confuse a desire for water with a desire for something containing hydrogen atoms.
> 4. An animal cannot have a (pure) desire for R if it cannot distinguish R from S. Our capacity to distinguish one object from another sets an upper limit on the kinds of objects that can be objects of desire. If the rabbit cannot distinguish iceberg lettuce from romaine, then it cannot be in an internal state that makes iceberg lettuce reinforcing but not romaine. Hence, the rabbit cannot possibly do something because it wants iceberg lettuce. Getting iceberg lettuce cannot explain a change in the rabbit's behavior, and hence cannot figure as a structuring cause

of present behavior, if the rabbit cannot distinguish this kind of lettuce from other kinds.

Such are the intentional aspects of basic, cognitively pure desires. As these desires become integrated into a richer network of beliefs and desires, they generate (derived) motivational states that have an even greater articulation in their intentional structure. We will examine the way this occurs in the final chapter.

5.5 *The Plasticity of Purposeful Behavior*

Nothing has been said, and nothing should be said, about the causal details of the process constituting behavior—the *way* M (the movements themselves) or N (some more remote result) is produced by D and B. We have spoken of a rat pressing a bar. In this case the behavior is constituted by the production of a certain result: N, depression of the bar. What particular bodily movements, M, are used to produce N is left open. This effect may be achieved in a great many different ways. The rat can press the bar with his right paw, with his left paw, with his teeth, or by sitting on it. In each case the rat is doing the same thing: pressing the bar. Even when it presses it with the same paw, in what appears to be the identical way, there are likely to be a great many differences at the neural and muscular level. Aside from identifying them as *bar-pressing* movements, as movements that have a certain upshot or result, there is no way of identifying the movements a rat learns to execute as the result of this kind of learning. As Taylor (1964, p.206) puts it, what is learned, even in rigidly constrained conditioning, is not movement but actions (I would say *behavior*)—processes that are classified in terms of their *product* or *result*, a result that can typically be reached in a great many different ways.

Behavior whose associated product is some enviromental change or condition—like pressing a bar, closing a door, or fetching a beer from the fridge—can obviously be done in many different ways. The way D and B bring about N, the particular pattern of bodily movements that is utilized to achieve this effect, many never be the same. But even if we confine ourselves to behavior that has as its associated product some bodily movement—like waving your arm, wiggling your ears, or walking—there are, generally speaking, a multitude of different ways these movements can be produced. Neuroscientists distinguish between a FAP (fixed action pattern), the stereotypical production of some particular motor *result* —a limb movement, say—and an FMP (fixed motor pattern), the electrical activity in the motor neurons that brings about that result, FMPs are comparatively rare. Cricket songs come close; the neural activity involved in the production of these songs is tightly controlled in regard to the number and the timing of motor impulses (Ewing and Hoyle 1965). Hoyle (1984, p. 405) describes an even move impressive case: The courtship behavior of a tiny male grasshopper produces stereotypic motor output accurate to within a millisecond of the firing of individual nerve impulses. However, most FAPs—even in insects—are not fixed with regard to the electrical activity in the motor neurons causing the movements. Careful measurement reveals that of the many thousands of visually identical stepping movements of a locust, for example, no two steps exhibit the same underlying pattern of electrical activity in the motor neurons causing the movements (Hoyle 1984, p. 405). And what is true of insects is even more obviously true of human beings—if not at the level of specific limb movements, then at the level of individual acts. (How many different ways are there of doing one thing, such as waving to a friend, scratching one's nose, or eating an apple?)

This is merely to say that an appeal to reasons—to what we believe and desire—explains, not the *particular* process by means of which B and D produce N (or M), for this may differ greatly from one instance to the next, but B and D's producing N (or M) *however* this may be managed on individual occasions. We can explain the fall of a leaf to the ground or the flow of a river to the sea by citing the influence of gravity without caring about why the leaf or the water took the particular route it took in reaching its destination. The particular route leaves and water take in reaching their destination depends on the location of obstacles, the wind, and a great many other factors. These may differ from case to case. What gravity helps us understand is not *why* they get there the *way* they get there, but, simply, why they get *there* (to the ground or to the sea) rather than elsewhere.

And so it is with explaining behavior. Explanations in terms of an agent's reasons are attempts to explain why B and D reached a certain destination, why they produced N (say) rather than something else. This is as it should be, since the behavior *is* the production of N. Such explanations make no attempt to explain why B and D cause N in this way rather than that way—why, for instance, one pattern of movements is used today and a different pattern of movements tomorrow. Clyde's wanting a beer and thinking there is one left in the refrigerator explains his going to the refrigerator, a process having that particular upshot. They do not explain his taking *that* particular route. There may be, but then again there may not be, a cognitive explanation for the detailed aspects of Clyde's trip to the refrigerator. Perhaps his detour by the cupboard can be explained by the fact that he wanted to pick up a glass. Perhaps his hesitation at the doorway can be explained by the fact that he was waiting for the dog to move. But there will surely be a great many things about his trip (details having to do with the pattern of leg movements that brought him to the kitchen, for instance) that will have no cognitive explanation whatsoever. Clyde had a reason to go to the kitchen, but no reason to get to the kitchen in *that* particular way. And even when there are reasons for going in *that* particular way, they are generally not the same as the reasons for going to the kitchen.

When Clyde goes to the refrigerator for his beer, much of the operation is carried out under the guidance of sensory feedback of which Clyde is largely unaware. *That $B + D$ produce N* may be determined by the intentional properties of B and D, but *how* they produce N must obviously be determined, in part at least, by continually updated information bearing on the conditions, some of them constantly changing, in which N is to be realized. Remove two legs from a cockroach and, automatically, an entirely different sequence of motor commands is issued to the remaining four legs in order to get the bug where it wants to go (Gallistel 1980).[13] The roach's wanting to reach a dark spot when it senses light and vibration (if we suppose that these are the roach's reasons for scurrying under the refrigerator) certainly doesn't explain why one sequence of motor commands is issued rather than another. It only explains why the roach scuttled away to a dark spot, why commands having *that outcome* were issued. Similarly, an expert marksman holds a pistol virtually immobile in spite of the fact that many parts of his body exhibit movement. The key to pistol stability (as electromyographic and kinematic studies show; see Evarts 1980) is that for each movement of the trunk or limbs there is a corresponding counterbalancing movement that stabilizes the position of the pistol in space. The marksman's desire to hit the target explains why he holds his arm still. This desire does not explain the enormously complex system of compensatory movements by means of which the motor control system *keeps* the arm still. The same is true of Clyde on his trip to the refrigerator.

The factors that are causally responsible for one thing's causing another—in this case, for B and D's causing N—need not be responsible, causally or otherwise, for *the way* the effect is produced. A chief executive officer can get his employees to do certain tasks without knowing or caring *how* they do them. Indeed, as we all know, a hierarchical arrangement of executive responsibility is an efficient way to organize command structures. It is also an effective way to design the mechanisms responsible for behavior. Even in the simplest sort of instinctive behavior—the defensive maneuvers of a moth or the pattern of leg movements in a roach, for instance—the details of the behavior are left to lower-level structures. The moth's sensitive auditory system is charged with the job of detecting the bat and issuing a

13. Gallistel (1980, p. 10), following Bruner (1970) and Bartlett (1958), finds the basis of intelligence, or at least a precursor of intelligence, in the nervous system's highly adaptable implementation of general patterns of action: "Thus, the neural machinery that organizes the sequences of stepping movements in the cockroach already manifests some elementary properties of intelligence."

Sure, you design clever subroutines to cover
funny particular contingencies; but still,
They have to make M (or M) happen

134   Chapter 5

command: Scram! What particular sequence of movements actually occurs in the execution of this command will depend on a great many variables— the position of the moth, the direction from which the bat is approaching, the speed of approach, and so on—which are of no concern to higher-level control structures.

This division of labor is exploited by the sort of learning from which our reasons—*what* we believe and *what* we desire—acquire an explanatory relation to our behavior. Learning produces a command structure in which N is produced by B and D. The intentional properties of B and D—the fact that B indicates or has the function of indicating F, and the fact that D is for R—explain (or so I have argued) why they produce N. Other factors must come into play to determine, on specific occasions, *how* they manage to produce N, why this itinerary rather than that itinerary is adopted to reach the destination. Given the initial state and position of the animal, given the obstacles in the way, and given the presence of similarly motivated animals nearby, perhaps, on this occasion, N can be brought about only by a completely novel sequence of movements, a sequence never yet executed in the production of N. Animals (Nissan 1950) trained to secure food by pushing a white panel (whether it is on the right or the left) will execute a altogether novel movements, movements required to push the *white* panel, when the device is turned on its side so that the white panel is *on top*. But this completely novel *way* of producing N does not mean that the content of D and B (what the animal believes and wants) do not explain the process, and hence the behavior, having N as its product. For the process, the behavior being explained, is the production of N (e.g., pressure on the white panel), and that stays the same even when there is a dramatic change in the way that result is brought about.

This selection of alternative means to reach a given end is sometimes called response generalization. This term can be misleading. It suggests that the animal has acquired something in learning (a response) and then generalized it. For example, a rat learns to run a maze to reach the goal. When the maze is flooded, the rat *swims* to the goal (Lashley 1924). When unable to run, the rat *rolls* to the goal. To suggest that this is an instance of response generalization is to suggest that what the rat learned to do in the first instance was to *run* to the goal. He then "generalized" this response. But there is no particular reason to suppose that this is what the rat learned to do. The rat learned to go to the goal box in order to get food. What was rewarded was *getting to the goal*, not getting to it in this way rather than that way. Even if, during learning, the rat always ran to the goal, there is no reason to think that *this way* of getting to the goal was part of what was learned. Gallistel (1980, p. 112) formulates the problem, the problem of how to describe what is learned during learning, this way:

One of the toughest problems in the analysis of learned behavior is to find appropriate units for the behavioral analysis. Does the organism learn to make a particular pattern of muscular contractions and relaxations, as conditioned reflex theories imply? Or does the learning experience operate at a higher level, a level that specifies, say, the direction a limb should move relative to some object, not the particular pattern of muscular activity to be used in accomplishing that movement?

He goes on to describe how Wickens's (1938, 1939) classic experiments on response generalization illuminate this problem. In these experiments, human subjects had their forearm strapped to a board with the palm downward. Their middle finger rested on an electrode that was capable of delivering mildly painful shocks. Subjects were conditioned to withdraw their finger from the the electrode at the sound of a buzzer. The conditioned response was involuntary in the sense that subjects could not inhibit the response when directed to do so. After thorough conditioning, the subject's arms were once again strapped down, only this time with the palm *upward*. In order to withdraw the finger from the electrode at the sound of the buzzer, the subjects now had to execute quite different movements. Different muscles had to be brought into play in order to perform the same action (withdrawing the finger from the electrode). Most of Wickens's subjects made a rapid finger withdrawal response the next time the buzzer sounded—clear evidence that what they had learned was not a way of withdrawing the finger from the electrode (though throughout the conditioning process subjects were only allowed to withdraw it in one way), but something already more general, more abstract: a process defined by its *result* (getting the finger away from the electrode) rather than by any particular way of producing that result. Though N was always brought about via M during learning, what the subject learned was to produce N, not to produce it via M. This is why reasons, when they help to explain behavior, explain why N is produced, not why it is produced in the way it is.

The determination—and, hence, the explanation—of those motor processes actually selected to reach a goal is not the job of the cognitive and conative mechanisms that determine that the goal is to be sought. In some cases these details are the job of lower-level mechanisms in a hierarchically organized control structure (e.g., the mechanism responsible for the particular leg movements Clyde executes in going to the kitchen); in other cases they are the job of other elements at the same level of control—i.e., other motives and beliefs.

Reasons explain *behavior*, the production of N—something more abstract than the particular motor patterns used to bring about those results that constitute the behavior in question. The rabbit's being thirsty explains its going to the water bottle and licking at the spout, and nothing more specific about this behavior, because, in the last analysis, the rabbit's having its thirst quenched was the result of its going to the bottle and licking at the spout, not of its *hopping* to the bottle or licking it from the right side rather than the left.

Reasons, though they can explain why an animal runs, cannot explain why the neural and muscular events that take place in the course of running occur. If we suppose that cockroaches and millipedes have reasons for some of the things they do (to reach a dark spot or to find food, for instance), then these reasons will explain, at most, why they go where they go, but not why they go *how* they go. The same is obviously true of all cognitive explanations of behavior. One's fear of a drop in the stock market explains why one sells, not why, in calling one's broker, one held the phone in one way rather than another. There may be no reason, no belief, desire, fear, or intention, that explains this behavior.

Chapter 6

The Interactive Nature of Reasons

However it may be with rats and pigeons, most of the reasons for deliberate human behavior have little or nothing to do with benefits conferred for performing feats of discrimination. I don't buckle my seat belt because I was rewarded each time I did it in the past. Nor was I conditioned to behave in this way in order to avoid aversive stimuli. There was, as I recall, sometimes an annoying stimulus—either an electronic buzz or a passenger's nagging—that I could avoid or eliminate by buckling up. These reminders, I admit, helped me develop the habit. Nevertheless, when I now buckle up, I (often enough anyway) buckle up for a reason that has nothing to do with what happened to me in the past. I buckle my seat belt in order to avoid serious injury in case of an accident—something, I am happy to report, I have never experienced. Perhaps a dog's leap over a barrier can be explained by the past administration of electric shocks, but my behavior in an automobile can't be explained in the same way.

I refrain from smoking, brush my teeth, avoid certain foods, look both ways before I cross a street, read the newspaper, and teach my classes for similar reasons—reasons that have little or nothing to do with rewards received or punishments actually administered for these behaviors in the past. I have certain beliefs about the situation I am in, certain desires about the situation I would like to be (or stay) in, and some ideas about how best to go from here to there. These, together with a few collateral factors (e.g., nervousness, shyness, a headache, a sprained ankle, fatigue) pretty much determine what I do and don't do. None of this has much to do, or so it seems, with how I acquired the concepts I apply in holding these beliefs (e.g., discrimination learning) or the rewards I received (if there ever were such) for performing similarly (if I ever did) in the past.

This is to say that the model we have so far developed for understanding the explanatory role of reasons is too simple to capture the enormously rich interplay of beliefs, desires, and behavior in cognitively and conatively developed animals such as humans. This is most certainly true, and, therefore, most certainly a reasonable complaint. Up to this point we have looked exclusively at *pure* conative states, states whose intentional object (goal) was not derived, as many of our goals are derived, from the beliefs we hold about ways to get, or ways to avoid, things we want (or fear) in some more fundamental way. We have also concentrated, almost exclusively, on beliefs of a rather primitive sort—beliefs about perceptually salient features of one's immediate environment. Such beliefs do not exhibit, as many of our beliefs do exhibit, the interdependent, holistic character of meaning in mature, tightly integrated representational systems. But though, given this narrow focus, the complaint is entirely reasonable, it is not, I think, a reasonable *criticism* of what has so far been done. To reject or ignore this model because it is too simple is like rejecting Copernican astronomy because it doesn't account for the return of Halley's comet, the shift in the perihelion of Mercury, or the wobble in the Earth's axis.

Nevertheless, something must be said, if not about the details, then about the overall structure in which these details must eventually find a place. Such is the intent of this final chapter.

6.1 Choice, Preference, and Decision

An obvious respect in which the model is too simple is that it says nothing about behavior that is the expression of *multiple* conative and cognitive elements: desires for X competing with desires for Y, beliefs about risks being balanced against beliefs about gains, desires being modified in the light of beliefs about their means of satisfaction, and so on. Once we enter this world, we are talking about phenomena like choice, preference, decision, and problem solving. We are talking about the economics, as it were, of behavior: ways of allocating resources in the production of output so as to maximize satisfaction of needs and desires.

I cannot hope to say anything useful about the actual way systems manage these complex administrative tasks. But I see no reason why I *should* say very much about them. It is enough, perhaps, to show (if it can be shown) that the general framework provided is *receptive*, or at least not unreceptive, to such ramifications. If there is reason to think that the basic building blocks can be combined to give a realistic portrait of purposeful, intelligent behavior, then this is, if not support for this account of intentional action, at least a way of neutralizing objections against it.

So let me begin by looking at behavior that is determined by two or more motivational states. If we oversimplify a bit and think of fear as being or involving a desire for a thing's absence or avoidance, then, on the account of desire given in chapter 5, an animal's behavior can clearly be motivated by two or more desires: a desire for food, say, and a fear for its own safety.[1] These different desires help to explain different *facets* (see

1. This is a classic approach-avoidance conflict situation. There has been an enormous amount of empirical work done on such behavior; see, especially, that of Neal Miller (1944,

section 1.5) of the animal's behavior. A jackal wants to share in the feast and that is why it waits *there*, near the dead antelope. It also wants to stay out of reach of the tiger's sharp claws, and that is why what it does there is *wait*. In the past, the tiger has always left a few scraps, and that fact— together, perhaps, with a few scars from an earlier, premature attempt to snatch a mouthful—has modified the kind of movements produced by the representation of a dead antelope and the desire for food (hunger). What the jackal wants (food), and what it fears, doesn't want, or wants to avoid (a swipe from a tiger's paw), may be just the kind of results that, through learning, helped to shape the causal processes that are unfolding (or refusing to unfold) in the scene I have described. Given our account of an internal state's goal or objective, to explain the jackal's behavior in terms of its *desire* for food and its *fear* of the tiger (not to mention its *knowledge* of their whereabouts) is to explain this behavior in terms of internal processes (whose product is the jackal's movements) that have been shaped by the animal's past encounters with food and tigers. It is, among other things, the jackal's past experience with tigers and food that, by helping to explain why processes having *these* movements as their product are now occurring, help to explain why the jackal is now behaving the way it is. They, together with its internal representations of where the antelope and the tiger are, help explain why it *waits* and, perhaps more specifically, why it waits *there*.

Of course, if the jackal has, as we say, an *instinctive* fear of tigers—a motivational state such that, independent of any past experience (on the part of the individual jackal), it will not, even when highly motivated (i.e., very hungry), approach closer than within a few yards of the tiger—then we can still explain facets of its behavior by talking about its (instinctive) fear of tigers; however, this is not a genuine *intentional* explanation. It is like explaining why an insect keeps three feet (forming a stable tripod) firmly planted on the ground when it lifts its other feet by saying it does so in order to avoid falling over or because it wants to keep its balance. There are, surely, *reasons why* bugs do this. That is to say, there is undoubtedly *an* explanation for such behavior. But this should not be taken to mean that there is, in this explanation of the insect's behavior, a reference to *the bug's* reasons for behaving in this way. There is also a reason why my car, before it has had a chance to warm up in cold weather, hesitates when I depress

---

1959), who, in applying principles derived from Hullian drive theory (Motivation = Drive × Habit) was able to predict behavior in approach-avoidance conflicts. I do not, of course, wish to endorse any particular theoretical account of such behavior. It is enough for my purposes if such accounts are *compatible* (as I think they are, in letter if not in spirit) with the very general picture proposed here of the way belief and desire figure in the explanation of behavior.

the accelerator. There is a reason why it behaves this way, but it isn't *the car*'s reason for behaving this way. The car doesn't have a reason for hesitating. Neither does the bug have a reason (e.g., in order to keep its balance) for keeping three feet planted on the ground.

Furthermore, besides the jackal's multiple motivational states, there is, as already noted, something *in* it that indicates the presence and the whereabouts of both an antelope carcass and a tiger, and these indicators are, together with the jackal's fears and desires, working together to guide the jackal's movements. The tiger leaves to get a drink and the jackal approaches the carcass. The tiger returns and the jackal retreats. The tiger drags the antelope to its lair and the jackal either follows at a safe distance or, losing hope, wanders off. To explain the coordination between the jackal's position and movements and those of the tiger and the antelope, one must suppose that there is a complex network of internal indicators functioning to keep the jackal informed of the whereabouts and the movements of the two remaining actors in this drama, a complex network of internal indicators that are making a causal contribution to determining the jackal's movements. To explain details of the jackal's motivated (by fear and hunger) behavior by appealing to what it *believes* or *knows* is to explain this behavior in terms of what these indicators have, through learning, acquired the function of indicating about the jackal's surroundings. When things are working right and the indicators indicate what they have the function of indicating, we speak of what the animal *knows* or *sees*—words that suggest that the representational mechanisms are working satisfactorily. They are doing their job, indicating what they are supposed to be indicating. When something goes wrong, we speak of what the animal thinks or believes—words that suggest that things are not, or may not be, the way the animal represents them as being.

This does not tell us *how* an animal develops strategies for negotiating compromises between competing desires or what kind of mechanisms there might be for implementing these strategies. Often, when desires come into conflict, there is an original or novel solution to the control problem. An animal has learned to do one thing (*M*, say) when it wants *X* and a different thing (*N*) when it wants *Y*. It confronts a situation in which it wants both *X* and *Y* and finds itself unable to do what is necessary to get both. It sometimes relinquishes one in order to get the other, thereby exhibiting a preference. Sometimes it forgoes both in order to reach some third result. The jackal doesn't run directly *to* the food (*M*), nor does it run directly *away* from the tiger (*N*). It sits and waits at a safe distance. It is easy to imagine that such "compromises" in the kind of movements produced by co-occurring desires (and beliefs about the jointly occurring conditions) are a completely novel solution to a behavioral problem. A routine for producing *M* (approach) in one set of circumstances (food) and a routine for producing N (retreat) in another set of circumstances (tiger) somehow join forces in still a third set of circumstances (food + tiger) to produce, not M *and* N (which is impossible), and not M *or* N (neither of which would be beneficial), but some third option, Q. How this novel third result is synthesized out of control structures already available is, at the biological level, a complete mystery—especially when one realizes that it may be a solution that is optimal from the point of view of securing at least partial satisfaction of both desires. If a choice was always made between the production of M and the production of N, we could imagine a high-level switching mechanism, sensitive to other channels of information and to collateral motivational variables, controlling the activation of already established (through learning) dispositions. But the production of novel responses, the essence of intelligent behavior, cannot be thought about in such simple, mechanical terms.

Part of the explanation for such creative responses must lie in the cognitive differences in these situations. After all, the representation of a tiger's being *near* the food is, we are supposing, a new element in the situation. Furthermore, we can easily imagine that the jackal exploits previously acquired but not-yet-applied bits of knowledge (perhaps acquired by watching older, more experienced jackals in similar situations) in figuring out what to do. We will look more closely at such possibilities in the following sections. For the moment we need only observe that the jackal's behavior, however it may actually be produced, is behavior that, *if* it can be explained by what I have been calling *pure* desires (for food and the avoidance of tigers), is constituted by internal states that have had their causal roles (in the production of movement) shaped by the jackal's past commerce with tigers and food. This, and not some particular story about exactly how this occurs, is what the present account implies about the way such reasons figure in the explanation of behavior. This much, I submit, is plausible no matter how many beliefs and desires go into the mix.

6.2 New Means to Old Ends

Besides wanting things I have never had, I can do things I've never done to get the things I've never had. How, on the present account of things, could my wanting R explain my doing M when I never had R and, hence, never received R for doing M? To make matters worse, how could it explain my doing M if I've never done M before, much less received R for doing it?

Archie joined the army, but he hasn't yet been promoted. He *wants* to be promoted. He works hard to be promoted. Maybe, if he keeps up the good work, he *will be* promoted. But he hasn't *yet* been promoted. So how, on the present account of things, could his desire for a promotion, something he has never had, explain his behavior? The past receipt of food may help to explain why a rat is now pressing the bar, but past promotions *cannot* explain why Archie is now polishing his boots.

Even if we suppose that Archie has had, if not *military* promotions, other types of promotions, the sort of behavior for which those promotions functioned as rewards may be quite different from the behavior he now exhibits to get his promotion to Private First Class. He didn't have to execute snappy salutes or keep his boots polished in order to get "promoted" from the fourth to the fifth grade. How, then, could those past rewards, assuming we can count them as promotions, help explain this behavior—something they must do if, on the present account of things, Archie is polishing his boots *in order* to get promoted?

To keep things manageable, let us suppose that Archie *has* been promoted, in some relevant sense of "promotion," but is now displaying altogether novel behavior (for him) in order to secure a promotion. He has never been one for spit and polish, starched shirts, parade-ground drill, and snappy salutes, but he now does all these things, and more, and he does them because he wants to be promoted and thinks this is the way to do it. We will return, in the next section, to the more complex case where the behavior in question, whether novel or not, is explained by desires for things one has never had or experienced.

We noted earlier that rats rewarded for *running* a maze will, if the need arises, *swim* through the maze or *roll* through it to reach the goal box. A rat that learns to press a bar to get food will, if no longer able to press with its paw, press with its nose. Response generalization, as this phenomenon is called, occurs even at the involuntary level. We saw earlier that persons conditioned to withdraw a finger (involuntarily) to avoid electric shock will, when necessary, execute altogether different movements, movements that are equally involuntary, to achieve the same result. This is simply to say that, normally, what animals learn to do in order to secure rewards and avoid punishments is to produce a certain result—getting to a goal box, depressing a lever, withdrawing a finger—rather than to secure those results *in some particular way*.

This fact has important implications. One implication is that when an animal displays novel behavior—behavior that was not, as such, reinforced in the past—this does not prevent our explaining it in terms of a history of reinforcement and, hence, in terms of what its present internal states are *for*. The rat is swimming to the goal box. It has never done this before. If you want to know why the rat is *swimming* to the goal box, the answer lies *partly* in the present—in what it knows, what it can *see*, about present conditions in the maze. But if you want to know why the rat is swimming *there, to the goal box*, if you want an explanation of *this facet* of its behavior, then the answer lies, according to the present account, in the past. It lies in the fact that reaching the goal box was rewarded by food. What the rat learned to do was to *go to* the goal box, and it learned to do this by being rewarded with food when it got there. And what the rat is now doing is, in one sense, exactly what it learned to do: going to the goal box. In explaining the rat's behavior by saying that it is swimming to the goal box *in order to get* food, because it *wants* food, because it has this *purpose, objective,* or *goal,* we are explaining, not why the rat is *swimming* there, but why it is swimming *there.* The novel aspect of the behavior—the fact that the rat is swimming, not walking, running, or rolling, to the goal box—is explained by the animal's altered cognitive situation. But it is doing something novel (*swimming*) as a means of doing something not at all novel (going to the goal box), and it is the latter behavior that has, as its structuring cause, the past receipt of food. That is why we can now explain the rat's behavior, at least *this facet* of its behavior, by alluding to the animal's present desire *for food.*

The explanation of Archie's behavior exhibits interesting parallels with that of the rat and, indeed, with that of any animal that, having learned to behave in one way to get what it wants, now behaves in new and often creative ways to achieve the same result. In saying this I do not mean to denigrate purposeful human behavior. I certainly do not mean to suggest that it is, in every respect relevant to its explanation, the same as that of a rodent. Obviously much more is going on in Archie's case than in the rat's. Archie is more resourceful than the rat in finding ways to reach his goal box (pleasing the authorities) that dispenses the goodies (promotions) that it is his desire to secure. Nevertheless, there are, in broad outlines at least, intriguing similarities. Archie knows that exhibiting a mastery of addition and subtraction, spelling, or whatever impressed his grade-school teachers and got him promoted from one grade to the next is not going to impress his company commander. *That* isn't the way to get promoted to Private First Class. A different means must be used to impress *this* authority, the source of the rewards that Archie seeks. So, just as the rat's *swim* cannot be explained by the rewards it received for negotiating a dry maze, Archie's *snappy salutes* cannot be explained by his past promotions. He doesn't salute because he was once rewarded with a promotion for saluting. This behavior is not *conditioned* behavior. But neither does the rat swim because it was rewarded with food for swimming. So, in the same respect, the rat's behavior is not *conditioned* behavior. Nevertheless, just as the rat, in swimming, is doing something—going to the goal box—that will (or did) bring it rewards (food), so Archie, in saluting, is doing something— impressing his superiors—that will (or did) bring him rewards (promotion). What is explained by the past results is not the novel or original facets of the behavior, but what it is about the behavior that makes it the same behavior as that which occurred in the past. What explains the rat's going to the goal box, something it does (this time) by swimming, is the rat's desire for food, something that derives from the past receipt of food for doing that. What explains Archie's efforts to impress the authorities, something he does this time by polishing his boots, is his desire for a promotion, something which (in the past) was the reward for such behavior. Archie's adoption of different means to reach his goal is best explained, as it was in the case of the rat, by his altered cognitive situation.

What, then, *does* explain Archie's adoption of novel means to reach a desired end? Why does he shine his boots, rather than practice the multiplication tables, to impress his superiors? It is for the same reasons, presumably, that the rat adopts novel means to reach the goal box in a flooded maze. Archie and the rat *know* something, and they are now applying it, perhaps for the first time, to a novel situation. This knowledge—a knowing *that* one thing leads (or might lead) to another—may well be the result of *observational* learning or imitation, forms of learning that can easily lead to novel (for the individual) forms of behavior.

Dispositions can change without this ever becoming apparent. A substance can become brittle without ever breaking. A powder can become soluble without ever dissolving. And learning can occur without the learning, and hence this altered set of dispositions, manifesting itself in overt behavior. Active responding and reinforcement are clearly not necessary for the acqustion and modification of response patterns. We all know this. I watch you work a vending machine. You get a can of cola. I'm not thirsty at the moment, so I don't *do* anything. I don't practice working the machine, nor am I rewarded (by a can of cola) for working it. Nonetheless, my dispositions are permanently altered. When I *want* a can of cola, I will know what to do. I will behave differently than I would have before I observed you work the machine.

Psychologists used to speak of latent learning. In a famous experiment, Tolman and Honzik (1930), following Blodgett (1929), showed that rats could learn to run a maze *without* reinforcement. The fact that the rats had learned their way to the goal box did not become apparent until food was placed there. *Then* it became apparent that rats receiving no reinforcement for reaching the goal box nonetheless learned as much about how to get there as rats that were rewarded for getting there. Once they knew that food was going to be there, these rats got there as quickly as the ones that were, during training, rewarded for getting there. The conclusion Tolman and Honzik reached was that, although rewards or the expectation of rewards may be necessary to make an animal perform in a certain way, it is not necessary for learning itself. This is a difference that, today, we are used to hearing expressed as the difference between competence and performance.

This conclusion should strike most people as obvious. It did not strike early learning theorists as obvious. Thorndike (1911), for instance, could find no evidence that a cat, allowed to watch another cat escape from a puzzle box, learned anything. When placed in the box, the observing cat did no better than a naive cat. Similar negative results were obtained with chicks, dogs, and monkeys, and Thorndike concluded that nonhuman animals cannot learn by observation.

Thorndike was wrong. A great deal of what animals learn is observational and and imitative learning (see, particularly, Bandura and Walters 1963). We learn that M leads to R in conditions F, and we learn this, not by ourselves producing and being rewarded for producing M in conditions F, but by observing others bringing about M in conditions F, or simply by observing that M, whether or not it is produced by another organism, is often or perhaps always accompanied by R in conditions F. Such knowledge of one's surroundings, knowledge of how one thing depends on or brings about another, is acquired in the normal course of development. It is often acquired when there is no immediate practical need for such knowledge. You don't *now* have a desire for R, or you are not in circumstances F. Hence, you have no reason, even if you are able to do so, to produce M. But this knowledge can be stored and used later. It may be particularly useful when circumstances F are circumstances in which familiar methods of obtaining R do not work. Then, when you find yourself in such circumstances, you may be forced to produce M—something that, for you, is an altogether novel response—in order to get what you want. I learn to work a coffee machine by watching you work it. This is something I learn whether or not I ever have a need to use this knowledge, whether or not I ever get coffee for myself from the machine. When I forget my thermos, though, I am now in a position to display altogether novel (for me) behavior to satisfy my desire for coffee.

It is for this reason that a desire for a promotion—or, more generally, a desire for R—can help explain behavior that has never before been exhibited in the pursuit of R. It is the agent's knowledge (in this case, *explicit* knowledge—see section 5.2) that doing M in conditions F will yield R that, when the desire for R and the belief that F co-occur, explains the novel production of M. The acquired piece of background knowledge gives the desire a new means of expression—a new causal path, as it were—to its own satisfaction.

This happens to us every day without our ever being aware of it. Though at one level of description I do the same thing every day (e.g., get out of bed, shave, or comb my hair), at another level of description I do it differently each day. The motor control system, operating largely below the conscious level and in response to altered conditions, adopts different means every day to produce the simplest voluntary movement. I move my arm each day, but at a neuronal level of description I probably never move it in exactly the same way. I have a reason to move my arm (to shut off the alarm) but no reason for moving it in this particular way. Doing things one has never done before, never *had* to do before, in order to get a promotion is just another illustration of this plasticity of behavior. The only difference is that in the case of Archie's promotion, and a great many other purposeful behaviors, we observe the plasticity being mediated by conscious processes exploiting acquired knowledge about alternative means to reach desired ends.

6.3 New Ends

I have been talking about animals that do novel things to get something they want. I have tried to show that this does not preclude the desire from helping to explain the novel behavior. The past receipt of R for producing a certain result does not, of course, explain the novel way D (the desire) brings about this result. It explains, merely, D's production of *this result*. Collateral knowledge—knowledge about how, in these *different* circumstances, this same result might be produced—explains the different *way* D produces what it produces.

But this doesn't tell us how we can do things out of a desire for something we have never had. What if Archie has *never* been promoted to (or from) *anything*. Couldn't he still *want* to be promoted? Couldn't he still do things for that reason?

Could a rat do something out of a desire for peanut butter if it never *had* peanut butter, never tasted or smelled the stuff? Yes, but presumably only if it *thought* that peanut butter would (or might) get it something it wanted in some more fundamental way.

Some desires are cognitively mediated. By this I mean, not that the desire isn't real enough, but that its object, what it is a desire *for* (call this *r*), depends on one's beliefs about what *r*, in turn, leads to. Just as knowledge that *r* will lead to R in circumstances F can lead one to exhibit novel forms of behavior having *r* as its product, such knowledge can lead one to have desires for whatever results (*r*) are deemed useful in obtaining what one desires (R). When the desire for *r* is derived, in this way, from a prior desire for R and a belief about the relationship between R and *r*—a belief to the effect that *r* is a means, perhaps the only means, or perhaps just a possible way of obtaining R—then I shall call the desire for *r* a cognitively derived or mediated desire.

Obviously one can have cognitively derived desires for things one has never had. Most of the things I want, at least most of the things I talk about wanting, are things my desire for which are cognitively mediated. I think they will make me rich, make me happy, give me pleasure, give my loved ones pleasure, or make things better in some way for me and those I care about. If I didn't *think* these things, I wouldn't want them. I think, in fact I *know*, that money (and here I should be understood as speaking about *lots* of money, something I have never had) is a powerful instrument. I know, at least I keep being told, that it can't buy everything, but it is certainly an effective way of getting a great many things that most of us want. That is why we want it—the *only* reason we want it.

Harold has never smoked a cigarette, but he now finds himself entering a store in order to buy them. His reason for going to the store is to buy cigarettes. Why does he want a cigarette? To smoke it. Why does he want to smoke a cigarette? Perhaps because he thinks that inhaling the smoke will give him a pleasant experience (his older friends seem to enjoy it). Maybe he thinks it will make him appear older and wiser to his companions, more attractive to the girls, or more rebellious to his parents and teachers. It may be just an experiment to see what it is like to smoke a cigarette. Wanting to smoke (r) is a derived desire because the objective of this motivational state is derived from what Harold knows or believes about the relationship between r and certain other things (R) he desires: sensory pleasures, respect and admiration of friends, interest of females, displeasure of parents and teachers, or simple curiosity (even information is reinforcing). After twenty years of smoking, the desire for a cigarette may take on a different quality, something more nearly like the pure (cognitively unmediated) desire for food and water; however, the desire for the first puff, if one does something in order to satisfy this desire, derives its motivational force—and hence its explanatory significance—from the beliefs one has about the *ends* to which that result will, or might, be an effective means.

As we saw in chapter 5, desire is a contributory cause of movement. In the case of pure desires, what explains a desire's (D's) causal role in the production of movement—what explains its helping to bring about M— is the fact that it is *for R*. This fact, plus the fact that M produces R, explains why D was recruited as a cause of M and, hence, why it is now *causing* M. It was recruited for this job because M results in R, a result that D makes reinforcing. In explaining behavior by describing what an agent wants (when these wants are pure) we are merely describing what the current internal states empowered as structuring causes of behavior. Cognitively mediated desires, however, are explanatory artifacts. They are, so to speak, *constructions* out of the cognitive and conative elements from which they derive their goal and motivational force (hence, their explanatory efficacy). We can explain Harold's behavior, his purchase of his first pack of cigarettes, by describing his desire to smoke a cigarette; however, this desire, a cognitively derived desire, borrows its object (smoking a cigarette) from the belief he has about what smoking a cigarette will (or might) accomplish and borrows its motivational efficacy, its power to produce movements, from the desire for these consequences. Take away Harold's desire to impress his friends or the belief that smoking will impress them and one is left, not with an inexplicable desire for a cigarette, but with no desire at all.

This is not to say that one can't want R and have no coherent or rational explanation for the desire. There are things one wants, as we say, for their own sake. One doesn't have to explain or justify the desire for food, companionship, and shelter. And one can want to listen to music, not because it is relaxing, not because it will get one X or help one avoid Y, but simply because one is in the mood for music and wants to hear some. I am not denying the existence of things that one finds *intrinsically* desirable, desirable for their own sake. This, indeed, is what the conception of a *pure* desire was meant to capture. What I am denying, and what my account of pure desires commits me to denying, is that a pure desire can figure in the explanation of behavior if one has never experienced a gratification of that desire. For if one has never experienced R, one has not, *a fortiori*, experienced R as a result of producing M. This being so, the receipt of R could not be the structuring cause of the process ($=$ behavior) having M as its product. Therefore, the fact that D is *for* R could not figure in the explanation of this behavior.

Nor do I wish to deny that one might develop a desire, a genuine, unmediated desire for something that *at first* one wanted only in a derived way or didn't want at all. Clyde ate asparagus the first time to please his parents. But now, years later, he loves asparagus and will go out of his way to get it. Once one has tasted asparagus (or whatever one counts as the reinforcing result), the taste and smell of it can permanently modify control structures. Asparagus, or eating asparagus, can become the objective, as this was defined in chapter 5, of an internal state that (together with a variety of beliefs) contributes to the production of movements involved in eating, ordering, shopping, and so on. *Now* Clyde eats in this restaurant and patronizes that supermarket because he wants fresh asparagus. Why does he want it? He likes it. And why does he like it? He just does. Not all the time, of course. He doesn't eat it for breakfast. But he does get a craving now and then. And even without the craving, it is for him a preferred vegetable. This explanation for his behavior no longer appeals (as it did originally) to a desire that derives *its* content from a belief about what eating asparagus might accomplish. Now that Clyde has eaten asparagus, his *eating asparagus* can help to explain things that it couldn't before. Hence, the desire *for* asparagus, the desire to eat asparagus, an internal state that now helps to determine motor output, can have its role in the production of output *explained* by the fact that it enabled this result to be reinforcing.

The interplay between beliefs and desires is a reciprocal process. We just witnessed the way a richer system of beliefs gives rise to a host of new desires, desires *for* whatever is *thought* to satisfy one's pure (or *less* derived) desires. Such derived desires inherit all the conceptual complexity, and hence all the intentional structure, of the beliefs from which they are derived. I want to be on the corner of State and Madison at exactly 10:30 A.M. because I want to see you and think that is where you will be at that time. In this case my desire to be at a certain place at a certain time is a desire I could never even have (let alone satisfy) without the representational resources implied by the belief from which this desire is derived.

Conversely, though, the development of more discriminating desires may require (and certainly encourages) the collateral development of more sophisticated representational techniques for servicing these desires. If I want to be on the corner of State and Madison at 10:30, it behooves me to have a variety of ways, the more the better, for representing times and places. The greater the representational power, the better the chances of producing change *when* and *where* it will be effective, when and where it will satisfy the desires for which it was undertaken. There is no point in chasing the herd (in fact a point in *not* chasing the herd) if none of them can be caught; no point in digging here, in the flower bed, if the bone was buried next to a tree; and no point in making or having appointments for 10:30 if one can't tell time. One has to learn to identify the signs, learn *when* and *where* conditions are optimal for initiating movements, in order to avoid futile expenditures of energy. This is especially true in creatures like ourselves, creatures whose desires are often such that they can be satisfied only by movements that are precisely coordinated with specialized, and often changing, circumstances—circumstances that, because of their specialized character, we have had to *learn* to identify. Crickets may be able to initiate copulation with anything emitting the right sequence of chirps and trills, sequences that the crickets are genetically programmed to recognize and respond to, but we enjoy no such infallible sign of sexual receptivity or interest. We have to negotiate a much more intricate web of cues and signals to achieve a comparable degree of success in our reproductive efforts. And most of these cues and signals have to be *learned*.

Aside, however, from cognitively derived desires, the reciprocal influence of cognitive and conative factors becomes evident with an increasing refinement of desire: desires that develop, not just for R, but a certain form of R or R under a special set of conditions. We want, not just R, but an FR, where F is a special form of R or the special conditions in which we prefer R. One develops a taste for a special kind of mushroom, for a blend of Virginia, latikia, and perique tobaccos, for a mixture of romaine and head lettuce, for dry French wines, for classical symphonic music, for mystery stories, or for nubile redheads. Since one has developed a preference for this particular kind of mushroom, tobacco, wine, and so on, one is obviously able to make the relevant discriminations—to distinguish between FRs and non-FRs. Nevertheless, regular and reliable satisfaction of these more refined desires typically requires the development of techniques for identifying FRs. In order to avoid prolonged investigation or repeated sampling of less desirable items (sampling that often involves an expenditure of energy to *secure* the sample), one needs, particularly in the case of gustatory preferences, a visual, olfactory, or tactile way of identifying the things one prefers. Modern packaging techniques, not to mention the use of language in identifying the contents of the package, tends to conceal this reciprocal dependency between cognitive and conative development, between the way knowing more makes you want more and wanting more forces you to know more. The mutual dependency is, however, merely a manifestation at the cognitive level of something that is already familiar at the evolutionary level: the way new cognitive resources are developed to serve a change in the circumstances—and hence in the needs—of a species. The pests evolve a way of resisting, or avoiding, each new development in poison.

6.4 Cognitive Holism

Besides enlarging the number and variety of conative resources available for explaining behavior, the development of a richer network of beliefs also changes the character of the beliefs *in* that network. A belief having the putative fact that F as its content, an internal state whose function it is to indicate that condition F exists, will inevitably *change* this content as it becomes more tightly integrated with other states having corresponding indicator functions. A spy, working alone in the field, may have a certain information-gathering function. But as *more* spies are deployed, and their information-gathering activities start to overlap and become interdependent, the responsibilities of each may change.

This so-called holistic character of belief has been much discussed and debated in recent philosophy (see especially Davidson 1980, 1982). The present view of belief, a view that indentifies *what* we believe with what it is the function of certain elements to indicate, not only implies that beliefs *have* this holistic character, it reveals *why* they have it. As beliefs become integrated into more tightly structured cognitive systems, their indicator functions become more interdependent. Not having to do as *much*, they are free to become more *specialized*. As a result of this increasing specialization, they begin to exhibit a finer-grained intentionality. This, in a nutshell, is why a rat's belief that a light is on might differ from my belief that the light is on while remaining, in an important sense, a belief that the light is on.[2] It

2. This section represents a movement on my part toward something closer to what is called (Block 1986) a two-factor theory of meaning, a theory in which the meaning of internal elements is a combination of (1) their relations (usually causal or informational relations) to

also helps explain how it is possible to develop concepts for features and conditions of our environment, the so-called *theoretical* properties, which we have so far ignored (see, e.g., Papineau 1984, p. 560).

Since the meaning or representational content of an element is what it has the function of indicating rather than what it actually succeeds in indicating, the meaning can change if this function changes. And the function can change without a change in what the element actually indicates. Consider the way this might happen in very simple cases. Suppose that an animal has learned to identify certain environmental conditions, F and G, because of their relevance to need-satisfying activities. In accordance with the account given in chapter 4, I shall assume that there are internal indicators—call them $B[F]$ and $B[G]$—whose function (derived from the learning process) is to register the presence of these two conditions. $B[F]$ represents something as being F; $B[G]$ represents it as being G. F and G can be thought of as particular shapes, colors, sounds, or smells. Or they may be thought of as particular patterns of color, shape, and sound— e.g., a warning call, a threatening profile, or a friendly gesture. Or they may be even more specific features of the environment—e.g., the cluster of properties used to identify individual members of the group (Mother) or important locations (my house). Whatever they are, F and G are properties the animal has learned to identify in order to more effectively satisfy its needs and ensure its safety.

Some things the animal now does it does, in part, because it represents its surroundings as being in condition F, and other things it does it does because it represents them as being in condition G. Suppose, then, that— because of its exposure to an environmental contingency, a correlation, between F and G—the animal learns to associate these two conditions— learns, let us say, that *whenever* F obtains, G also obtains: whenever a neighbor emits *that* distinctive call, an eagle is circling overhead; whenever the lioness (a dangerous enemy when hungry) looks like *that*, she has just

---

the *external* situations they represent and (2) their functional (or conceptual) role in the production of output (including their *internal* relations to each other). Earlier (1981) I favored something that was more nearly a one-factor theory. Though compositionality (and, hence, indirectly, functional role) played a part in distinguishing extensionally equivalent concepts, I emphasized the information-carrying factor to the exclusion of the functional- or conceptual-role component of meaning.

I still think the primary component of meaning is the set of external relations, the *indicator* (or, as I earlier expressed it, the *informational*) relations an element exhibits. Without this, no amount of "role playing" can transform a meaning-less element into one with meaning. There is noting to make the functional role, no matter how elaborate, a *conceptual* role. Nonetheless, once the meaning of an element is identified (as I now think it must be) with its indicator *function*, it becomes easier to see how internal elements, by becoming more interdependent, could affect each other's indicator function and, hence, each other's meaning.

eaten and hence is not hungry; whenever a flower looks like this and smells like that, it is rich in pollen and nectar. This piece of knowledge can change the way B[F] starts to *function* in controlling movements. For circumstances can easily be imagined in which this internal representation of F starts to assume some of the control duties formerly performed by the representation of G. If concealment is mandatory in conditions G (an eagle in the sky), it is *now*, after learning, also mandatory in condition F, when a distinctive "warning" call is emitted by neighbors. B[F] now begins to cause those evasive movements whose production was formerly the job of B[G]. Once this occurs, a subtle shift can occur in the meaning of that element, B[F], whose function it was to indicate F. Though retaining this original function, it can, after learning, acquire an additional function: the function of indicating G. Assuming that there is an external, objective correlation between F and G, B[F] always, in fact, indicated G when it indicated F. Prior to learning, though, because it did not have the function of indicating G, B[F] did not *represent* G. But the internal association between B[F] and B[G] brought about by learning can change the indicator function of B[F]; it can do so by changing what B[F] causes *as a result of what it indicates about G*. B[F] acquired the function of indicating F by being given a job to do because it indicated F. When B[F]'s job description changes, and it changes because of what it indicates about G, then B[F] acquires the *additional* function of indicating G. Hence, the indicator function of B[F] changes. What it *represents* or *means* changes.

Whether or not an element acquires this added indicator function, and hence changes its meaning, is a question about whether its newly acquired control duties, the initiation of those movements formerly controlled by other representational elements, were acquired *as a result of* its indication of what these other elements indicate. An element that began its career as a representation of F can change its meaning—can acquire, if you will, an additional component of meaning—by having its causal role modified by its indication of G. When the warning call of a neighbor makes a vervet monkey behave the way it normally does to an aerial threat (e.g., an eagle), the internal representation of this acoustic stimulus acquires an additional significance: it becomes a representation of a *warning* call, a representation (at one remove, so to speak) of an eagle.[3] When this happens, the internal element changes its function, and hence its meaning, for the same reason the function of a dog may change from being merely a pet to also being a

3. I assume, for the sake of the illustration, that the monkeys *learn* to associate the various warning calls with different sorts of threats (eagles, snakes, leopards, etc.). In point of fact, this behavior is (or facets of this behavior are) probably instinctive. As Gould and Marler (1987) observe, this behavior, like many other behaviors, is an interesting mixture of instinctive and learned elements. Animals are genetically programmed to learn some things.

watchdog if it is kept, in part at least, *because* of its aggressive and noisy response to intruders.

As a result of being integrated into a network of associated concepts, a concept can change in this way. It can grow—sprout new dimensions of meaning (intension), as it were—without losing its underlying character, while suffering no appreciable change in its extension. It still indicates all the same things, but it now has a different—perhaps a more specialized, perhaps a more variegated—indicator *function*.

Pigeons, I am told, can learn to identify trucks in photographs. Besides being pictures *of trucks*, the pictures do not seem to have much in common. They are, for example, taken from different angles, of different parts of the truck, from different distances. The pigeons are better at this task than small children. Do the pigeons believe that X (the thing whose picture they are shown) is a truck? Is that why they peck the target (as they have been taught to do when they see a picture of a truck)? Do they have the concept of a truck? We might be willing to credit this concept to a child if it performed as well in such discriminatory tasks. Why are we tempted to credit the child with a belief and reluctant to do so with the bird? There is, or course, the obvious fact that children are often given ways of responding to trucks that involve words that, in a public language, *mean* truck. It is, therefore, easier to assign (no doubt prematurely in many cases) the representational properties of their overt responses (the words they use) to the internal causes of these responses (their internal beliefs). Aside from this difference, though, children (and adults, of course) often know things about trucks that pigeons don't: that trucks require fuel to run, that they are used to carry heavy loads, that they travel on highways, and so on. None of these things is essential to their being trucks, is something we could plausibly use to *define* the word "truck". Some trucks don't run at all. Some never carry, and are not used to carry, heavy loads. They are, nonetheless, *trucks*. These connections between the concept of a truck and other concepts (load, highway, fuel, etc.) constitute a system of knowledge and enable our internal representations of trucks to function in indicator-related ways, as the pigeon's representations cannot. We expect to see trucks stop *at service stations*; we *hear* (and by hearing, identify) trucks passing on the road; we know there is a driver in the cab and an engine under the hood; we know that a truck is probably equipped with a very loud horn and with air brakes. Some people know these things; other people know different things. But the point is that a structure whose primary or original function (in a child, say) may have been to indicate trucks in something like the simple way pigeons have of identifying trucks acquires, as a result of this vast network of associations, a variety of other indicator functions. And its function is, in turn, partially taken over by structures whose primary functions may be quite different. This system of interconnected functions then modifies what the individual elements in that network mean.

This is why it would be misleading to say that a pigeon, though better at identifying trucks than a child, believes what the children believe: *that* they are trucks. Given the bird's impressive performance on discrimination tasks, there must be something in its head that indicates which objects are trucks. This element (as a result of learning) may even have acquired the function of indicating which objects are trucks. Nevertheless, this element lacks the cluster of collateral functions, or the network of relations to elements having collateral functions, that helps to define *our* concept of a truck. Thus, no matter how we choose to express the way the pigeon represents trucks, it would be at best misleading (and at worst simply wrong) to say that it represents these objects *as trucks*. Whatever the pigeon thinks about these objects, it is probably best expressed, if it can be expressed at all, in some other way.

It is this fact, I submit, that makes us want to deny to nonlinguistic animals the same concepts, the same beliefs, that we have. Even with such elementary observational notions as "red" and "triangular", the animal, lacking language, presumably lacks the network of associations that give its internal color and shape indicators (indicators it must surely have to per-form the discriminatory tasks animals routinely perform) the allied set of indicator functions that these representational structures have acquired in the course of human cognitive development. Red may not mean STOP in any sense that would be of interest to a lexicographer, but it does mean this in a sense that is relevant to distinguishing my belief that the object is red from a rat's belief that the object is red. And my concept of red exhibits a particularly intimate relationship to my concept of color—a relationship that (Premack 1978) may be altogether lacking in animals because, though possessing something whose function it is to indicate *red*, they lack a concept of (something whose function it is to indicate) *color*.

This leaves us with a view of concepts that is closer to contemporary "exemplar," "holistic" and "prototype" theories than it is to classic ideas (Smith and Medin 1981; Rosch 1978). The picture that emerges is a picture of a dynamic process of conceptual change, a change brought about by the increasing articulation a concept receives in virtue of its inclusion in an expanding network of concepts. This is not to say that whenever we change the network—whenever, for example, we add a new concept or establish a new link between concepts already in the network—every element undergoes a corresponding change in meaning. Something changes, of course, but it need not be the indicator function of the struc-tures already inhabiting that network. What changes is what these struc-tures, in virtue of their connection to the newly added structure, indicate about those conditions the new structure has the function of indicating. But this alone is not enough to change the concepts (meanings) in that network, since their identity depends, not on what they in fact indicate, but on what it is their function to indicate. An organization can grow larger (employ more people) without necessarily changing the functions of the other employees.

This leaves us, to be sure, with a fuzzy boundary. Just when does a structure acquire or change its indicator function? When does an element whose primary function it is to indicate F come to have the additional function of indicating G? Such questions have reasonably clear answers when the functions in question are what I called (in chapter 3) assigned functions, for in this case *we*, by our intentions and use, determine a thing's function, and we can presumably tell when we change our intentions or the way we use something. But things are less clear with intrinsic functions. If sea turtles now use their front flippers to dig in the sand (to bury their eggs), and we suppose that these flippers originally evolved for purely locomotory purposes, at what point (if any) can we say that these flippers changed their function? When did the sesamoid bone in the panda's wrist *become* a thumb (Gould 1980)?

There is no clear dividing line between the way something functions and its function. After a thing functions in that way long enough so that it is clear that it is being selected or being used in a way that depends on its continued performance of that task, then we can say that it has acquired the function of performing that task. In the case of indicators and their function, these questions will not always (or perhaps ever) have precise answers. But this result, far from being an objection to this account of meaning, is, I submit, one of its virtues. For this is precisely the sort of thing one should expect to find in the case of beliefs and the concepts on which they depend. In terms of associated concepts, what else, exactly, *must* one believe to believe that fire engines are red, that there is a bird on the branch, or that there is a truck in the driveway?

Bibliography

Alcock, J. 1984. *Animal Behavior: An Evolutionary Approach*. Sunderland, Mass.: Sinauer Associates.

Alkon, D. 1983. Learning in a marine snail. *Scientific American* 249: 1.

Anscombe, G. E. M. 1958. *Intention*. Ithaca, N.Y.: Cornell University Press.

Armstrong, D. M. 1973. *Belief, Truth and Knowledge*. Cambridge University Press.

Bandura, A., and R. H. Walters. 1963. *Social Learning and Personality Development*. New York: Holt, Rinehart & Winston.

Bartlett, F. C. 1958. *Thinking*. New York: Basic Books.

Bennett, J. 1973. Shooting, killing and dying. *Canadian Journal of Philosophy* 2: 315–323.

Blakemore, R. P., and R. B. Frankel. 1981. Magnetic navigation in bacteria. *Scientific American* 245: 6.

Block, N. 1978. Troubles with functionalism. In *Perception and Cognition*, ed. W. Savage (Minneapolis: University of Minnesota Press).

Block, N. 1986. Advertisement for a semantics for psychology. In *Midwest Studies in Philosophy*, vol. 10, ed. P. French et al. (Minneapolis: University of Minnesota Press).

Blodgett, H. C. 1929. The effect of the introduction of reward upon maze performance of rats. *University of California Publications in Psychology* 4, no. 8: 113–134.

Boorse, C. 1976. Wright on functions. *Philosophical Review* 85: 70–86.

Braithwaite, R. B. 1953. *Scientific Explanation*. Cambridge University Press.

Brand, M. 1984. *Intending and Acting: Toward a Naturalized Action Theory*. Cambridge, Mass.: MIT Press. A Bradford Book.

Bruner, J. S. 1970. The growth and structure of skill. In *Mechanisms of Motor Skill and Development*, ed. K. Connolly (New York: Academic).

Catania, A. C. 1984. *Learning*. Second edition. Englewood Cliffs, N.J.: Prentice-Hall.

Churchland, P. M. 1981. Eliminative materialism and propositional attitudes. *Journal of Philosophy* 78: 2.

Cummins, R. 1975. Functional analysis. *Journal of Philosophy* 72: 741–765.

Cummins, R. 1983. *The Nature of Psychological Explanation*. Cambridge, Mass.: MIT Press. A Bradford Book.

Cummins, R. 1986. Inexplicit information. In *The Representation of Knowledge and Belief*, ed. M. Brand and R. Harnish (Tucson: University of Arizona Press).

Cummins, R. 1987. Why adding machines are better examples than thermostats: Comments on Dretske's "The Explanatory Role of Content." In *Contents of Thought: Proceedings of the 1985 Oberlin Colloquium in Philosophy* (Tucson: University of Arizona Press).

Davidson, D. 1963. Actions, reasons and causes. Reprinted in Davidson 1980.

Davidson, D. 1967. The logical form of action sentences. In *The Logic of Decision and Action*, ed. N. Rescher (University of Pittsburgh Press). Reprinted in Davidson 1980.

Davidson, D. 1971. Agency. Reprinted in Davidson 1980.

Davidson, D. 1980. *Essays on Actions and Events*. Oxford University Press.

Davidson, D. 1982. Rational animals. *Dialectica* 36: 318–327.

Davidson, D. 1987. Knowing one's own mind. *Proceedings and Addresses of the American Philosophical Association* 60: 3.

Davis, L. 1979. *Theory of Action.* Englewood Cliffs, N.J.: Prentice-Hall.

Dennett, D. 1969. *Content and Consciousness.* London: Routledge and Kegan Paul.

Dennett, D. 1978. *Brainstorms.* Cambridge, Mass.: MIT Press. A Bradford Book.

Dennett, D. 1981a. Three kinds of intentional psychology. In *Reduction, Time and Reality,* ed. R. Healey (Cambridge University Press).

Dennett, D. 1981b. True believers: The intentional strategy and why it works. In *Scientific Explanation,* ed. A. F. Heath (Oxford University Press).

Dennett, D. 1983. Intentional systems in cognitive ethology: The "Panglossian paradigm" defended. *Behavioral and Brain Sciences* 6, no. 3: 343–355 and ("Response") 379–388.

Dennett, D. 1985. *Elbow Room.* Cambridge, Mass: MIT Press. A Bradford Book.

Dennett, D. 1987. Evolution, error, and intentionality. In D. Dennett, *The Intentional Stance* (Cambridge, Mass.: MIT Press).

Dethier, V. G. 1976. *The Hungry Fly.* Cambridge, Mass: Harvard University Press.

Dretske, F. 1972. Contrastive statements. *Philosophical Review* 81: 411–437.

Dretske, F. 1981. *Knowledge and the Flow of Information.* Cambridge, Mass: MIT Press. A Bradford Book.

Dretske, F. 1983. Précis of *Knowledge and the Flow of Information. Behavioral and Brain Sciences* 6, no. 1: 55–63.

Dretske, F. 1985. Mentality and machines. *Proceedings and Addresses of the American Philosophical Association* 59: 1.

Dretske, F. 1986. Misrepresentation. In *Belief,* ed. R. Bogdan (Oxford University Press).

Dretske, F. 1987. The explanatory role of content. In *Contents of Thought: Proceedings of the 1985 Oberlin Colloquium in Philosophy* (Tucson: University of Arizona Press).

Eibl-Eibesfeldt, I. 1975. *Ethology.* Second edition. New York: Holt, Rinehart & Winston.

Eibl-Eibesfeldt, I. 1979. Human ethology: Concepts and implications for the sciences of man. *Behavioral and Brain Sciences* 2, no. 1: 1–58.

Enc, B. 1979. Function attributions and functional explanations. *Philosophy of Science* 46, no. 3: 343–365.

Enc, B. 1982. Intentional states of mechanical devices. *Mind* 91 (362): 161–182.

Enc, B. 1985. Redundancy, degeneracy and deviance in action. *Philosophical Studies* 48: 353–374.

Engle, B. T. 1986. An essay on the circulation as behavior. *Behavioral and Brain Sciences* 9, no. 2: 285–318.

Evans, G. 1981. Semantic theory and tacit knowledge. In *Wittgenstein: To Follow a Rule,* ed. C. Leich and S. Holtzman (London: Routledge and Kegan Paul).

Evans, M., R. Moore, and K.-H. Hasenstein. 1986. How roots respond to gravity. *Scientific American* 255, no. 6: 112–119.

Evarts, E. V. 1980. Brain mechanisms in voluntary movement. In *Neural Mechanisms in Behavior,* ed. D. McFadden (New York: Springer-Verlag).

Ewing, A., and G. Hoyle. 1965. Neuronal mechanisms underlying control of sound production in a cricket, *Acheta domesticus. Journal of Experimental Biology* 43: 139–153.

Flynn, J. P. 1972. Patterning mechanism, patterned reflexes, and attack behavior in cats. *Nebraska Symposium on Motivation* 20: 125–153.

Fodor, J. 1980. Methodological solipsism considered as a research strategy in cognitive psychology. *Behavioral and Brain Sciences* 3, no. 1: 63–110.

Fodor, J. 1984. Semantics, Wisconsin style. *Synthese* 59: 1–20.

Fodor, J. 1987a. *Psychosemantics.* Cambridge, Mass.: MIT Press. A Bradford Book.

Fodor, J. 1987b. A situated grandmother. *Mind and Language* 2, no. 1: 64–81.

Follesdal, D. 1985. Causation and explanation: A problem in Davidson's view on action and mind. In *Actions and Events: Perspectives on the Philosophy of Donald Davidson*, ed. E. LePore and B. McLaughlin (New York: Basil Blackwell).

Gallistel, C. R. 1980. *The Organization of Action: A New Synthesis*. Hillsdale, N.J.: Erlbaum.

Gallup, G. G., Jr. 1974. Animal hypnosis: Factual status of a fictional concept. *Psychological Bulletin* 81: 836–853.

Garcia, J., and R. A. Koelling. 1966. Relation of cue to consequence in avoidance learning. *Psychonomic Science* 4: 123–124.

Garfinkel, A. 1981. *Forms of Explanation: Rethinking the Questions of Social Theory*. New Haven, Conn.: Yale University Press.

Goldman, A. 1970. *A Theory of Human Action*. Englewood Cliffs, N.J.: Prentice-Hall.

Goodman, N. 1976. *Languages of Art*. Indianapolis: Hackett.

Gould, J. L. 1979. Do honeybees know what they are doing? *Natural History* 88: 66–75.

Gould, J. L. 1982. *Ethology, The Mechanisms and Evolution of Behavior*. New York: Norton.

Gould, J. L., and P. Marler. 1987. Learning by instinct. *Scientific American* 256, no. 1: 74–85.

Gould, S. J. 1980. *The Panda's Thumb*. New York: Norton.

Greene, H. W. 1973. Defensive tail display by snakes and amphisbaenians. *Journal of Herpetology* 7: 143–161.

Grice, P. 1957. Meaning. *Philosophical Review* 66: 377–388.

Grier, J. W. 1984. *Biology of Animal Behavior*. St. Louis: Mosby.

Griffin, D. R. 1984. *Animal Thinking*. Cambridge, Mass.: Harvard University Press.

Groves, P. M., and K. Schlesinger. 1979. *Introduction to Biological Psychology*. Dubuque: Wm. C. Brown.

Gwinner, E. 1986. Internal rhythms in bird migration. *Scientific American* 254, no. 4: 84–92.

Hanson, N. R. 1958. *Patterns of Discovery*. Cambridge University Press.

Haugeland, J. (ed.) 1981a. *Mind Design*. Cambridge, Mass.: MIT Press. A Bradford Book.

Haugeland, J. 1981b. Semantic engines: An introduction to mind design. In Haugeland 1981a.

Haugeland, J. 1985. *Artificial Intelligence: The Very Idea*. Cambridge, Mass.: MIT Press. A Bradford Book.

Hinton, G. E., and J. A. Anderson, eds. 1981. *Parallel Models of Associative Memory*. Hillsdale, N.J.: Erlbaum.

Honderich, T. 1982. The argument for anomalous monism. *Analysis* 42, no. 1: 192.

Hornsby, J. 1980. *Actions*. London: Routledge and Kegan Paul.

Hoyle, G. 1984. The scope of neuroethology. *Behavioral and Brain Sciences* 7, no. 3: 367–412.

Huber, F., and J. Thorson. 1985. Cricket auditory communication. *Scientific American* 253, no. 6: 60–68.

Hull, C. L. 1943. *Principles of Behavior*. New York: Appleton-Century-Crofts.

Jeannerod, M. 1981. Input-output relations in goal directed actions. *Behavioral and Brain Sciences* 4, no. 4: 628–629.

Kim, J. 1976. Events as property exemplifications. In *Action Theory*, ed. M. Brand and D. Walton (Dordrecht: Reidel).

Kuo, Z.-Y. 1970. The need for coordinated efforts in developmental studies. In *Development and Evolution of Behavior: Essays in Memory of T. C. Schneirla*, ed. L. R. Aronson et al. (San Francisco: Freeman).

Lashley, K. S. 1924. Studies of the cerebral function in learning. V. The retention of motor habits after destruction of the so-called motor areas in primates. *Archives of Neurology and Psychiatry* 12: 249–276.

Lehrman, D. S. 1953. A critique of Konrad Lorenz's theory of instinctive behavior. *Quarterly Review of Biology* 28, no. 4: 337–363.

Lewontin, R. 1983. Darwin's revolution. *New York Review of Books* 30: 21−27.

Loar, B. 1981. *Mind and Meaning*. Cambridge University Press.

Loeb, J. 1918. *Forced Movements, Tropisms, and Animal Conduct*. Philadelphia: Lippincott.

Lorenz, K., and N. Tinbergen. 1938. Taxis and Instinkthandlung in der Eirollbewegung der *Graugans*. *Zeitschrift für Tierpsychologie* 2: 1−29.

Mackie, J. L. 1979. Mind, brain and causation. In *Midwest Studies in Philosophy*, vol. 4, ed. P. French et al. (Minneapolis: University of Minnesota Press).

Mazur, J. E. 1986. *Learning and Behavior*. Englewood Cliffs, N.J.: Prentice-Hall.

MacDonnel, M. F., and J. P. Flynn. 1966. Sensory control of hypothalamic attack. *Animal Behavior* 14: 399−405.

McClelland, J. L., and D. E. Rumelhart. 1985. Distributed memory and the representation of general and specific memory. *Journal of Experimental Psychology: General* 114: 159−188.

McGinn, C. 1979. Action and its explanation. In *Philosophical Problems in Psychology*, ed. N. Bolton (London: Methuen).

McGinn, C. 1982. *The Character of Mind*. Oxford University Press.

Meehl, P. E. 1950. On the circularity of the law of effect. *Psychological Bulletin* 47: 52−75.

Menzel, E. W. 1978. Cognitive mapping in chimpanzees. In *Cognitive Processes in Animal Behavior*, ed. S. Hulse et al. (Hillsdale, N.J.: Erlbaum).

Miller, N. E. 1944. Experimental studies of conflict. In *Personality and the Behavioral Disorders*, volume 1, ed. J. McV. Hunt (New York: Ronald).

Miller, N. E. 1959. Liberalization of basic S-R concepts: Extensions to conflict behavior, motivation and social learning. In *Psychology: A Study of a Science*, vol. 2, ed. S. Koch (New York: McGraw-Hill).

Millikan, R. G. 1984. *Language, Thought, and Other Biological Categories: New Foundations for Realism*. Cambridge, Mass.: MIT Press.

Millikan, R. G. 1986. Thoughts without laws: Cognitive science with content. *Philosophical Review* 95, no. 1: 47−80.

Nagel, E. 1961. *The Structure of Science*. Indianapolis: Hackett.

Nissan, H. W. 1950. Description of the learned response in discrimination behavior. *Psychological Review* 57: 121−131.

O'Keefe, J. 1976. Place units in the hippocampus of freely moving rat. *Experimental Neurology* 51: 78−109.

Olton, D. S. 1978. Characteristics of spatial memory. In *Cognitive Processes in Animal Behavior*, ed. S. Hulse et al. (Hillsdale, N.J.: Erlbaum).

Paige, K. N., and T. G. Whitham. 1985. Report of research published in *Science*. *Scientific American* 252, no. 4: 74.

Papineau, D. 1984. Representation and explanation. *Philosophy of Science* 51, no. 4: 550−572.

Porpora, D. 1980. Operant conditioning and teleology. *Philosophy of Science* 47: 568−582.

Postman, L. 1947. The history and present status of the law of effect. *Psychological Bulletin* 44: 489−563.

Premack, D. 1959. Toward empirical behavioral laws. I. Positive reinforcement. *Psychological Review* 66: 219−233.

Premack, D. 1965. Reinforcement theory. In *Nebraska Symposium on Motivation*, ed. D. Levine (Lincoln: University of Nebraska Press).

Premack, D. 1978. On the abstractness of human concepts: Why it would be difficult to talk to a pigeon. In *Cognitive Processes in Animal Behavior*, ed. S. Hulse et al. (Hillsdale, N.J.: Erlbaum).

Preyer, W. 1885. *Specielle Physiologie des Embryo*. Leipzig: Grieben.

Pylyshyn, Z. 1984. *Computation and Cognition*. Cambridge, Mass.: MIT Press.

Ramsey, F. P. 1931. *The Foundations of Mathematics, and Other Logical Essays*. London: Routledge and Kegan Paul.

Rachlin, H. 1976. *Behavior and Learning*. San Francisco: Freeman.

Raven, P. H., R. F. Evert, and H. Curtis. 1981. *Biology of Plants*. New York: Worth.

Ringen, J. 1985. Operant conditioning and a paradox of teleology. *Philosophy of Science* 52: 565−577.

Robinson, H. 1982. *Matter and Sense*. Cambridge University Press.

Rosch, E. 1978. Principles of categorization. In *Cognition and Categorization*, ed. E. Rosch and B. B. Lloyd (Hillsdale, N.J.: Erlbaum).

Rothenbuhler, W. C. 1964. Behavior genetics of nest cleaning in honey bees. IV. Responses of F1 and backcross generations to disease-killed brood. *American Zoologist* 4: 111−123.

Ryle, G. 1949. *Concept of Mind*. London: Hutchinson's University Library.

Searle, J. 1980. Minds, brains and programs. *Behavioral and Brain Sciences* 3, no. 3: 417−457.

Sheridan, M. R. 1984. Planning and controlling simple movements. In Smyth and Wing 1984.

Sherrington, C. 1906. *The Integrative Action of the Nervous System*. New York: Scribner.

Shik, M. L., F. V. Severin, and G. N. Orlovsky. 1966. Control of walking and running by means of electrical stimulation of the mid-brain. *Bifizika* 11: 659−666.

Skillen, A. 1984. Mind and matter: A problem that refuses dissolution. *Mind* 93 (372): 514−526.

Smith, E. E., and D. L. Medin. 1981. *Categories and Concepts*. Cambridge, Mass.; Harvard University Press.

Smyth, M. M., and A. M. Wing, eds. 1984. *The Psychology of Human Movement*. New York: Academic.

Sober, E. 1984a. *The Nature of Selection*. Cambridge, Mass.: MIT Press. A Bradford Book.

Sober, E., ed. 1984b. *Conceptual Issues in Evolutionary Biology*. Cambridge, Mass.: MIT Press. A Bradford Book.

Sober, E. 1987. Apportioning causal responsibility. Forthcoming.

Sorensen, R. A. 1985. Self-deception and scattered events. *Mind* 94 (373): 64−69.

Sosa, E. 1984. Mind-body interaction and supervenient causation. *Midwest Studies in Philosophy*, vol. 9, ed. P. French et al. (Minneapolis: University of Minnesota Press).

Sperry, R. W. 1956. The eye and the brain. Reprinted (from *Scientific American*) in *Perception: Mechanisms and Models* (San Francisco: Freeman).

Staddon, J. E. R. 1983. *Adaptive Behavior and Learning*. Cambridge University Press.

Stampe, D. 1975. Show and tell. In *Forms of Representation*, ed. B. Freed et al. (Amsterdam: North-Holland).

Stampe, D. 1977. Toward a causal theory of linguistic representation. In *Midwest Studies in Philosophy*, vol. 2., ed. P. French et al. (Minneapolis: University of Minnesota Press).

Stampe, D. 1986. Verification and a causal account of meaning. *Synthese* 69: 107−137.

Stampe, D. 1987. The authority of desire. *Philosophical Review* 96: 335−381.

Stellar, J. R., and E. Stellar. 1985. *The Neurobiology of Motivation and Reward*. New York: Springer-Verlag.

Stich, S. 1983. *From Folk Psychology to Cognitive Science*. Cambridge, Mass.: MIT Press. A Bradford Book.

Stoutland, F. 1976. The causation of behavior. In *Essays on Wittgenstein in Honor of G. H. von Wright* (*Acta Philosophica Fennica* 28) (Amsterdam: North-Holland).

Stoutland, F. 1980. Oblique causation and reasons for action. *Synthese* 43: 351−367.

Taylor, C. 1964. *The Explanation of Behavior*. London: Routledge and Kegan Paul.

Taylor, R. 1966. *Action and Purpose*. Englewood Cliffs, N.J.: Prentice-Hall.

Thalberg, I. 1972. *Enigmas of Agency*. New York: Allen and Unwin.

Thalberg, I. 1977. *Perception, Emotion and Action*. Oxford; Basil Blackwell.

Thomson, J. J. 1971. The time of a killing. *Journal of Philosophy* 68: 115−132.

Thomson, J. J. 1977. *Acts and Other Events*. Ithaca, N.Y.; Cornell University Press.

Thorndike, E. L. 1911. *Animal Intelligence*. New York: Macmillan.

Tinbergen, N. 1951. *The Study of Instinct*. Oxford University Press.

Tinbergen, N. 1952. The curious behavior of the stickleback. *Scientific American* 187, no. 6: 22–26.

Tolman, E. C., and C. H. Honzik. 1930. Introduction and removal of reward and maze performance in rats. *University of California Publications in Psychology* 4: 257–275.

Tuomela, R. 1977. *Human Action and its Explanation* (*Synthese* Library, vol. 116). Dordrecht: Reidel.

Weiner, B. 1985. *Human Motivation*. New York: Springer-Verlag.

Wilson, G. 1980. *The Intentionality of Human Action*. Amsterdam: North-Holland.

Wickens, D. D. 1938. The transference of conditioned excitation and condition inhibition from one muscle group to the antagonistic group. *Journal of Experimental Psychology* 22: 101–123.

Wickens, D. D. 1939. A Study of voluntary and involuntary finger conditioning. *Journal of Experimental Psychology* 25: 127–140.

Woodfield, A. 1976. *Teleology*. Cambridge University Press.

Wright, C. 1986. How can the theory of meaning be a philosophical project? *Mind and Language* 1, no. 1: 31–44.

Wright, L. 1973. Functions. *Philosophical Review* 82: 139–168.

Wright, L. 1976. *Teleological Explanations*. Berkeley: University of California Press.

von Wright, G. H. 1971. *Explanation and Understanding*. London: Routledge and Kegan Paul.

Index